STUDIES IN SOCIETY NO. 5

IMPERIALISM AND SOCIAL REFORM

STUDIES IN SOCIETY

1. CHILDREN UNDER FIVE
by J. W. B. Douglas and J. M. Blomfield

2. TECHNICAL EDUCATION AND
SOCIAL CHANGE
by Stephen F. Cotgrove

3. THE BLACKCOATED WORKER
by David Lockwood

4. THE JEWISH IMMIGRANT
IN ENGLAND, 1870-1914
by Lloyd P. Gartner

STUDIES IN SOCIETY

Edited by Ruth and David Glass

IMPERIALISM AND SOCIAL REFORM

English Social-Imperial Thought

1895–1914

BY

BERNARD SEMMEL

PH.D.

Ruskin House

GEORGE ALLEN & UNWIN LTD

MUSEUM STREET LONDON

FIRST PUBLISHED IN 1960

PRINTED IN GREAT BRITAIN
in 11 *on* 12 *point Bell type*
BY C. TINLING AND COMPANY LIMITED
LIVERPOOL, LONDON AND PRESCOT

To My Mother

PREFACE

Curiously, very little scholarly attention has been given to so important a field of study as modern 'social-imperialism,' and that has gone, almost exclusively, to its German, Italian, and French variants. Both the subject of British social-imperialism and that of the development of social-imperial thought, generally, have been badly neglected, a circumstance which may be regarded as justifying a special study. This book grew out of a dissertation submitted in 1955 for the doctorate in history at Columbia University. My interest in the subject stemmed from an earlier study of the strange union of socialism and imperialism in the thought of leading Fabians in the period between the wars. The ideas owe much to discussions with the late J. Bartlet Brebner, under whom it was prepared, and whose loss is keenly felt by students of modern English history. The present work is an expansion and considerable revision of the unpublished dissertation.

The original dissertation was read by, and profited from the comments of H. L. Beales, of the London School of Economics and Political Science, who was Visiting Professor at Columbia University, in 1954-55; Professors Herman Ausubel, R. K. Webb, and David Landes of Columbia University; and a friend, Martin Albaum. Of course, none of these persons ought to be held responsible for the book's deficiencies. I was enabled to prolong a stay in England to consult materials not elsewhere available and to complete the preparation of the book because of a most timely grant from the Rockefeller Foundation, for which I am greatly appreciative. For equally timely help and encouragement, I should like to thank Professor D. V. Glass of the London School of Economics and Political Science.

I should like to make special mention of the advice and assistance, at every stage, of my wife, Maxine Guse Semmel. It was in the course of talks with her that the ideas took shape, and her painstaking help on editorial matters was of the utmost value. She also typed several drafts of the manuscript.

Sections of the book have appeared in *Economica*, the *British Journal of Sociology*, and the *Canadian Journal of Economics and Political Science*, and I wish to thank the editors for permission to reprint material which first appeared in those journals.

Bernard Semmel

London, November, 1959

CONTENTS

I

SOCIAL-IMPERIALISM

> When the extra-group struggle with inferior races abroad
> has run to its end; then, if not sooner, the population question
> will force on a severer struggle for existence between
> civilized communities at home. Whether this struggle takes
> the form of actual warfare, or of still keener competition for
> trade and food-supply, that group in which unchecked internal
> competition has produced a vast proletariat with no limit of
> endurance, or with—to use a cant phrase—no 'stake in the
> State,' will be the first to collapse. It is extra-group com-
> petition which will more and more force the nations of
> Europe in the direction of socialism. . . .

> KARL PEARSON in *Socialism*
> *and Natural Selection*, 1894

'Social-Imperialism' is a term used by a number of scholars
during recent years. One of them, Franz Neumann, described it
as an attempt on the part of the governing classes to provide a
mass base for imperialism, an attempt 'to incorporate the
working classes into an imperialistic system.' 'Concessions to
the masses,' such as 'the extension of the franchise or material
benefits,' Neumann explained, 'were employed to secure popular
support for aggressive expansion.'[1] The economist J. A.
Schumpeter, in a famous essay written in 1919, defined social-
imperialism as an imperialism in which 'entrepreneurs and other
elements woo the workers by means of social welfare concessions which appear to depend on the success of export mono-
polism.' Social-imperialism, Schumpeter continued, was an
attempt to revive the people's imperialisms of ancient times, to
create a warrior nation modelled after the ancient Assyrians or
the Arabs of the early middle ages.[2] Both Schumpeter and
Neumann asserted that such a 'people's imperialism' was an
impossibility in the modern world; they insisted that it would
be resisted by the industrial working class. Both, however,

[1] Franz Neumann, *Behemoth: The Structures and Practice of National
Socialism* (London: Gollancz, 1944), pp. 153–5.
[2] Joseph A. Schumpeter, *Imperialism and Social Classes* (Oxford:
Blackwell, 1951), f.n. pp. 114-115, and *passim*.

admitted that a temporary mood of imperialism could be fostered among the workers.[1] During the past three-quarters of a century, there have been several efforts, some more, some less successful, to revive such a people's imperialism, to demonstrate to the masses of the more industrially advanced nations of western Europe that their interests would be furthered by the advantages their nation-state gained over other nation-states. This work is an investigation of the ideological background of one such effort.

Imperialism and social-imperialism have been the subject of several inquiries in the past half-century—though they have not received all the attention they merit. The Marxists have probably written the most about imperialism and its relation to capitalist production. Some Marxist writers—Hilferding, Lenin, Renner, for example—have made pregnant suggestions concerning the phenomenon of social-imperialism which have proved stimulating for more recent writers, and it was probably the Austrian socialist Karl Renner who first employed, in 1917, the term 'Sozialimperialismus.'[2] But the Marxists have taken their cue from the writings of the English Liberal economist, John A. Hobson. For Hobson, writing after the Boer War, imperialism was promoted by certain business interests which profited enormously thereby, to the great loss of the rest of the nation. Manufacturers of war materials, industrialists who required export markets, capitalists with idle funds—all these, and only these, gained by imperialism. 'The economic root of

---

[1] Neumann, *op. cit.*, p. 155; Schumpeter, *op. cit.*, pp. 34, 115.

[2] See Rudolf Hilferding, *Das Finanzkapital, Eine Studie über die jüngste Entwicklung des Kapitalismus* (Vienna, 1910), *passim*, especially pp. 468-477; also Karl Renner, *Marxismus, Krieg und Internationale* (Stuttgart, 1917), pp. 323-350, where Renner discussed the 'error' of 'Sozialimperialismus' and the 'positive interest of the working class' in international socialism. See also Joseph Schumpeter, *Business Cycles* (New York, 1939), II, fn. p. 696. Schumpeter cryptically noted that 'a glimpse of a view that now seems to the writer to be nearer the truth than either the Marxist or his own theory is embodied in Karl Renner's concept of Social Imperialism.' It is difficult to understand Schumpeter's meaning from this solitary remark especially since Renner simply offered the conventional socialist objections to social-imperialism.

Imperialism,' Hobson wrote, 'is the desire of strong organized industrial and financial interests to secure and develop at the public expense and by the public force private markets for their surplus goods and their surplus capital.' Hobson put the chief onus for modern imperialism upon the owners of capital who wished more profitable investments than were available at home. For Hobson, imperialism was the result of the maldistribution of the national product which left huge surpluses in the hands of the possessing classes. A more just distribution, he urged, would remove this surplus income and at the same time broaden the home market sufficiently to enable it to absorb the goods and the capital which had heretofore been destined for shipment abroad. 'Trade Unionism and Socialism are thus the natural enemies of Imperialism,' wrote Hobson, 'for they take away from the "imperialist" classes the surplus incomes which form the economic stimulus of Imperialism.' Hobson hinted at social-imperialism when he suggested that the 'tendency of Imperialism is to crush Trade Unionism and to "nibble" at or parasitically exploit State Socialism.'[1]

Basing themselves largely upon Hobson's Radical anti-imperialism, the so-called 'Neo-Marxists'—Rosa Luxemburg and Rudolf Hilferding, in particular—subjected imperialism to the closest scrutiny in the years which preceded the war of 1914. For them, imperialism was the latest, and probably the last, stage of capitalist development. In this stage, free competition no longer existed—trusts, cartels, monopolies were the rule. New technological advances, they argued, had resulted in a fall in the rate of profits (as a result of the increasing proportion of capital invested in machinery rather than in labour). Capital therefore had been compelled to turn to undeveloped areas in order to realize more satisfactory returns. In addition, agreeing with Hobson, they asserted that capitalism's fatal tendency toward irrational accumulation, a tendency associated with a vast working class living on the bare minimum of subsistence, has resulted in a tremendous capacity to produce goods without the simultaneous development of domestic markets to absorb this production. Hence the necessity for markets abroad. All this

[1] J. A. Hobson, *Imperialism; A Study* (London: Allen & Unwin, 1938), pp. 106, xv, 81-84, 89-90, 140-145. Originally published in 1902.

gave rise to imperialism and wars, from which the capitalists alone benefited, although the Marxists were willing to admit that the working class might possibly achieve some 'temporary' advantage.[1]

Lenin repeated the doctrines of Hobson and the Neo-Marxists and added some words on social-imperialism. The receipt of 'monopolistically high profits' by the capitalists, he wrote, 'makes it economically possible for them to corrupt certain sections of the working class, and for a time a fairly considerable minority, and win them to the side of the bourgeoisie of a given industry or nation against all the others. The intensification of antagonisms,' of competition, 'between imperialist nations for the division of the world increases this striving,' he added. Lenin further suggested that this 'bond between imperialism and opportunism' had 'revealed itself first and most clearly in England' since 'certain features of imperialist development were observable there much earlier than in other countries.'[2] Lenin quoted at some length from remarks which were made by Cecil Rhodes, in 1895, as an example of this tendency in Great Britain:

'I was in the East End of London yesterday and attended a meeting of the unemployed. I listened to the wild speeches, which were just a cry for "bread," "bread," "bread," and on my way home I pondered over the scene and I became more than ever convinced of the importance of imperialism. . . . My cherished idea is a solution for the social problem, i.e., in order to save the 40,000,000 inhabitants of the United Kingdom from a bloody civil war, we colonial statesmen must acquire new lands to settle the surplus population, to provide new markets for the goods produced by them in the factories and mines. The Empire, as I have always said, is a bread and butter question. If you want to avoid civil war, you must become imperialists.'

The Marxist proponents of proletarian socialist internationalism were not the only enemies of imperialism or social-

---

[1] Hilferding, op. cit.; Rosa Luxemburg, The Accumulation of Capital (New Haven, 1951), passim, especially pp. 446-453. Luxemburg's work originally published in 1913.

[2] N. Lenin, Imperialism; The Highest Stage of Capitalism (New York, 1939), p. 126. Rhodes is quoted on p. 79.

imperialism, as we have seen in Hobson's case. From a slightly different standpoint, Joseph Schumpeter, in a brilliant and highly stimulating essay on imperialism, suggested that far from being an inevitable stage in the development of capitalism, capitalism was by its essential nature anti-imperialist. Were not the Cobdenites, the spokesmen of the rising British capitalism of the nineteenth century, the opponents of militarism and imperialism? Modern imperialism was not a product of rational, economic factors, but of irrational sentiments which had managed to survive from feudal, pre-capitalist times. Placing his opposition to the position of the Marxists in their own language, Schumpeter wrote: 'Imperialism thus is atavistic in character. . . . In other words, it is an element that stems from the living conditions, not of the present, but of the past—or, put in terms of the economic interpretation of history, from past rather than present relations of production.'[1] Schumpeter explained modern imperialism as an alliance between 'expansive interests' within capitalism, selfish interests constituting a minority of the capitalists, and the survivals of feudal, pre-capitalist classes. Imperialism, he held, was rooted in the irrational sentiments still lodged in the breasts of the feudal and military classes.

Schumpeter developed his theory of imperialism largely upon the basis of English politics up until the war of 1914. He published his essay in 1919 and he had the recent conflict between England and Germany very much in mind. Schumpeter's sympathies were with England, the home of the most highly developed capitalism, rather than with a Germany in which the industrial machine was still under the control of pre-capitalist classes. He noted with interest the conflict within British capitalism between the advocates of a tariff and the defenders of free trade—a conflict concerning which we will have much to say. Schumpeter was convinced that protection, too, was a pre-capitalist survival, was 'not an essential characteristic of the capitalist economy.'[2] He agreed with the supporters of protectionist-imperialism that imperialism, if it were properly launched, required a protectionist base, but added that protection harmed both the workers and the capitalists (meaning here the rentier,

---

[1] Schumpeter, *Imperialism*, p. 84, and *passim*.
[2] *Ibid*, p. 101.

B

the beneficiary of industrial loan capital, as opposed to the entrepreneur, who, however, only benefited in so far as the tariff affected his own industry). Only the large landowners stood to benefit unreservedly from protection, he asserted. Most assuredly, Schumpeter added, the working class could only lose from a policy of protection and imperialism.

Imperialism was also subjected to analysis by one of the principal groups of German social-imperial theorists—the *Katheder-Sozialisten*. Curiously, the 'Socialists of the Chair' appear to have accepted many of the pre-suppositions and con-clusions of the Marxists, the nation-splitting international socialists whom they regarded as one of their principal enemies (along with the cosmopolitan Cobdenite Free Traders). The German historical school which had provided the doctrinal basis for Bismarckian protectionism and social-imperialism of the 1880's agreed, for example, that capitalism needed external markets if it were to survive, though it emphasized the common interest of industrialist and worker in that survival. Gustav Schmoller, the leader of the so-called 'younger' historical school and the leading *Katheder-Sozialist*, asserted that only three world-states—the British Empire, Russia and the United States —possessed territories so vast and populations so numerous that they would be able to rely entirely upon internal markets and not be compelled to seek new markets abroad.[1] This argu-ment, of course, had the effect of excusing German imperialism without at the same time justifying that of Germany's principal competitors. But much of this same reasoning underlay the widespread support given Joseph Chamberlain's campaign to create a protected imperial market, a campaign which forms a central thread in our subject. It was, as we shall see, an English disciple of the school of Schmoller, W. J. Ashley,[2] who also accepted many Marxist arguments in his analysis, though like-wise turning them into an anti-Marxist direction, who was to advocate this view during the tariff controversy. However, this use of Marxist argument, and even Marxist terminology, in an effort to defeat the goal of proletarian internationalism, was to become a hallmark of continental, rather than British, social-imperialism, as we shall note.

[1] See discussion in Luxemburg, *op. cit.*, pp. 295-296.
[2] See Chapter XI, *infra*.

The roots of British social-imperialism lie in the nineteenth century history of the working class. Although there is some disagreement on the part of a few historians, the condition of the working man in the early decades of industrialism is generally acknowledged to have been miserable. Karl Marx had told the grim story in *Das Kapital*—but his principal source of information, it is important to observe, was recorded testimony before parliamentary committees. In these blue-books, the facts were all set down—stories of eighteen hours a day of work for women, of little children being dragged, still half-asleep, to draughty, damp, dark, factories after only four hours of sleep, of children who were strapped if they could not maintain the rapid pace of the shop. Wages were so frightfully low that frequently the entire family was compelled to work if all were to survive. The great critics of mid-Victorian *laissez-faire*, Thomas Carlyle, John Ruskin and Charles Dickens had attempted to awaken the consciences of Englishmen to these sordid conditions. The spokesmen for the new industrialism, on the other hand— radical leaders like John Bright and Richard Cobden—had defended the factory-system, citing the 'laws' of political economy; they suggested not only that mill-hands owed their unhappy position to intemperance or to lack of thrift but that the factory owner was in some fashion an altruistic servant and even a saviour of the community. The Marxist opponents of capitalism declared that the wages of the working men had been set at the lowest amount necessary for bare survival. The defenders of the factory-system replied by citing Ricardo's Iron Law of Wages: higher wages, they argued, would only encourage large families and depress the labour market of the future. The socialists pointed to the irrational tendency of capitalism to accumulate more and more wealth in fewer and fewer hands. The defenders of the new capitalism insisted that such savings were the heart-blood of the economic system upon which the welfare and employment of the entire community depended.

These economic conditions had their counterpart in political affairs. In 1832, the new middle classes had gained admittance into the governing class, but the working class was still excluded, despite repeated efforts to enfranchise them. In the 'thirties and 'forties, there were in England 'two nations,' which Disraeli described in his novel, *Sybil*:

'Yes,' resumed the younger stranger after a moment's interval. 'Two nations; between whom there is no intercourse and no sympathy; who are as ignorant of each other's habits, thoughts, and feelings, as if they were dwellers in different zones, or inhabitants of different planets; who are formed by a different breeding, are fed by a different food, are ordered by different manners, and are not governed by the same laws.'

'You speak of——' said Egremont, hesitatingly.

'THE RICH AND THE POOR.'[1]

In the 'thirties and 'forties, the Chartist movement organized the British working classes to seek the vote—a vote which everyone understood would be used to gain a greater share of the produced wealth. Chartism failed in 1848, but the chief political aim of Chartism was realized less than twenty years later in 1867, when the British working man was finally enfranchised, at the conclusion of nearly two decades of unexampled British prosperity.

What was true in Great Britain was true, in varying degrees, throughout Western Europe. (Western Europe, in mid-century, was not, however, as far advanced, industrially, as its insular offshoot.) Just as the repressions of the working class had led to Chartism in England, so it had led to socialism on the continent. The harshness of the factory-system drove working men into opposition; in many instances, in Germany in particular, the standard of socialism flew above the battalions of 'working men' even before the factory system had established itself. French working men attached themselves to the doctrines of Louis Blanc and Proudhon. Ferdinand Lassalle rallied the German workers. By the 'seventies, however, the almost universally acknowledged leader of European socialism was Karl Marx, and each year thousands of recruits flocked to the banner of the Marxist parties. Marx addressed himself to the 'international' working man, for, he had insisted, the proletarian had no country. The working men of all countries were brothers united in seeking the destruction of the capitalists of all countries. Everywhere the proletarian was exploited. 'Workmen of the world, unite. You have nothing to lose but your chains.' These were the final words and the chief message of the *Communist Manifesto*. There was

---

[1] Benjamin Disraeli, *Sybil, or The Two Nations* (London: 1954), p. 173.

sufficient truth in the phrase, as we have seen, for the socialist doctrine to seize hold of large sections of the working classes of Europe. It was Nietzsche who spoke of 'the two opposing parties' which faced each other in every European country. They were, he wrote, 'the socialist and the national—or whatever they may be called in the different countries of Europe.'[1]

England proved able to withstand socialism until the 'eighties. At that time, economic depression and widespread unemployment signalled the end of the blissful decades of trade prosperity. Many factors were no doubt at work in the trade fall-off, but many in Great Britain blamed the growing competition in foreign markets—and in the home market itself—of new and powerful trade rivals, in particular Germany and the United States. Trade depression activated the latent sentiments of Chartism—and London meeting-halls began to ring with the same phrases which had converted the working classes of the continent. In 1881, Henry George, the American social re-former, was welcomed to England and stirred men to ask along with him how there came to be such great poverty amid such evident signs of progress. In 1882, a Cambridge man, Henry Mayers Hyndman, formed the Social Democratic Federation, the first Marxist society in Great Britain. In 1883, the Fabian Society was formed—and soon that famous group, which was to be dominated by Sidney and Beatrice Webb and Bernard Shaw, began its work of investigation and publication. The Dock Strike of 1889 spurred the trade union movement to organize the unskilled, ill-paid trades and initiated the startling growth in unionized workers during the 'nineties and afterwards. In 1893, the first popularly-based party of English, non-Marxist socialism appeared with the establishment of the Independent Labour Party under the leadership of Keir Hardie. During the 'nineties the annual conferences of the Trades Union Congress regularly passed socialist resolutions; there was little or no opposition. In 1900, the socialist societies—the I.L.P., the S.D.F., the Fabians —joined with the trade unions in founding a Labour Representation Committee. Three years later this Committee was to pro-claim itself independent of the two old parties, and in 1906, after winning 30 parliamentary seats, it adopted the name of Labour

[1] Quoted in Crane Brinton, *Ideas and Men; The Story of Western Thought* (New York, 1950), p. 473.

Party. England at last found itself face to face with the socialist
difficulties which were besetting the continent.

The main-body of English socialism was not Marxist, but it
was internationalist. Its internationalism stemmed not only from
socialist feelings of world-wide solidarity against capitalism but
from the *laissez-faire* cosmopolitanism of British Radicalism.
The suspicion that the growing socialist working class would
prove untrustworthy in an international conflict was widespread
among the middle classes. The Labour and Socialist International
—to which the British Labour Party, the I.L.P., the Fabian
Society and the S.D.F. were all affiliated—continued to assure
European governments that this, in truth, was the case. The
socialists of each nation repeated the doctrine of Marx and Engels
that the working classes of all nations were brothers and that
their enemy was international capitalism. The average middle-
class Englishman may have half believed that it was the purpose
of the working-class socialists not only to expropriate his
property in the United Kingdom, if they got the chance, but to
sit supinely by as the Germans, or French, or Russians expro-
priated British property in Asia or Africa and possibly even in
the homeland itself.

The aristocracy in England and throughout Europe was of
course thoroughly nationalist and patriotic. Even the French
aristocracy which hated the republic still consented to serve it in
military and diplomatic capacities, in those positions where they
could advance the 'eternal' national interest of France rather
then the transient political interests of the Third Republic. As
for the middle-classes, the nationalism of the nineteenth century
can be regarded as peculiarly their own. Although the suffrage
had been granted to the better part of the urban working classes
in 1867, the working class had still not been admitted to power,
to the responsibility of governing. The 'depression' of the
'seventies, the revival of socialism in the 'eighties, the organization of the unskilled workers in the 'nineties, combined to give
the working class a new consciousness of both its strength and,
at the same time, of its political helplessness. The working class
had still to be 'satisfied.'[1]

[1] The chief sources for general background material are the seven
volumes of Élie Halévy, *A History of the English People in the Nineteenth Century* (London: E. Benn, 1949); R. C. K. Ensor, *England,*

All this posed a serious problem for the late nineteenth-century governing classes. In the new world of the twentieth century—the American Civil War and the Franco-Prussian War had already demonstrated—international conflicts were going to be fought by mass national armies. Could the hundreds of thousands of able-bodied, loyal soldiers the mass armies required be obtained from an unpatriotic and stunted working class? This seemed an especially serious problem to the *fin-de-siècle* statesmen who heard repeated warnings about war as a natural law of history, the struggle for existence, and the 'survival of the fittest' from the Social-Darwinists—and who saw in Imperial Germany a 'national organism' determined to prove itself the fittest.

What was to be done? Many in England pointed to the 'state socialism' introduced by the German Chancellor Bismarck in the 'eighties. Bismarck's 'system,' constructed to win the support of all classes for the 'national' interest, had been inaugurated by the tariff of 1879, enacted to protect agrarian interests and to promote the growth of heavy industry. This tariff protection secured for Germany an iron and steel industry which was to outstrip British output by the turn of the century. Observers had also testified that the Bismarckian system had resulted in increased wages and greater employment for the German working class. In 1878, Bismarck had secured the passage of laws which outlawed the Social-Democrats and banned the socialist press, though the party could still contest elections. Growing social discontent had nonetheless resulted in the increase in the number of Social-Democrats in the Reichstag. Bismarck then embarked upon a social programme designed to undermine this growing German socialism. In 1883, Bismarck secured the passage of the Sickness Insurance Law; in 1884 and 1885, of Accident Insurance Laws; and finally in 1889, of an Old Age Insurance Law. The various features of Bismarck's programme became, successively, the goals of British social reformers—and of social-imperialists.[1]

1870-1914 (Oxford University Press, 1936); Max Beer, *A History of British Socialism* (London: Allen & Unwin, 1919-20); G. D. H. Cole, *A Short History of the British Working Class Movement, 1789-1947* (London: Allen & Unwin, 1952).

[1] See W. H. Dawson, *Bismarck and State Socialism; An Exposition of the Social and Economic Legislation of Germany since 1870* (London, 1890).

Social-imperialism was preached on other parts of the continent. In France, it had its exponents in Charles Maurras and
Georges Sorel; in Italy, Corradini and the socialist Labriola
espoused its doctrines; in Germany, it had a host of advocates.
Both German and Italian social-imperialism adopted Marxist
ideological concepts and terminology—inevitable in countries
where Marxism had made important gains among the working
class. The Germans and Italians described their countries as
'proletarian' nations, poor and over-populated, late arrivers on
the international scene, who had found most of the colonial
plums already in the possession of other nations. Just as the
socialists were urging the proletarians within each nation to
battle that nation's plutocratic capitalists if they wished to
solve the social problem, so the social-imperialists turned that
advice down national lines and urged war by the proletarian
nation—whether Germany or Italy—against the plutocratic
nations—usually Great Britain.[1]

Social-imperialism was designed to draw all classes together
in defence of the nation and empire and aimed to prove to the
least well-to-do class that its interests were inseparable from
those of the nation. It aimed at undermining the argument of
the socialists and demonstrating that, contrary to the Marxist
allegation, the workers *had* more to lose than their chains.

In his *The Economic Consequence of the Peace*, Keynes described
the economic structure of pre-1914 Europe:

'Europe was so organized socially and economically as to secure
the maximum accumulation of capital. . . . Society was so
framed as to throw a great part of the increased income into the
control of the class least likely to consume it.[2]

---

[1] Aspects of continental social-imperialism are discussed in: Neumann,
op. cit.; G. A. Borgese, *Goliath* (London: Gollancz, 1938); Gaudens
Megaro, *Mussolini in the Making* (London: Allen & Unwin, 1938);
W. C. Buthman, *The Rise of Integral Nationalism in France* (New
York, 1939); M. De Roux, *Charles Maurras et la nationalisme de
l'Action Française* (Paris, 1927); Richard Humphrey, *Georges Sorel,
Prophet Without Honor* (Cambridge, Mass., 1951); Ralph Bowen,
German Theories of the Corporative State (New York, 1947).
[2] John Maynard Keynes, *The Economic Consequences of the Peace*
(London: Macmillan, 1920), p. 16.

If the factory-owner had spent in wasteful fashion what he had accumulated, industrial progress would have been halted. But he did not play the part of the prodigal—nor did he forget the parable of the talents: he saved and he re-invested his savings to expand the industrial plant and, therefore, in the long run, the stock of commodities available for consumption. If this stock had been shared more equitably by the first generation in the factories, there would have been comparatively little to go about—and all of it would have been consumed. In effect, the first few of the factory generations were sacrificed in order to produce a larger stock of commodities to be shared in the future. By the end of the nineteenth century, there was, finally, enough produced so that the capitalist could respond to the demands of the proletarian Oliver Twists for 'more' without endangering investment capital. That the capitalist actually did so doomed the prophecies of Marx.

The Marxist theory of increasing misery was proving false and, most especially in the decade before 1914, the condition of the working class had much improved through most of Europe. The governments of Europe, during the decades before the war, had erected barriers against socialist internationalism by their programmes of social reform which gave the workers a further stake in national well-being. The Italian working class, to cite one example, which had attempted to sabotage the ill-fated Ethiopian War of 1896, joyously supported the successful war against Turkey to acquire Libya in 1911. One Socialist even described it as imperialism in the primary interest of the Italian working classes. What had intervened was a decade of Giolittian social reform, a system of national insurance, and a promise of universal suffrage, all of which had sapped the revolutionary ardour of Italian socialism.

A growing awareness of the immense popularity of imperialism among the British working classes had brought many politicians of both political parties, by the time of the Boer War, to share the view which Austen Chamberlain recorded in his journal during the first decade of the century. 'The democracy,' Chamberlain observed, 'want two things; imperialism and social reform.' The Conservative party was successful when—under Disraeli—it combined the two; its success ended when it failed to satisfy the aspirations of the working class in the matter of social reform. 'We can only win by combining them again,' Chamberlain had concluded.[1] Disraeli had 'combined' the two— he had called himself both a social reformer and an imperialist— but had made no attempt to integrate them. In the first decade of the twentieth century, several attempts were made in Great Britain not only to combine these ideals but at the same time to demonstrate their interdependence, to say that the realization of one was not possible without the realization of the other.

The dominant form of British social-imperialism was that of Joseph Chamberlain and the adherents of the programme of Tariff Reform and imperial preference. Bismarck had welded the policies of nationalism and social reform in an effort to 'dish' the socialists by the use, among other instruments, of protection. With this example at hand and mindful of the minor successes among the working class of their Fair Trade protectionist predecessors, the Tariff Reformers appealed for working class support on the grounds that the condition of the working man was dependent upon the prosperity of British industry which required tariff protection against foreign rivals and that only imperial preference could prevent the disintegration of the empire, whose unity, strength, and markets were essential to the welfare of the working class. Since the adoption of a pre-ferential system would mean a sacrifice in the form of higher food prices for the working man, the working man was offered 'compensation' in the form of more work at better pay and the promise of old-age pensions financed from tariff revenues. This was the social-imperial argument advocated by the bulk of the Unionist party from 1903 to 1912 and presented to the working man in many millions of leaflets and in many thousands of street-corner speeches.

The social-imperial system of Joseph Chamberlain and the Tariff Reform League served as a basis for the more abstract conceptions of others further removed from the hurly-burly of politics. Among these were Viscount Milner, who had served as British High Commissioner in South Africa during the Boer War; the noted economic historian and distinguished church-man, William Cunningham; W. J. Ashley, who held the chair of commerce at the newly established University of Birmingham;

[1] See Austen Chamberlain, *Politics from Inside* (London: Cassell, 1936), pp. 41-42.

and the economist and political geographer, H. J. Mackinder. All were Unionists and regarded the Chamberlain programme as the best political device to meet the new conditions of the twentieth century. The Chamberlain programme seemed to them the best immediate solution to such problems as the undermining of British industrial and commercial hegemony by foreign rivals, the impairment of key British industries, the loosening of imperial ties and the threatening dissolution of the empire, the challenge of German power, the menace of socialism and open class struggle, and the demand for social reform by a working class entering political maturity. Yet despite this substantial area of agreement, they all developed their theories and arguments in a highly individual manner.

There were socialists who shared much of the outlook and many of the goals of these Unionist social-imperialists, although they did not necessarily give detailed support to the Chamberlain programme. These 'imperial socialists'—some Marxists have called them 'social-chauvinists'—included the Fabian leaders George Bernard Shaw, Sidney and Beatrice Webb, and Clifford Sharp, the editor of the Fabian weekly *New Statesman*, established in 1913, and Robert Blatchford, the editor of the popular socialist weekly, *The Clarion*. The Fabians and Blatchford—nationalists, militarists, and imperialists—regarded the Cobdenite opponents of the social-imperialists as their principal enemies. Hostile to *laissez-faire* in all its phases, they found themselves in theoretical agreement with the tariff proposals of Chamberlain, although some distrust for the class motives of the Unionists' tariff and revenue-raising programmes, as well as their own commitment to the socialist organization of industry, made political support of the Chamberlain programme difficult. The Fabians—like Mackinder among the Tariff Reformers—regarded the setting of a national minimum for all citizens as a basis for imperial strength.

The programme of the Liberal Party constituted a rival species of social-imperialism, though less explicitly advocated as such by triumphant pre-war Liberalism. The Liberal programme of 1906-14 was certainly not that of the Cobdenite anti-imperialists. It was a combination of Radical social reform and imperialist foreign and military policy. The Liberal-Imperialist integration of imperialism and social reform had been outlined

during the early years of the century: in a word, it emphasized
the necessity for breeding an imperial race in Great Britain if the
Empire were to remain both British and strong. Representing
those interests which continued to be dependent upon Free
Trade, the Liberal-Imperialists offered—through the agency of
the Budget of 1909—to make available part of the fruits of this
'Free Trade imperialism' in exchange for continued working-
class support for the economic system which made such benefits
possible.

That imperialism and interest in social reform had become
deep and widespread in the decades before the war of 1914, is
proved by the three elections of the first decade of our century
—one in 1906 and two in 1910—in which both parties made
fever-pitched appeals based upon these motifs. A key issue in
each of these electoral campaigns was Tariff Reform's challenge
to Free Trade, and the interests committed to each trade policy
sought support on grounds that their programme would
strengthen the Empire and would best provide for needed social
reforms. Imperial preference was presented to the electorate as
a means of maintaining a colonial market essential for employment and a protective tariff was pictured as a device for providing revenues for social reform. Similarly, beneath the surface
of the social reform programme of the Liberals was the theme
of the need to breed an 'imperial race.' There were efforts upon
all political levels to demonstrate the interdependence of
imperialism and social reform, to show that each was essential
if the other were to be realized.

This social-imperial thinking of the period between the Boer
War and the war of 1914 was closely allied to the 'non-
Spencerian' Social-Darwinism of the 'nineties, as it was set
forth in the writings of Benjamin Kidd and, more especially, of
Karl Pearson. Although most social-imperialists were not
conscious manipulators of Social-Darwinist arguments and
phrases, the link was substantial. In Karl Pearson's Social-
Darwinism, we can see a fairly fully-developed 'scientific' social-
imperialism.

II

SOCIAL-DARWINISM:
BENJAMIN KIDD AND KARL PEARSON

> This seems the appropriate moment to lay bare the sophism
> of a certain school of English sociologists which has entered
> into the very bones of the nation. 'Nature shows us,' say they,
> 'that in this world-struggle the strongest only will survive
> and flourish at the expense of the weaker neighbour.' The
> English people are steeped in this doctrine, which they believe
> to be in strict keeping with the latest discoveries of science,
> especially with the latest theories of the great English
> thinkers, such as Darwin and his followers, which, above all,
> they feel to be in keeping with the temperament of the race.
> It is this doctrine which has really created the Imperialist
> frame of mind in the nation. . . .
>   VICTOR BÉRARD, 1906

Herbert Spencer, a social-evolutionist before Darwin's *Origin
of Species*, had originally based his views entirely on Lamarckian evolution. After 1859, he added Darwin's 'natural selection'
to his armory of ideas—and even bestowed upon it the description which it was to bear most frequently, 'the survival of the
fittest.'[1] Spencer was a Liberal—a Radical and an individualist.
He employed the Darwinian theory to supplement the Malthu-
sian argument of the classical economists, to prove that the
individualistic competitive society of Victorian England had been
ordained by nature and was the sole guarantor of progress.[2]
This application of Darwinism to society which saw the struggle
for existence as the economic competition between individuals
within a society soon found a rival in another view of social

[1] See Herbert Spencer, *The Man Versus the State* (London: Watts,
1892), pp. 67-8. See excerpt from letter of A. R. Wallace to Charles
Darwin, July 2, 1866 and Darwin's reply, in Francis Darwin, ed.,
The Life and Letters of Charles Darwin (London: J. Murray, 1887),
III, pp. 45-7.

[2] Spencer, *op. cit.*, pp. 65-72; F. W. Headley, a prominent zoologist,
maintained the view that scientific Darwinism made socialism
impossible in his *Darwinism and Modern Socialism* (London, 1909);
(see especially pp. 300, 308-9, for references to Pearson's socialism).

evolution. Was it not as reasonable to view progress as the result of an evolutionary struggle between groups of men, between tribes or nations or races, the fittest group predominating in the ceaseless warfare which constituted the evolutionary process? Darwin himself had anticipated this view, as had Walter Bagehot, but individualistic England had preferred the Social-Darwinism of economic competition outlined by Herbert Spencer.[1] By the end of the nineteenth century, however, the non-Spencerian view was finding more and more favour as a justification of British imperialism.[2]

The controversy between what might be called 'internal' and 'external' Social-Darwinism actually ante-dated the Darwinian hypothesis. Certain mid-Victorian opponents of the 'dismal science' of political economy—Thomas Carlyle, Charles Kingsley, and Charles Dickens, for example—had opposed the stern individualism of the Radicals which, they felt, resulted in the brutalization of the British working man, but at the same time these critics of internal *laissez-faire* were unbendingly severe in their attitude toward 'inferior' races outside the national pale. Carlyle's racist tract, 'Essay on the Nigger Question,'[3] in which he defended slavery, written ten years before Darwin's *Origin*, can be regarded as 'premature' external social-Darwinism, as can his position in the celebrated Eyre case, during the period between 1865 and 1868. On this occasion, Carlyle and Ruskin, Kingsley, and Dickens all insisted that it was not worth considering the injustices perpetrated against Jamaican 'niggers' as long as English working men continued to groan under the oppression of the factory system. On the other hand, the Cobdenite Radicals—including John Stuart Mill, Darwin, Spencer, Huxley and John Bright—good Malthu-

[1] See David G. Ritchie, *Darwinism and Politics* (New York, 1889), pp. 7-8, 45, *passim*; Robert Mackintosh, *From Comte to Benjamin Kidd; The Appeal to Biology or Evolution for Human Guidance* (New York, 1899), *passim*.

[2] See Friedrich Brie, *Der Einfluss der Lehren Darwins auf den britischen Imperialismus* (Freiburg in Baden, 1927); Pearson is discussed on pp. 14-15; Victor Bérard, *British Imperialism and Commercial Supremacy* (London, 1906), p. 279.

[3] Thomas Carlyle, 'The Nigger Question,' [1849] in *Critical and Miscellaneous Essays* (London, 1901), pp. 348-383.

sians and internal Social-Darwinists—took for granted the necessity of the factory system and the internal economic struggle but protested the brutal suppression of the Jamaican coloured men by the British Governor Eyre.[1]

By the end of the century, with the growing acceptance of evolutionary concepts, the debate was being waged under auspices which Carlyle, a disbeliever in Darwinian evolution, would never have accepted. Yet the arguments of the two sides were much the same. In England, internal Social-Darwinism, drawing sustenance from the doctrines of *laissez-faire*, was challenged by the new collectivist spirit of the 'eighties. The state had received a new meaning and importance at the hands of the Neo-Hegelian philosophers Green and Bradley. Free Trade, the bastion of Radical cosmopolitanism, was threatened in the 'eighties by the emergence of the rival notion of a protected national economy. In the battle between social-imperialism and Cobdenite liberalism, we will find that external Social-Darwinism provided one of the ideological foundations of social-imperialism while internal Social-Darwinism was a bulwark of Liberalism. The two leading exponents of British external Social-Darwinism were Benjamin Kidd and Karl Pearson, both of whom took up the position of Ruskin and Carlyle and asserted that England's first concern—if she meant to maintain her world position—was with the welfare of her own people at the expense, if need be, of other, 'inferior' peoples.

BENJAMIN KIDD

Benjamin Kidd was a minor civil servant in the Inland Revenue department when the publication of his *Social Evolution*, in 1894, made him famous. The book was a financial success and Kidd was able to resign his position and to devote himself exclusively to writing. His published writings, during the following twenty

---

[1] See John Stuart Mill, *Autobiography* (London: 1908), pp. 169–71; J. A. Froude, *Thomas Carlyle; A History of His Life in London, 1834-81* (London, 1902), II, pp. 351–354, 390; E. T. Cook and A. Wedderburn, editors, *The Works of John Ruskin* (London: Allen & Unwin, 1905), XVIII, pp. 550-554; Leonard Huxley, *Life and Letters of Thomas Henry Huxley* (New York, 1901), I, pp. 300-305.

years, were few in number and largely repeated his views of
1894; thus he remained a man of one book. The success of this
book, however, was enough to make him one of the leading
figures in British sociology and to place him, for a time, in the
forefront of political life.

In *Social Evolution*, Kidd had attempted to provide a central
conception which would unify the various social laws and which
would even predict the future. Spencer had attempted to create
such a unifying conception on behalf of 'evolutionary science' but,
Kidd insisted, he had failed signally. The Marxists, on the other
hand, whom Kidd regarded as his principal enemy, had just such
a unifying synthesis and a most dangerous one. The new
socialist religion was spreading and 'the worker is beginning to
discover that what he has lost as an individual, he has gained as
a class; and that by organization he may obtain the power of
meeting his masters on more equal terms.' 'Even national lines
of demarcation are disappearing,' Kidd declared. 'Society is
being organized by classes into huge battalions, the avowed
object of which is the making of war on each other.'[1] How had
this happened? Kidd placed the blame upon the internal Social-
Darwinism of the Spencer school:

'The evolutionist may be convinced that what is called the
exploitation of the masses, is but the present-day form of the
rivalry of life which he has watched from the beginning, and that
the sacrifice of some in the cause of the future interests of the
whole social organism is a necessary feature of our progress. But
this is no real argument addressed to those who most naturally
object to be exploited and sacrificed, and who in our modern
societies are entrusted with power to give political effect to
their objections.'

What then was the remedy? Certainly something had to be done,
given not only the sorry plight of the working classes (Kidd
cited the conclusions of a recently completed survey of London's
poor by Charles Booth) but the explosive fact that these
impoverished groups were in possession of political power.
Kidd's conclusion was that it had now become vitally necessary
to subordinate individual interests to those of the group.[2]

[1] Benjamin Kidd, *Social Evolution* (London, 1894), pp. 2-3, 11.
[2] *Ibid.*, pp. 67, 69-70, 74.

Kidd did not repudiate internal Social-Darwinism entirely, however. He saw the internal struggle for existence in a special light. The whole direction of social development in the nineteenth century, he explained, had been 'to raise the rivalry of existence to the highest degree of efficiency as a cause of progress.' How had this happened? The granting of the vote to virtually everyone had brought a 'great body of the people' into the 'rivalry of life' on virtually 'equal terms', on 'a footing of equality of opportunity.' The future had to 'complete the process of evolution in progress, by eventually bringing all the people into the rivalry of life, not only on a footing of political equality, *but on conditions of equal social opportunities.*' Kidd saw this process as already under way. Legislation, whose characteristic feature was 'to raise the position of the lower classes *at the expense of the wealthier classes,*' had already been passed. Spencerian individualists had fought against such state interference but in vain. In the future, the state would continue to intervene into the affairs of the nation. Such future moves as the establishment of the eight-hour day, the graduated income tax, and the provision of education for all would tend 'ultimately to place the workers more on a footing of equality in the rivalry of life with those above them.'[1]

Was the struggle for existence, upon which the improvement of the race depended, doomed to disappear? No, there was a 'rivalry of nationalities,' a struggle between different races. External Social-Darwinism would replace the internal competition of *laissez-faire* England. In this struggle, Kidd believed, the Anglo-Saxon race had a good chance to triumph. Kidd vaunted the Anglo-Saxons: 'In the North American Continent, in the plains of Australia, in New Zealand, and South Africa,' he wrote, 'the representatives of this vigorous and virile race are at last in full possession.' With all its faults, the Anglo-Saxon race had 'honestly endeavoured to carry humanitarian principles into its dealings with inferior peoples.' This was, indeed, a characteristic of the race. The races of Europe had different qualities. For example, the Celts, the stock to which the French belong, had high intellectual powers: the French had a 'light, yet agile and athletic grasp of principles and ideas.' The leading mental

---

[1] *Ibid.*, pp. 165, 227, 233-234.

C

characteristic of the Teutons, on the other hand, the stock to which both the Germans and the English belonged, was 'painstaking, conscientious endeavour.' The English and the Germans consequently had a higher 'social-efficiency' than the French, a greater sense of social discipline. Hence the string of defeats suffered by France at the hands of England during the eighteenth century and her resounding defeat by Germany in 1870.

What were the qualities which led a nation to greatness? Kidd was convinced that they were not of an intellectual order. Such qualities as 'reverence,' 'great mental energy, resolution, enterprise, powers of prolonged and cencentrated application, and a sense of simple-minded and single-minded devotion to conception of duty' were decisive in the struggle for existence. Without these, 'high intellectual development may even lower social efficiency to a dangerous degree, and so contribute to the decided worsting, in the evolution which is proceeding, of the people possessing it.' Reason and intellect were Kidd's *bêtes noires*. One of his major objections to socialism was its 'rational' foundation. Reason—and socialism—were entirely self-seeking, concerned with self-gratification and paying no heed to the future interests of the race. Kidd explained the stability of the French birth-rate to a 'self-assertive rationalism' which had resulted in voluntary birth control in complete disregard of the race and he condemned this 'racial self-effacement.'[1]

Only a super-rational sanction could justify the subordination of the immediate interests of the present to the larger interests of the future. Kidd was convinced that only religion provided that sanction. Religious impulses had set altruistic, humanitarian sentiments into being. Socialism aimed 'at exploiting' those sentiments 'in the interests of the existing generation of individuals,' rather than at harnessing them as 'a developmental force operating largely in the interests of future generations.' Marxism was really as '*anti*-social' as individualism, since both represented 'the extreme logical expression of rationalistic protest by the individual against the subordination of his interests to the process of progressive development society is undergoing from generation to generation.' Religion was

[1] *Ibid.*, pp. 45-46, pp. 277-287.

opposed to 'the materialistic socialism of Marx' as well as to individualism.[1]

Kidd had selected as his chief enemies both individualism and socialism, recognizing both as inherently subversive of the foundations of the edifice of external Social-Darwinism which he had erected. Much of his book was in the form of a running debate with the individualism of Herbert Spencer and Kidd's final un-Spencerian conclusion was that 'it is this quality of social efficiency that nations and peoples are being continually, and for the most part unconsciously, pitted against each other in the complex rivalry of life.'[2] Kidd's social-imperialism was still tentative and hesitating. His successors were to venture far beyond. But in his charting of the future course of social reform and the conflict between the 'races' of Europe, in his raising of the banner of social efficiency, he anticipated much which the next twenty years would bring to England.[3]

KARL PEARSON: SOCIALIST AND DARWINIST

In the mid-'seventies of the last century, evolution was a principal subject of debate in Imperial Germany, as indeed it had been in most of the civilized nations of Europe since the publication of Darwin's *Origin of Species* in 1859. The leader of the German opposition to Darwinism was Rudolf Virchow, the formulator of the cellular theory. Virchow employed a wide variety of arguments in his attack upon the evolutionists. In one of his addresses, in September 1877, he made use of what was regarded by his friends as well as his opponents as an *argumentum ad hominem*. Virchow asked his audience, in a Germany where socialism was about to be outlawed, to 'picture to yourself the theory of descent as it already exists in the brain of a socialist.' 'Ay, gentlemen,' he continued, 'it may seem laughable to many, but it is in truth very serious, and I only hope that the theory of descent may not entail on us all the horrors which similar theories have actually brought upon neighbouring countries.' 'At all times,' Virchow concluded, 'this theory, if it is logically

[1] *Ibid.*, p. 241.   [2] *Ibid.*, p. 327.
[3] See Benjamin Kidd, *Individualism and After* (Oxford, 1908), pp. 20, 24-5, 29, and *passim*; and *The Control of the Tropics* (New York, 1898), pp. 17, 58, 59-60, and *passim*.

carried out to the end, has an uncommonly suspicious aspect.'[1]

The leading German Darwinist, Ernst Haeckel, defended the theory of evolution against Virchow's charge. He suggested that it was impossible to imagine 'this English hypothesis' in the brain of a socialist, since it was 'aristocratic, certainly not democratic, and least of all socialist' in concept.[2] Darwin himself commented on the subject in a letter, written in December 1879: 'What a foolish idea,' he exclaimed, 'seems to prevail in Germany on the connection between Socialism and Evolution through Natural Selection.'[3] Some years later, Huxley pointed to the haziness of Virchow's suggestion. Huxley wrote that he had tried 'to comply' but that he had 'utterly failed to call up the dread image,' adding that he supposed that this was so 'because I do not sufficiently sympathise with the Socialists.'[4]

Studying in Germany during the period when echoes of the Virchow-Haeckel debate could still be heard in academic circles was a young Englishman who was to realize in his subsequent writings and activities Virchow's nightmare of Darwinism in the brain of a socialist. Karl Pearson—who was to make an international reputation as the author of *The Grammar of Science*—had studied at the University College School and had been Third Wrangler in the Mathematical Tripos of 1879 at Cambridge and was now completing his education at the Universities of Heidelberg and Berlin. At Berlin, Pearson attended lectures on Darwinism by the celebrated Du Bois Reymond and was greatly impressed. He appears also to have come into contact with the ideas of the two leaders of German socialism—Marx and Lassalle—and to have been similarly persuaded of their truth. When he returned to England to become a barrister like his father before him, he was, to judge from his writings of the period, both a convinced evolutionist and a fervent socialist. More that this he had already begun to merge his two faiths into a rather special variety of Social-Darwinism.

[1] Quoted in Ernst Haeckel, *Freedom in Science and Teaching* (London, 1892), pp. 89-90; see also G. C. Stabling, *Sozialismus und Darwinismus* (New York, 1879), p. 3 and *passim*.

[2] Haeckel, *op cit.*, p. 92.

[3] Quoted in Darwin, *op. cit.*, III, pp. 236–7.

[4] T. H. Huxley in Preface to Haeckel, *op. cit.*, p. xix.

Young Pearson, once more in England, proceeded with his study and practice of the law. But the law seemed rather narrow to a young man with wide interests and through the efforts of his friends, and with his success in the Cambridge Mathematical Tripos sustaining him, he was offered and persuaded to accept the Goldsmid Professorship of Applied Mathematics and Mechanics at University College, London, in 1884. In his new post, Pearson determined to employ his mathematics to 'prove' Darwinian theory correct. In the course of these efforts, he played a leading role in creating the subject of biometrics— statistical biology—and helped to establish, in 1901, the journal devoted to the subject, *Biometrika*. During the 'eighties, Pearson also lectured at London working-men's and socialist clubs on the ideas of Marx and Lassalle.[1]

Pearson's socialism—as revealed in his early lectures—was not easily classifiable. He appears to have been an adherent of Marxist economics. In an address to London working men during the 'eighties, he spoke of Marx as 'the great economist'[2] and defended the labour theory of value, which had already been brought under considerable attack. Pearson even accepted Marx's view of surplus value—although he preferred to call the concept 'surplus labour'—which was at the heart of the Marxist argument concerning the exploitation of labour.[3] He was full of Marxist-sounding phrases and modes of thought. For example, he asserted that he looked toward 'the failure of the old economic system, owing to the sweeping industrial and commercial changes which are in progress';[4] and he believed that 'our legislation, our government, has been a scarcely disguised warfare of classes.'[5] Yet, if he agreed with much of Marxian economic analysis, he departed from the Marxists upon the matter of goals and programme of action.

[1] Details of Pearson's life have been obtained through several sources: E. S. Pearson, *Karl Pearson, An Appreciation of Some Aspects of His Life and Work* (Cambridge University Press, 1938); G. Udney Yule and L. N. G. Filon, 'Karl Pearson, 1857-1936,' in *Obituary Notices of Fellows of the Royal Society* (London, 1936), II, No. 5, pp. 73-110; *D. N. B., 1931-1940*, pp. 681-4.
[2] Karl Pearson, 'The Moral Basis of Socialism' (1887), in *The Ethic of Free Thought* (London, 1901), p. 325.
[3] *Ibid.*, pp. 325-8, 318.   [4] *Ibid.*, p. 310.   [5] *Ibid.*, p. 306.

Pearson denounced certain socialists for teachings which he regarded as 'not only very foolish, but extremely harmful.' 'So far from aiding true Socialism' the teaching of these socialists 'stirs up class-hatred, and instead of bringing classes together, it raises a barrier of bitterness and hostility between them:'[1] This denunciation of class struggle and eulogy of class unity was at the opposite pole of Marxism. Pearson also displayed a most un-Marxist opposition to revolution. 'You may accept it as a primary law of history,' he said, '*that no great change ever occurs with a leap,* no great social reconstruction, which will permanently benefit any class of the community, is ever brought about by a revolution.'[2] What ought a socialist to do then? A 'true Socialist must be superior to class interests. He must look beyond his own class to the wants and habits of society at large.'[3] What method can he employ? He must educate the governing class toward a 'higher social morality.'[4] Pearson also rejected working class internationalism in favour of patriotism. He was very much a national socialist.[5]

Karl Pearson's use of Marxist analysis directed toward such a non-Marxist goal as class harmony and his opposition to revolutionary change and internationalism bring to mind the views of the German school of *Katheder-Sozialisten,* the Socialists of the Chair, who, under the leadership of Gustav Schmoller, helped to construct Bismarck's social programme.[6] It is entirely possible that Pearson had come into contact with the thinking of this group while he studied in Germany. The moderate character of Pearson's 'socialist' programme was also similar to theirs. Pearson urged the nationalization of land and capital by the conversion of all freeholds into leaseholds of up to 100 years, a method he believed would lead to little real injury to the present

---

[1] Karl Pearson, 'Socialism in Theory and Practice' (1884), in *op. cit.,* p. 345.

[2] *Ibid.,* p. 347.   [3] *Ibid.,* p. 350.

[4] *Ibid.,* p. 346; see also Karl Pearson, *The Grammar of Science* (London, 1900), p. 368.

[5] For Pearson on patriotism, see Karl Pearson, *National Life from the Standpoint of Science* (London, 1905), p. 53. Lecture delivered November 1900.

[6] For the *Katheder-Sozialisten,* see J. A. Schumpeter, *History of Economic Analysis* (London, 1954), pp. 800-24.

owners.[1] Pearson may also have picked up in Germany the outlook of the group toward the state, a view which was quite alien to the dominant English liberalism of Pearson's day—and even to the thinking of contemporary English socialism.

Pearson urged 'veneration for the State,' a veneration which he asserted 'has been stifled by a not unjustifiable contempt for existing government.'[2] He posited as the 'moral basis' of his new socialist society, not religion, but a 'rational motive for conduct' —'service to Society.' Whatever was social was moral; the anti-social was immoral.[3] In effect, Pearson was making the state the focus of his morality, of his religion, of his conception of socialism: 'If the welfare of society be the touchstone of moral action, then respect for the State—the State as *res publica*, as commonweal—ought to be the most sacred principle of the new movement.'[4] This was a doctrine which he regarded as of decisive importance. Pearson insisted that an 'offence against the State ought to be looked upon as a far graver matter than the offence against the individual.'[5] 'The legislation or measures of police, to be taken against the immoral and anti-social minority,' he continued, 'will form the political realization of Socialism.'[6] Most shocking to individualist-minded Englishmen was Pearson's view that 'Socialists have to inculcate that spirit which would give offenders against the State short shrift and the nearest lamp-post.' 'Every citizen,' he concluded, 'must learn to say with Louis XIV, "*L'état c'est moi!*"'[7]

Karl Pearson's socialism was the keystone of his Social-Darwinism, a very different doctrine in his hands than that of the first of the English Social-Darwinists, Herbert Spencer. As early as the 'eighties, Karl Pearson was finding his way to his non-Spencerian Social-Darwinism. In later years, he described his goal to have been a proof that 'Socialism, despite Häckel, despite Herbert Spencer, *is* consonant with the whole teaching of modern Science,' by which he meant the science of evolution.[8] In 1887, he told an assemblage of working men of 'the course of

[1] Pearson, 'Socialism in Theory and Practice,' pp. 351-2.
[2] Pearson, 'The Moral Basis of Socialism,' p. 306.
[3] *Ibid.*, pp. 304-5.   [4] *Ibid.*, p. 308.   [5] *Ibid.*, p. 307.
[6] *Ibid.*, p. 311.   [7] *Ibid.*, pp. 307-8.   [8] *Ibid.*, p. 305.

evolution and the struggle of group against group'[1] and linked his view of the struggle for existence with socialism: 'To give all a like possibility of usefulness,' he asserted, 'to measure reward by the efficiency and magnitude of socially valuable work, is surely to favour the growth of the fittest within the group, and the survival of the fittest group in the world-contest of societies.'[2]

But this was rather tame offspring from the awesome union of socialism and Darwinism concerning which Virchow had darkly prophesied. The maturing of Pearson's thought was to prove less unworthy of Virchow's fears. In 1894, Pearson wrote an article for the *Fortnightly Review* in which he defended socialism against the attacks of certain Darwinists. These Darwinists—in particular, Spencer and Benjamin Kidd, to whose *Social-Evolution*, published some weeks before, this article was a response—had suggested that, in trying to limit the struggle between members of a group, socialism would endanger the forward march of progress. This was nonsense, Pearson proclaimed. It was not the intra-group struggle but pure 'physical selection'—disease, climate, strain—which weeded out the unfit within a society. Under socialism, physical selection would operate even more strongly since all would be obliged to work for their living and weaklings would no longer be protected by inheritances. The most important biological mechanism to insure progress was the 'extra-group' struggle between nations. If competition within the group were not severely limited, 'social stability' would be endangered, and, in case of war, 'we should be crushed' because 'we have proceeded on the assumption that it is better to have a few prize cattle among innumerable lean kine than a decently-bred and properly-fed herd.'[3]

In November 1900, Karl Pearson delivered a lecture in which he presented the first full-blooded exposition of his Social-Darwinism. England was then in the midst of the Boer War and Pearson was filled with patriotic feeling and enthusiasm for combat. He began his talk with a paean of praise for the struggle for existence, a struggle which meant 'suffering, intense

[1] *Ibid.*, p. 303; also see Pearson, *Grammar of Science*, p. 364.

[2] Pearson, 'The Moral Basis of Socialism,' p. 305.

[3] Karl Pearson, 'Socialism and Natural Selection,' in *The Chances of Death and Other Studies in Evolution* (London, 1897), I, p. 113; see also pp. 107-30, *passim*.

suffering,' but which was the mechanism of all progress. 'This dependence of progress on the survival of the fitter race, terribly black as it may seem to some of you,' he continued, 'gives the struggle for existence its redeeming features; it is the fiery crucible out of which comes the finer metal.' When wars cease, 'mankind will no longer progress' for 'there will be nothing to check the fertility of inferior stock; the relentless law of heredity will not be controlled and guided by natural selection.'[1]

Pearson accused the early Darwinists, like Spencer and Haeckel and Huxley, of having 'obscured' the issue when they 'painted evolution as the survival of the fittest *individual* and spoke of his struggle against his fellows.' Man was a 'gregarious animal' whose safety depended upon his 'social instinct.'[2] The truly elevating struggle was not that between individuals but 'the struggle of tribe against tribe, of race against race.' Spencer and Huxley had forgotten 'that the herd exists owing to its social instincts, and that human sympathy and racial and national feelings are strong natural forces controlling individual conduct', stronger, indeed, than economic forces emerging from the laws of supply and demand.[3] Pearson upheld 'the scientific view of a nation,' a 'natural history view of mankind.' A nation, he said, was 'an organized whole,' which was 'kept up to a high pitch of external efficiency by contest, chiefly by way of war with inferior races, and with equal races by the struggle for trade-routes and for the sources of raw material and of food supply.'[4]

Pearson's socialism found its full place in the compound. The nation, in order for it to be properly organized for struggle, had to be a *'homogeneous* whole,' not 'a mixture of superior and inferior races,' he said, writing as a good nationalist, and equally important, 'we must not have class differences and wealth differences so great within the community that we lose the sense of common interest.' 'No tribe of men work together,' Pearson maintained, 'unless the tribal interest dominates the personal and individual interest at all points where they come

[1] Karl Pearson, *National Life*, pp. 26-7.
[2] *Ibid.*, p. 49.   [3] *Ibid.*, p. 55.
[4] *Ibid.*, p. 46; see also Karl Pearson, *The Function of Science in the Modern State* (Cambridge, 1919); pp. 2-8, 14. Originally published in 1902.

into conflict.'[1] Class oppression could be disastrous in case of war since 'the oppressed' may feel that they 'will hardly get worse terms from a new master.'[2]

The struggle, furthermore, was of decisive importance, most especially for the working classes. Those who would give up the fight were reminded that 'the daily bread of our millions of workers depends on their having somebody to work for,' that 'our strength depends . . . upon our colonies' which were only maintained 'by respect for the present power of our empire,' that if 'war or competition' diminished British trade, 'it is the Lancashire operative who feels the pinch.' 'The day when we cease to hold our own among the nations,' Pearson proclaimed, 'will be the day of catastrophe for our workers at home.'[3] As early as the 'eighties, when he addressed the London working men, Pearson's message had been the same. 'Some of you may be indifferent to the great empire of England,' he told the working men, 'but let me assure you that, small as in some cases is the comfort of the English working classes, it is on the average large compared with that of an inferior race. . . .'[4] In 1894, he wrote in a fortnightly journal: 'No thoughtful socialist, so far as I am aware, would object to cultivate Uganda *at the expense of its present occupiers* if Lancashire were starving. Only he would have done this directly and consciously, and not by way of missionaries and exploiting companies.'[5]

In a conclusion and summation of his position, Pearson repeated his Darwinist assertion that 'science realizes that the nation is an organized whole, in continual struggle with its competitors.' 'You cannot get a strong and effective nation,' admonished the socialist Pearson, 'if many of its stomachs are half fed and many of its brains untrained.'[6] It was the duty of 'the true statesmen' to 'treat class needs and group cries from the standpoint of the efficiency of the herd at large.' The duty of a nation's leaders was 'to lessen, if not to suspend, the internal struggle, that the nation may be strong externally.'[7] 'This tendency to social organization, always prominent in progressive

[1] Pearson, *National Life*, pp. 50-1.
[2] *Ibid.*, pp. 49-50.   [3] *Ibid.*, pp. 47-8.
[4] Pearson, 'Socialism in Theory and Practice,' pp. 337-8.
[5] Pearson, 'Socialism and Natural Selection,' p. 111.
[6] Pearson, *National Life*, p. 54.   [7] *Ibid*, p. 56.

communities, may be termed, in the best and widest sense of the word, *Socialism.'*[1] It would be best, Pearson came to feel, to have his socialist state under the control of a dictator, free from the 'bias of class interest'; for the great danger in a democracy was that the leaders might attempt to secure 'the intra-racial dominance of a caste.' But however desirable a dictatorship might be in the guidance of the race, the selection of a dictator might prove too difficult and therefore democracy, although 'terribly cumbersome' might be the 'best practical solution,' Pearson reluctantly concluded.[2]

Pearson's union of socialism and Darwinism was a sword of two edges. Not only was the struggle—or at any rate the fruits of successful struggle—necessary for the welfare of the working classes, as Pearson told the working men, but the nation's leaders, he asserted, ought to recognize that unless class differences were substantially eliminated, unless the working classes were strong, healthy, and well trained, Britian could not succeed in this struggle for existence. This double warning appeared to call for the revival of a people's imperialism, under the leadership of a warrior-chieftain, and grounded upon a more equal sharing of the plunder.

As heady a drink as Karl Pearson's Social-Darwinism was, thus far most of its elements differ more in degree (though this cannot be underestimated) than in essential character from the view of other Social-Darwinists on the Continent or even in England, from, for example, Benjamin Kidd, whose *Social Evolution*, we have seen, Pearson had condemned. Kidd, too, an imperialist, a nationalist and a racist, though of milder degree, was disturbed about the class-divisive tactics of 'certain' socialists and concerned about readying the nation for conflict with other nations. Kidd, too, although much opposed to socialism, had spoken of the need for social-efficiency, for the improvement of the condition of the lower classes, for the subordination of individual goals to those of the entire society. In all fairness, it should be noted that Kidd's brew was heavily watered compared with Pearson's. Furthermore, Kidd was a traditionalist, a devout Christian. Pearson had damned all forms of irrationalism, especially Christian 'mythology,' and had virtually deified the

[1] Pearson, *Grammar of Science*, p. 365.
[2] Pearson, *Function of Science*, pp. 14-15.

state, making it the source of all morality. While Kidd had urged a return to the traditional, conservative idea of the state and had condemned the *laissez-faire* state of Spencer, it would have been impossible for him to have accepted Pearson's state where offenders were hung at the nearest lamp-post, or the principle of dictatorship. Nor, not being a 'socialist,' would he have suggested the virtually complete elimination of the intra-group struggle in favour of the extra-group struggle. In these matters, Pearson's 'socialism' might have been a differentiating factor.[1] There was yet a further step to be taken by Pearson, a step which was to sharply separate him from Kidd and other Social-Darwinists.

While Pearson had adapted his socialism to what might be called external Social-Darwinism, that which concerned itself with the struggle between races and nations, was this not a comparatively simple task? Other Social-Darwinists who were not socialists, we have seen, had also proclaimed the necessity of improving the condition of the lower classes in order to make them more efficient soldiers in time of war. Pearson was to spend the greater part of his mature life in the adaptation of his socialism to Spencerian or internal Social-Darwinism. Pearson, we recall, had berated the older evolutionists for emphasizing this internal struggle at the expense of the external struggle. He had never suggested that the internal struggle was not valid from a scientific point of view, was not in its way essential to progress. The problem was how to limit intra-group competition and still insure the progress which resulted from such competition. Pearson was to adapt Spencer's competitive and highly individualistic economic struggle of the free market to the needs and methods of his socialist state.

In the accomplishment of this task, Pearson was associated with the famous Victorian biologist—and a cousin of Charles Darwin—Francis Galton. Galton had become convinced that heredity was of greater significance than environment in determining individual characteristics and that action could be

---

[1] Pearson levelled an attack on Kidd's belief that religion was a necessary basis for ethics in Karl Pearson, *Reaction! A Criticism of Mr Balfour's Attack on Rationalism* (London, 1895), p. 6.

taken to regulate heredity.[1] His views did not receive much attention until the late 'eighties when the German biologist, August Weismann, published a series of papers which seriously questioned the widely-held Lamarckian view that characteristics acquired by an individual during his lifetime could be transmitted to his progeny and which espoused the doctrine of the immutability of germ plasm. Weismann's papers attracted widespread attention and provoked Herbert Spencer, who had based much of his sociology upon the inheritance of acquired characteristics, to earnest debate. Lamarckianism was at the root of Spencer's belief in an inevitable progress as a result of constant improvement of the species, generation by generation.[2] The adherents of Weismann and Galton insisted, on the other hand, that no man could be inherently more intelligent than his progenitors, that each generation had to be re-educated. Whereas liberals had urged the importance of environment, and hence of social reforms to improve the environment, conservatives who had opposed these reforms were delighted by the new doctrine's emphasis on the limited efficacy of environmental improvement when seen against the limitations imposed by inborn characteristics.[3]

Galton was convinced that the only way of assuring continued progress was by the science of 'eugenics'—a word he himself had coined. By the application of eugenic methods, Galton suggested, it would be possible to assure the England of the future of a population healthy and strong and intelligent, rather than sickly, weak, and incompetent. What was involved was 'the national efficiency of future generations,' and to secure this end Galton urged the formation of local associations to encourage pride in worthy stock and to promote eugenic principles.[4]

---

[1] His first book on eugenics was published in 1883. Francis Galton, *Inquiries into Human Faculty and its Development* (London, 1883).

[2] See August Weismann, *Essays on Heredity and Kindred Biological Problems* (Oxford, 1889), Vol. I, pp. 165-248, and *passim*; Herbert Spencer, *A Rejoinder to Professor Weismann* (New York, 1894), pp. 27, 29, and *passim*.

[3] See the work of an early adherent of these views, John Berry Haycraft, *Darwinism and Race Progress* (London, 1895), pp. 19-43, 54-7, 170, and *passim*.

[4] Sir Francis Galton, *Essays in Eugenices* (London, 1909), pp. 108-9.

Galton, in fact, proclaimed that eugenics had to be 'introduced into the national conscience, like a new religion.' Eugenics had, indeed, Galton insisted, 'strong claims to become an orthodox religious tenet of the future, for Eugenics co-operates with the workings of Nature by securing that humanity shall be represented by the fittest races.'[1] Galton, like Pearson, was, in positivist fashion, proclaiming the religion of science. Once sufficient information had been obtained, 'a "Jehad," or Holy War' would be declared 'against customs and prejudices that impair the physical and moral qualities of our race,'[2] Galton asserted. Then it would be possible to take action to encourage in every way possible procreation on the part of fitter stocks and discourage the procreation of the unfit. Galton wrote of the compilation of a 'golden-book' of the eugenically fit, the issuance of eugenic certificates, the financial support of the poor but eugenically favoured by the wealthy, and every kind of discouragement to child-bearing by the unfit. Galton, no socialist, confined his practical programme largely to the gathering and publicizing of eugenic data.[3]

How was the information to be gathered? More and more, Francis Galton looked towards Karl Pearson to perform this task. During the last decade of his life, Galton worked closely with Pearson. Pearson had been in the chair when Galton delivered, in 1904, his important address on eugenics to leading men in all fields of British intellectual life under the auspices of the Sociological Society.[4] Already it was bruited about that the old man thought of Pearson as his successor. In October 1904, Galton offered the University of London £1,500 for a three-year study of 'National Eugenics,' which was defined by the grant as 'the study of the agencies under social control that may improve or impair the racial qualities of future generations either physically or mentally.'[5] At Galton's death in 1911, his

---

[1] *Ibid.*, p. 42; see also pp. 68-70.   [2] *Ibid.*, p. 99.

[3] See C. P. Blacker, *Eugenics, Galton and After* (London: Duckworth, 1952), pp. 103-19. Galton, a product of mid-Victorian liberalism, appears to have had little contact with socialism although he was not antipathetic to the doctrine. See *ibid.*, pp. 94-6, 138-9, 295.

[4] See the Sociological Society, *Sociological Papers* (London, 1905), Vol. I (1904), pp. 45-50.

[5] Quoted in Yule and Filon, *op. cit.*, p. 77.

will created a Galton Professorship of Eugenics at the University of London and designated Karl Pearson as the first occupant of that chair, a chair he held until 1933.

There was certainly sufficient evidence in Pearson's earlier writings of his interests in the field of eugenics, a subject with which the last part of his life was entirely occupied; these early writings yield anticipations of views about matters of eugenic concern which already went far beyond Galton, and of methods, too, which appeared more extreme than those of the founder of eugenics. In a lecture on 'The Woman's Question' in 1885, he asserted that 'those nations which have been most reproductive have, on the whole, been the ruling nations in the world's history,' adding that a 'strongly developed sexual instinct may accordingly be a condition for race permanence.' On the issue of elevating the position of women: 'If child-bearing women must be intellectually handicapped, then the penalty to be paid for race-predominance is the subjection of women.'[1] This last was a most unusual attitude for a socialist—this elevation of 'race-predominance' as the ultimate criterion, which must banish women to the kitchen and nursery. In a lecture on 'Socialism and Sex' delivered in 1886, he expanded on these views, in a more conventionally socialist fashion. In Marxist manner, he suggested that under socialism, a 'different mode of ownership,'[2] there would be correspondingly a new kind of sex-relationship which would grant women 'economic independence.'[3] Women under socialism would have the 'duty to labour'[4] outside the home—until the coming of children—would be able to contract 'free sexual union,'[5] as sex-relationships would be separated from child-bearing, with the state taking an interest in child-bearing to prevent economic dependence on the part of the mother and regulating both 'quantity and quality' of children since this had such an important bearing upon 'the happiness of society as a whole.'[6] This suggestion that the state take upon itself the obligation of encouraging, regulating and supporting

[1] Pearson, 'The Woman's Question' (1885), in Ethic, pp. 373-4.
[2] Pearson, 'Socialism and Sex' (1886), in Ethic, p. 415.
[3] Ibid., p. 418.   [4] Ibid., p. 421.   [5] Ibid., p. 427.
[6] Ibid., p. 424; Pearson also wrote on this subject in his 'Women and Labour' (1894), in Chances of Death, I, p. 251.

this most vital kind of production constituted a far more ambitious objective than that of the non-socialist, Galton. In 1894, Pearson wrote 'that the superior and not the inferior members of the group should be the parents of the future, is far more likely to be realized in a socialistic than in an individualistic state.'[1]

After his acceptance of his role as Galton's ally in the propagation of the new eugenic religion after the turn of the century, Pearson once again addressed himself to the eugenic problem. As a result of improved conditions—as a result, for example, of medical progress—there had been a reduction of the death-rate. This was nothing short of calamitous: the 'death-rate is selective, and if we check Nature's effective but roughshod methods of race betterment, we must take her task into our own hands and see to it that the mentally and physically inferior have not a dominant fertility.'[2] Galton had emphasized the encouragement of the fit to reproduce; Pearson added certain prescriptions to discourage the reproduction of the unfit: the closing of casual wards, the barring of the 'undesirable alien,' the expatriation of 'confirmed criminals,' and the exclusion from the workhouses and asylums of the 'congenital pauper and the insane.'[3] 'Darwinism and medical progress,' Pearson told a meeting of doctors in 1912, 'are opposed forces.'[4] Even so-called 'reforms' were frequently harmful. The factory acts, for example, by depriving parents of the economic value of the child made them less concerned about bearing and rearing of offspring.[5] Neither medical progress nor legislative reform made for progress: 'No degenerate and feeble stock will ever be converted into healthy and sound stock by the accumulated effects of education, good laws, and sanitary surroundings.'[6] 'We have placed our money on Environment,' argued Pearson, 'when Heredity wins in a canter.'[7] The influence

[1] Pearson, 'Socialism and Natural Selection,' p. 138.
[2] Karl Pearson, Darwinism, Medical Progress and Eugenics (London, 1912), p. 29.
[3] Pearson, National Life, pp. 104-5.
[4] Pearson, Medical Progress, p. 27.
[5] Karl Pearson, The Problem of Practical Eugenics (London, 1912), pp. 24, 36.
[6] Pearson, Grammar of Science, pp. 26-7.
[7] Pearson, Practical Eugenics, p. 36.

of environment was not 'one-fifth that of heredity, and quite possibly not one-tenth of it.'[1]

More and more, race became the crucial question for Pearson. He continued to call himself a socialist—despite his opposition to the factory acts and his support of child labour!—but the term had acquired a new meaning for him: 'Those who believe that our increasing knowledge of what tends to improve or impair the racial qualities of future generations . . . will enable us to foresee and in part control social evolution are justified in calling themselves "Socialists," whether from the standpoint of politics, morality or religion.'[2] The problems of 'true socialism —the socialism of the future' were to answer such questions as 'what are the racial forces at work?—how can we modify or direct them toward furthering human evolution?'[3] The work of the true socialist had been transformed from the improvement of environment to the improvement of race. Pearson looked forward to the time 'when conscious race culture will cope with the ills which arise when we suspend the full purifying force of natural selection.'[4] 'The higher patriotism and the pride in race must come to our aid in stemming deterioration.'[5]

Nor was there any doubt of the ultimate purpose of this 'conscious race culture': to make the nation or race better able to survive in the struggle for existence. If 'we leave the fertile, but unfit, one-sixth to reproduce one-half the next generation,' Pearson warned, 'our nation will soon cease to be a world power.'[6] There was the real danger: as a result of the lowered death-rate and the voluntary reduction of offspring among the able, the coming generations of Britons would be—unless something were done—unfit for imperial responsibilities. As

---

[1] Karl Pearson, *Nature and Nurture: The Problem of the Future* (London, 1910), p. 27; see also Karl Pearson, *The Groundwork of Eugenics* (London, 1909), and Karl Pearson, *The Academic Aspect of the Science of National Eugenics* (London, 1911).

[2] Karl Pearson, *Social Problems: Their Treatment, Past, Present, and Future* (London, 1912), p. 4.

[3] *Ibid.*, p. 5.

[4] Karl Pearson, *The Scope and Importance to the State of the Science of National Eugenics* (London, 1911), p. 12.

[5] *Ibid.*, p. 25.

[6] Pearson, *National Life*, p. 106.

D

early as 1886, Pearson had urged the seizure of territories where white men could live, territories which would provide room for 'a high birth-rate' which would be 'levied on the physically and mentally fitter classes of the community,' 'the efficient classes,' as a means of increasing for many generations 'the vigour and power of the empire.'[1] In his *Grammar of Science* he had proclaimed it 'a false view of human solidarity, a weak humanitarianism' which regretted that 'a capable and stalwart race of white men should replace a dark-skinned tribe.'[2] As the international tensions within Europe increased, Pearson's racism was applied to the intra-European situation: 'if the German people dominate today the French; . . . if Spain and Holland disappear from the fore-rank of nations, can we throw light even for an instant on these momentous facts of history by such studies of mankind as are summed up in Philosophy, Anthropology, or Political Economy?' Such studies revealed nothing concerning the causes of victory or defeat in the struggle of nations for existence: the answer for 'Socialist' and Darwinist Pearson had become Race.[3]

Was this the vision which had passed before Virchow's mind when he suggested the nameless horrors which would come from the theory of evolution in the brain of a socialist? Horrible it must be to persons of the present generation who have had direct experience with a species of national socialism which also regarded democracy as 'cumbersome,' and was as concerned as Pearson with conscious race culture, with encouragement to child-bearing, with the elevation of the lower classes in the common interest of the tribe, with the necessity for imperialism, with the beneficial character of war. Pearson's contemporaries, that is, the leading statesmen and intellectuals of *antebellum* Great Britain, the men to whom Pearson was primarily addressing himself, on the whole ignored the warnings of the eugenicists, with the exception, curiously enough, of certain of Pearson's fellow socialists, especially the leaders of British 'national' socialism, the Fabians—perhaps one more confirmation of Virchow's fears.

[1] Pearson, *Ethic*, p. 428 fn.
[2] Pearson, *Grammar of Science*, p. 369.
[3] Pearson, *Scope and Importance*, p. 6.

H. G. Wells, for example, then a Fabian socialist, had been present at Galton's exposition of the eugenic religion before the Sociological Society. Wells was sufficiently impressed with what he heard to advocate 'the sterilization of failures.'[1] Bernard Shaw agreed fully with Galton and Pearson that 'nothing but a eugenic religion can save our civilization from the fate that has overtaken all previous civilizations.'[2] Sidney Webb, in a Fabian tract, gave fulsome approval to Pearson. Webb shared the eugenicist's concern about the decline in the birth-rate, especially among the 'abler' classes, which had been accompanied by a corresponding increase among the 'thriftless and irresponsible.' He wrote, in 1907: 'Twenty-five per cent of our parents, as Professor Karl Pearson keeps warning us, is producing 50 per cent of the next generation. This can hardly result in anything but national deterioration; or, as an alternative, in this country gradually falling to the Irish and the Jews.' Webb further agreed with Pearson's Darwinist contention that the lower death-rate had intensified the effect of this 'adverse selection.'[3] Webb's solution, like Pearson's, was the 'endowment of motherhood': 'once the production of healthy, moral and intelligent citizens is revered as a social service and made the subject of deliberate praise and encouragement on the part of the government, it will, we may be sure, attract the best and most patriotic of the citizens.' This was the only way to avoid 'degeneration of type,' that is 'race deterioration, if not race suicide.'[4] Less virile, perhaps, than Pearson's statements, but certainly supporting his views.

---

[1] *Sociological Papers*, pp. 58-60.

[2] *Ibid.*, p. 74; Pearson suggested that Shaw 'went further than Galton certainly approved,' and warned Shaw to be a 'fabian' in his eugenics, cautioning that 'he who would practically reform mankind must not begin by alarming it.' See Karl Pearson, *The Life, Letters, and Labours of Francis Galton* (Cambridge University Press, 1930), Vol. IIIa, pp. 260-1. Shaw was at one time a lecturer of the Eugenics Education Society, *ibid.*, p. 427.

[3] Sidney Webb, *The Decline in the Birth Rate* (London, 1907), Fabian Tract No. 131, pp. 16-17.

[4] *Ibid.*, p. 19; another Fabian expression of agreement with Pearson's endowment of mothers was H. D. Harben, *The Endowment of Motherhood* (London, 1910), Fabian Tract No. 149.

English liberalism, on the other hand, had no stomach for Pearson's doctrines. L. T. Hobhouse, a prominent exponent of the dominant 'new' Liberalism, a professor of sociology at the University of London, asserted that 'progress is not racial, but social,' and was extremely critical of eugenic methods and purposes.[1] English conservatism, traditionalism, felt similarly. One such traditionalist appears to have grasped the full implications of Pearson's 'eugenic religion,' the culmination of his socialism and Darwinism. That was Benjamin Kidd, the first of the English sociologists to alter the direction of Social-Darwinism from its Spencerian path, who lived to regret his association with this 'science of power.' In a volume written after the beginning of the European war of 1914 (a war which saw the conversion of even Ernst Haeckel to a glorifier of war and the state),[2] and published posthumously after his death in 1916, Kidd denounced all Social-Darwinism which, he wrote, appealed to 'the half-informed pagan mind of our civilization.'[3] In particular, he denounced Karl Pearson, 'one of the ablest of the group of contemporary evolutionists' who was essentially a 'pagan' and spoke with 'the voice of Nietzsche's superman.' He condemned Pearson's lack of interest in the traditional liberties of Englishmen, making references to his 'nearest lamp-post' statement, and Pearson's lack of sympathy with Christian feeling.[4] In a view of brilliant anticipation of things to come, Kidd set his curse upon 'those who have imagined that the greatest revolution in the history of humanity' lay implicit in Pearson's eugenic religion 'could it only be applied to the world by the methods of the German General Staff!'[5]

[1] Leonard T. Hobhouse, *Social Evolution and Political Theory* (Oxford University Press, 1911), pp. 39, 40-79.

[2] Ernst Haeckel, *Eternity; World-War Thoughts on Life and Death, Religion, and the Theory of Evolution* (New York, 1916), pp. 129, 141, 152, 156-65.

[3] Benjamin Kidd, *The Science of Power* (London: Methuen, 1918), pp. 9-10.

[4] *Ibid.*, pp. 79-82.

[5] *Ibid.*, p. 74.

III

A PARTY OF NATIONAL EFFICIENCY: THE LIBERAL-IMPERIALISTS AND THE FABIANS

> They are tumbling over each other, Liberals and Conservatives, to show which side are the greatest and most enthusiastic Imperialists. . . . The people have found that England is small, and her trade is large, and they have also found out that other people are taking their share of the world, and enforcing hostile tariffs. The people of England are finding out that 'trade follows the flag' and they have all become Imperialists. They are not going to part with any territory. . . . The English people intend to retain every inch of land they have got, and perhaps they intend to secure a few more inches.
>
> CECIL RHODES, 1899

> MR. JACKSON. . . . What I have to tell you is I'm not going to have you loafing away your time here. I disapprove of loafing on principle. Both as a public man and as a private man I disapprove of it. There's far too much of it in England today. That's where the Germans are ahead of us. Young men who ought to be at business or in the professions idle away their time and live on their parents.
>
> ST. JOHN HANKIN, *The Return of the Prodigal*, 1905

Contemporary observers have commented on the militant patriotism, and even jingoism, which the Boer War had stimulated among all classes of Englishmen. Previous hopes of strengthening the ties between the scattered parts of Victoria's realm seemed dramatically realized when troops from all over the empire joined together to extend Britain's authority in South Africa. The idea of 'empire building' had become popular. The British government had previously seemed to turn a deaf ear to entreaties that it take positive action to enlarge its possessions. England appeared to have gathered her empire, to use the familiar phrase, 'in a fit of absence of mind.' By 1899, however, Great Britain was in full possession of her imperial senses.

Such a break in policy which the coming of the Boer War so dramatically presented, could not fail to seriously divide the nation. Many Liberals—in parliament and throughout the country—ranged themselves on the side of the Boers and against the Unionist government waging the war. But even within the party of 'peace, retrenchment, and reform' there was now a group of self-designated 'Liberal-Imperialists' who, under the leadership of the former Liberal prime minister, Rosebery, gave their full support to the government's policy. The popular reaction to the Jameson raid of 1895 had demonstrated the new spirit of the country. When the siege of Mafeking was lifted in May 1900, the mob rioting and street celebrations presented a picture of a nation whose combative instincts had been aroused. The election of October 1900 indicated that the entire electorate, less noisily perhaps but equally emphatically, had endorsed the imperialist policy of the government: the Unionist majority was 134. Writing in 1900, Victor Bérard, a French observer, proclaimed imperialism 'all-triumphant.'[1]

The Boer War had climaxed a period of growing British interest in extending her empire. Some years before the war, Britain's new imperial spirit could have been seen in the Sudan, in the exploits of Gordon and Kitchener and in the enthusiasm which they inspired at home. During the 'eighties and 'nineties the great powers had been engaged in carving out empires and spheres of influence in Africa and Asia, and statesmen were relating these moves to the future prosperity of the nation. The Liberal-Imperialist Rosebery, as early as 1893, had described British motives in African colonization as 'pegging out claims for the future.' In an address before the Colonial Institute he had declared:

'It is said that our Empire is already large enough, and does not need extension. That would be true enough if the world were elastic, but unfortunately it is not elastic, and we are engaged at the present moment, in the language of mining, "in pegging out claims for the future." We have to consider not what we want now, but what we shall want in the future. We have to consider what countries must be developed either by ourselves

[1] Victor Bérard, *British Imperialism and Commercial Supremacy* (London, 1906), p. 42, and *passim*.

or some other nation, and we have to remember that it is part of our responsibility and heritage to take care that the world, so far as it can be moulded by us, shall receive an English-speaking complexion, and not that of other nations. . . . We have to look forward beyond the chatter of platforms and the passions of party to the future of the race of which we are at present the trustees, and we should, in my opinion, grossly fail in the task that has been laid upon us did we shrink from responsibilities and decline to take our share in a partition of the world which we have not forced on, but which has been forced upon us.'[1]

Popular reaction to imperialism was assessed by Rosebery when he remarked, in a famous speech at Chesterfield on December 16, 1901, that 'the Liberal party should not dissociate themselves, even indirectly or unconsciously or by any careless words, from the new sentiment of Empire which occupies the nation . . . for the statesman, however great he may be, who dissociates himself from that feeling must not be surprised if the nation dissociates itself from him.'[2] During the period few politicians took this risk. There were few men in public life who still insisted that the inevitable tendency of the colonies was independence; fewer still asserted that the colonies were a millstone around the neck of the mother country. Such views, however, had been quite common some sixty, or even some twenty, years earlier. Imperialism, indeed, had won the day.

'Imperialism' is a word of comparatively recent origin,[3] first associated with the Second Empire of Louis Napoleon, before it became identified with some of the more extravagant notions of Benjamin Disraeli. A conventional starting point in the story of late nineteenth-century British 'imperialism' is 1876, when Disraeli persuaded a reluctant parliament to add 'Empress of India' to Victoria's royal title. In the 'eighties, imperialism was sometimes understood to mean the maintenance of the union with Ireland in opposition to the Home Rule ideas of Gladstonian

[1] Quoted in William L. Langer, *The Diplomacy of Imperialism* (New York: 1935), I, p. 78.
[2] Liberal League Publication, No. 37.
[3] Richard Koebner, 'The Concept of Economic Imperialism', *The Economic History Review*, Second Series, Vol. II, No. 1, 1949, pp. 1-29, discusses the development of meaning of the term.

Liberalism. More frequently, imperialism was taken to mean a desire to increase the unity of the 'self-governing' parts of the empire, and as such this sentiment was shared by leaders of both parties. The Imperial Federation League, which was established in 1884 to 'secure by Federation the permanent unity of the Empire,' included the Liberal W. E. Forster as well as Edward Stanhope, who was to become Salisbury's Colonial Secretary in 1886. Other members of the League were Froude, the Tory historian of Tudor England; Sir John Seeley, who held the chair of modern history at Cambridge from 1869 to 1894; Sir Charles Tupper who 'represented' Canada; Sir Charles Gavan Duffy and Sir Henry Parkes who spoke for Australia; but by far the most prominent of the politicians associated with the League was the Earl of Rosebery.

The formation of the Imperial Federation League was just one of the signs of the awakening of imperial sentiment.[1] In 1891, the United Empire Trade League was established. In 1893, the British Empire League was set up and later in that year the Imperial Federation (Defence) Committee. The United Empire Trade League posited an imperial *Zollverein*, a union of the empire on the basis of an imperial customs system, as its objective, and many imperialists of the 'nineties regarded this device as the most logical means for insuring imperial unity. As early as the 'eighties the *Statist* had offered a thousand guinea prize for the best essay on an imperial customs union. Growing concern with empire and with Britain's 'imperial mission' can be seen in the reception accorded Sir John Seeley's *The Expansion of England*, one of the most popular books of the 'eighties, and the Liberal-Imperialist Charles Dilke's *Problems of Greater Britain*. A more aggressive imperialism was perceptible in W. E. Henley, who made the *National Observer*, which he edited from 1888 to 1893, the literary organ of imperialism, and in Rudyard Kipling, who became the nation's most popular poet with his verses extolling the special mission of the British people and the 'white man's burden.' In 1894, Benjamin Kidd published his *Social Evolution* in which, as we have seen, he discussed the racial superiority of the Teutonic peoples and called for the sacrifice of individual interests in behalf of a

[1] See J. E. Tyler, *The Struggle for Imperial Unity* (1868-1895) (London: Longmans, 1938).

greater national and imperial ideal. Nor was imperialism found
only in political philosophy and literature. The mass-circulation
penny-press was enlisted in the cause of the empire and delivered
daily sermons on the subject to its growing readership. In the
'eighties, W. T. Stead, the friend and executor of Cecil Rhodes,
re-made the *Pall Mall Gazette* into an organ of imperialism.
Alfred Harmsworth's *Daily Mail*, founded in 1896, was marked
by its imperial jingoism. In 1900, Arthur Pearson founded a
competitor paper, the *Daily Express*, whose first leader, dated
April 24th, read: 'Our policy is patriotic; our policy is the
British Empire.'[1]

LIBERAL-IMPERIALISM

Liberal-Imperialism dated from the 'eighties and was
espoused during its early phase by the two most promising of
the younger leaders of the Liberal Party—Earl Rosebery and
Sir Charles Dilke. Both Rosebery and Dilke believed that it was
possible to be a Liberal without at the same time joining in the
Radical chorus, led by men like John Bright, of shouting the
praise of *laissez-faire* and the denunciation of Empire. Many
young Oxford men were attracted to this new vision of Liberalism by the Oxford Neo-Hegelian and Liberal, T. H. Green, who
can be said to have laid the philosophical foundations for Liberal-
Imperialism. Green had turned against the Benthamite
utilitarianism which had supported the atomistic individualism
of Cobdenism and had preached a new concept of the organic
nation which opened the door to social reform and to positive
state action in all areas, a gospel which he preached to Balliol
men of the generation of Asquith and Milner. A philosophical
follower of Green, Bernard Bosanquet, extended that doctrine and
struck out against Cobdenite cosmopolitanism and internationalism. Writing in 1899, Bosanquet declared that 'the Nation-State
is the widest organisation which has the common experience
necessary to found a common life,' and urged a new patriotism
and a subordination of the individual to the community.[2]

[1] Quoted in Sidney Dark, *The Life of Sir Arthur Pearson* (London,
n.d.), p. 88.
[2] Bernard Bosanquet, *The Philosophical Theory of the State* (London,
1899), p. 320 ff.

As we have noted, Rosebery, in the 'eighties, was perhaps the most prominent member of the Imperial Federation League and Dilke was penning his books of praise for 'greater Britain.' Dilke was to be eliminated from consideration for high party or governmental leadership because of an unfortunate divorce action. Rosebery was to fulfil his promise and to succeed the grand old man, Gladstone, as premier in 1894. At Gladstone's retirement from office, the Queen had been faced with a choice between Sir William Harcourt, who led the Radical, Gladstonian segment of the party, and Rosebery. She chose Rosebery because, as she wrote on March 4, 1894, she did not 'think it possible that Lord Rosebery will destroy well tried, valued and necessary institutions for the sole purpose of flattering useless Radicals.'[1] It is easy to understand why Archibald Philip Primrose, the fifth Earl of Rosebery, the flower of the Scottish peerage, was more to the taste of the Queen than Harcourt, a keener Radical than Gladstone himself. Rosebery did not have the cramped, non-conformist style which Victoria had learned to despise. For example, the Queen might recall that Rosebery's name had been expunged from the rolls of Christ Church, Oxford, when, as an undergraduate, he had refused to sell his stud of race horses, and the recollection could not fail to be comforting. The supporters of Harcourt were none too content with the situation and there were considerable difficulties for the Liberal government of 1894-95. The troubles did not cease after the Liberals were ejected from office. Rosebery, who does not seem to have had much of a taste for party politics, found it more comfortable to resign from the leadership of the Liberal party in October 1896.

Highly placed in the party were several followers of Rosebery's Liberal-Imperialism, some of whom had held office in his government. There were three who rose to particular prominence—Grey, Asquith, and Haldane. Sir Edward Grey, Rosebery's Under-Secretary of State for Foreign Affairs, was a country gentleman who, on the whole, preferred the ordinary, off-season pursuits of that class of Englishmen to politics. Yet he strongly impressed not only his Liberal-Imperial colleagues but also the Tory opposition with his grasp of Britain's diplomatic

[1] Quoted in Marquis of Crewe, *Lord Rosebery* (London: J. Murray, 1931), II, p. 443.

problems. Henry Herbert Asquith had been Rosebery's Home
Secretary. Asquith was of humbler background—his father had
been a Lancashire wool-spinner and weaver—and as a scholarship student at Balliol, he had capped a brilliant Oxford career
with two firsts and the presidency of the Union. He had been
called to the bar in 1876 and to the House of Commons, sitting
for East Fife, in 1886. In the years between his election to
Commons and his appointment, in 1892, to the Cabinet, he
scored success after success both in politics and in his private
legal practice. Everywhere he was regarded as a man to be
watched. After the fall of the Rosebery government, Asquith
once more returned to his private law practice, but kept an
active hand in political affairs. Another key Liberal-Imperialist
was Richard Burdon Haldane. Haldane, a member of a
distinguished Scottish family, first attended the University of
Edinburgh, and then Göttingen. His earliest interest was in
philosophy and he was to do much writing in this area throughout his lifetime. After Göttingen, he read for the bar, to which
he was called by Lincoln's Inn in 1879, and soon became known
as one of England's most learned and most able barristers. In
1885, he was elected M.P. for East Lothian, a seat he was to
hold until elevated to the peerage in 1911, on becoming
Lord Chancellor.

The coming of the Boer War intensified the cleavage within
the Liberal party between these followers of Rosebery and the
anti-imperialist Radicals. The Radical wing, the wing of Sir
William Harcourt, included two other leaders of the party, Sir
Henry Campbell-Bannerman, and the fiery chieftain of Welsh
liberalism, David Lloyd George. Both these men protested
against the war as a ramp for South African financiers and
condemned, in Campbell-Bannerman's words, the 'methods of
barbarism' by means of which the British government was
waging war. The imperialist-wing of Liberalism, on the other
hand, gave its full support to the policies of the government, of
its colonial secretary, Joseph Chamberlain, and of its representative in South Africa, Sir Alfred Milner. Asquith, Grey, and
Haldane had the greatest confidence in Milner, a Balliol
companion of Asquith's, whose competence, disinterested
patriotism and lofty imperial sentiment had won their highest
respect. The Liberal-Imperialist position toward the war was

set down by Rosebery as early as October 1899, when he proclaimed that 'in the face of this attack the nation will, I doubt not, close its ranks, and relegate party controversy to a more convenient season.'[1]

During the course of the war, the division within Liberalism widened. In the middle of 1901, Lord Rosebery wrote a letter to the City Liberal Club, of which he was then the president, which made many think that the Liberal party would once again be split as it had been in the 'eighties. Rosebery's letter was an expression of faith 'that there is a great Liberal force in the country, that it could effectively combine on a domestic policy, and that it is capable of indefinite extension.' But for all that, the Liberal party 'can only become a power when it has made up its mind on Imperial questions, which are at this moment embodied in the war.' These imperial questions, Rosebery continued, 'are supreme issues; none greater ever divided two hostile parties.' One of the Liberal schools of thought, 'blind as I think to the developments of the world, is avowedly insular.' The other 'places as the first article of its creed the responsibilities and maintenance of our free and beneficent Empire.' It was 'the evolution of our Empire and of Imperial feeling during the past 20 years which has produced this divergence.' The party, Rosebery concluded, 'cannot . . . contain these two schools of thought and remain an efficient instrument'; 'one school or the other must prevail if the Liberal party is once more to become a force.'[2]

During the next several days, there was speculation that the Rosebery letter was the signal for the establishment of a new party—or perhaps for the Liberal-Imperialists to join Joseph Chamberlain in the Unionist party which had united the opponents of Irish Home Rule in the 'eighties. The supporters of Chamberlain and those of Rosebery certainly agreed as to outlook on the Empire and agreed, in opposition to the *laissez-faire* position of orthodox Radicalism, upon the necessity for social reform. Wherein lay their differences, if any? The distinction between the two—Liberal-Imperialists and Liberal Unionists—was already clear and was destined to become clearer

[1] Quoted in T. F. G. Coates, *Lord Rosebery, His Life and Speeches* (London, 1900), II, p. 989.
[2] *The Times*, July 17, 1901, 7 c, d.

during the next several years. Chamberlain was a screw-manufacturer from Birmingham and his followers were largely drawn from the manufacturing areas of the midlands. For them, as we shall see, the crucial criterion of British economic strength was manufacturing, in Great Britain's power to out-produce her foreign rivals. For Rosebery, the president of the Liberal Club of the City of London and a Rothschild son-in-law, capital was a more important consideration than productive capacity. In a speech delivered at Chatham in January of 1900, Rosebery spoke of Britain's loss of prestige as a result of the war in South Africa. But such lost prestige could be regained, he was convinced, because 'this country has two supreme assets, to a degree which no other country in the world possesses; therefore I venture to use the word "supreme." They are our Navy and our capital (Cheers)—weapons of enormous importance in time of war and instruments of enormous weight in time of peace.' With 'that start of a Navy and capital, we should not be long in building up our prestige.'[1]

Rosebery's expression of faith in the power of British capital was central to the special world-outlook of Liberal-Imperialism. During the period of the Boer War, the outstanding theorist among the Liberal-Imperialists was Halford J. Mackinder, then Reader in Geography at Oxford, and an unsuccessful Liberal-Imperialist candidate in the election of 1900. In December 1899, Mackinder delivered a remarkable series of lectures to the Institute of Bankers in London in which this outlook was fully displayed. In the course of these lectures, Mackinder carefully differentiated between the interests of industry and those of finance. British industry was faced with the keenest foreign competition, he asserted, and soon British commerce might be in a similar position. This circumstance was a result of a tendency 'towards the dispersion and equalisation of industrial and commercial activity throughout the world.' However, the more dispersed the world's industry and commerce might be, 'the greater will be the need of a controlling centre to it.' Mackinder was convinced that London was destined to remain the banking centre of the world. 'It appears, therefore, quite possible,' he suggested, most significantly, 'that the financial importance of

[1] *The Times*, January 24, 1900, 7 b, c.

the City of London may continue to increase, while the industry, at any rate, of Britain, becomes *relatively* less.'[1]

The followers of Rosebery associated their imperialism with a faith in free trade, which, they felt, was responsible for Britain's imperial greatness and upon which British financial and commercial interests felt themselves completely dependent. In the 'nineties, Rosebery had stated his opposition to any form of tariff, insisting that protection would spur the hostility of all foreign countries. The Liberal-Imperialists dissociated themselves from any conception of empire bearing the taint of 'aggression and greed and violence' and preached an imperialism which was 'a passion of affection and family feeling, of pride and hope and helpfulness.'[2] They regarded schemes of imperial preference as 'shoddy Imperialism' in contrast to their own 'sane Imperialism'.[3] Protectionism, they believed, would pit the interests of the homeland against those of the other parts of the Empire, would 'impoverish and sterilize and extinguish the imperial sentiment among the great mass of the people,'[4] to use the words of Asquith, and that it would 'tend to make the Empire odious to the working classes.'[5] The Liberal-Imperialists remained Free Traders, they insisted, to preserve the Empire.

This conception of empire, Asquith explained, stimulated rather than paralyzed 'all those aspirations and efforts which Liberals included under the general name of social reform.' 'It was the work of statesmanship in this country,' he declared, 'to make the Empire worth living in as well as worth dying for.'[6] Rosebery presented the social-imperialist argument of Liberal-Imperialism in this fashion: 'An Empire such as ours requires as its first condition an imperial race—a race vigorous and industrious and intrepid.' He added: 'in the rookeries and slums which still survive, an imperial race cannot be reared.' 'Remember,' he urged his audience, 'that where you promote health and arrest disease, where you convert an unhealthy

---

[1] Halford Mackinder, 'The Great Trade Routes,' *Journal of the Institute of Bankers*, May, 1900, p. 271.

[2] Liberal League Publication No. 37, p. 8. In the future L.L.P.

[3] L.L.P. No. 144, pp. 3-4.   [4] L.L.P. No. 51.

[5] L.L.P. No. 46, p. 9. See L.L.P. No. 47, pp. 12, 15.

[6] Earl of Oxford and Asquith, *Fifty Years of Parliament* (London, 1926), II, pp. 2-3.

citizen into a healthy one, where you exercise your authority to promote sanitary conditions and suppress those which are the reverse, you in doing your duty are also working for the Empire.'[1] Speaking at Liverpool, February 14, 1902, Rosebery declared that 'the true policy of Imperialism' 'relates not to territory alone, but to race as well. The Imperialism that, grasping after territory, ignores the conditions of an Imperial race, is a blind, a futile, and a doomed Imperialism.' Rosebery urged action to provide housing suitable for 'citizens and subjects of an Imperial race';[2] he explained that 'a drink-sodden population . . . is not the true basis of a prosperous Empire.'[3] Elsewhere he declared that more widespread educational opportunities were a necessary basis of imperial strength— although R. B. Haldane made this aspect his particular forte.[4]

The issues of educational, housing and temperance reform were joined by Rosebery in the idea of 'efficiency,' which he defined in Glasgow, on March 10, 1902, as 'a condition of national fitness equal to the demands of our Empire—admini-strative, parliamentary, commercial, educational, physical, moral, naval, and military fitness—so that we should make the best of our admirable raw material.'[5] In this notion of 'efficiency,' the Liberal-Imperialists merged their desires for social reform and their wish to strengthen Britain's military and naval capabilities.

In early 1902, the followers of Rosebery established the Liberal League, an extra-party organization whose president was Rosebery and whose chief spokesmen were H. H. Asquith, R. B. Haldane, and Sir Edward Grey. The Liberal League programme was imperialism and social reform. Rosebery employed an address at Glasgow in March 1902, to introduce the Liberal League to the nation. On that occasion, he made it quite clear that he was not leading his followers out of the house of Liberalism in order to join the Unionists. In fact, he denounced the Unionist government as 'seven years lost for all social and

[1] Lord Rosebery, *Miscellanies: Literary and Historical* (London, 1921), II, pp. 250-251.
[2] L.L.P. No. 37, pp. 4, 21-22.   [3] L.L.P. No. 144, pp. 3-4.
[4] See R. B. Haldane, *Universities and National Life* (London: J. Murray, 1911); *National Education* (London: J. Murray, 1913).
[5] L.L.P. No. 37.

human causes; seven years lost for all measures which make for national health and national efficiency; seven years lost in our training and preparation for the keen race of nations, both in commerce and in dominion.'[1] Rosebery seemed determined, however, to form a party of national efficiency. Whether he hoped to set up an entirely new party or whether he hoped to shape the Liberal Party to his special ends was an undecided question in the early part of 1902.

THE FABIANS

Historians have generally accepted the view that socialists in the years before the war of 1914 had rejected nationalism and its appendages—imperialism, militarism, protectionism—in favour of a working-class internationalism. The Socialist International had indeed busied itself in the passing of resolutions, usually by unanimous votes, protesting national imperialisms in Asia or Africa, denouncing the increased military budgets of the great powers, defending free trade against grasping monopolists, and proclaiming workers in all lands brothers united against international capitalism. Yet, more and more, scholars have come to recognize that there was a vocal minority within the socialist movement which refused to be bound by these oft-repeated phrases of good will, who jeered at the ideals of internationalism and accepted—more or less completely—the goals of nationalism.[2] Among these socialists were the leaders

---

[1] Crewe, op. cit., II, p. 575.

[2] The pre-war German socialists who dissented from working class internationalism have been the object of special study by American scholars, probably because Germany was the enemy during the war of 1914 and because of the subsequent rise of Hitler's national socialism. See Carlton J. H. Hayes, 'Influence of Political Tactics on Socialist Theory in Germany, 1863-1914,' in C. E. Merriam and H. E. Barnes, eds., A History of Political Theories; Recent Times (London: Macmillan, 1924); John L. Snell, 'Socialist Unions and Socialist Patriotism in Germany, 1914-1918,' The American Historical Review, LIX, No. 1, October, 1953, pp. 66-76. The imperialistic views of certain Italian socialists have been discussed in Roberto Michels, Le proletariat et la bourgeoisie dans le mouvement socialiste italien particulièrement des origines à 1906 (Paris, 1921), pp. 338-351. Also A. William Salomone.

of the British Fabian Society—Sidney Webb and George Bernard Shaw—and they were supported in their stand by what was probably a majority of the active members of the Society. Though charges of nationalism and imperialism had been hurled against the chief Fabians by such prominent British socialists as J. Ramsay Macdonald and Graham Wallas—who, in fact, found themselves compelled to resign from the Society, giving as motive their disagreement with the society's views on war, colonies, and nationalist economics—with the significant exception of Élie Halévy,[1] there has been neglect of these charges on the part of historians of ideas, who have preferred to focus their attention on the influential Fabian programme of domestic reform.

Indeed, up until the time of the Boer War, in 1899, the Fabian Society had paid little or no attention to foreign or imperial questions. Their domestic programme—the traditional one of European socialism: national ownership and regulation of the vital sectors of the economy and a demand that the incomes of the wealthy be levelled and the living standards of the poorer classes be elevated—had been fully developed in the famous Fabian Essays, and in scores of tracts. Only one of the Fabian essayists, the journalist William Clarke, had made reference to matters of international policy.[2] Sidney Webb later described

Italian Democracy in the Making (Oxford University Press, 1945), *passim*. British 'national' or 'imperial' socialists have thus far escaped intensive inquiry. However, William P. Maddox, *Foreign Relations in British Labour Politics* (Oxford University Press, 1934), has discussed the nationalism and militaristic attitudes of certain British trade unionist members of parliament, especially those from the armaments industries; see pp. 44-45, 54, 209.

[1] Speaking of the Webbs, Halévy wrote: 'Convinced imperialists and looking to a national and militarist state to realize their programme of moderate collectivism, they had never felt anything but contempt for every formula of Liberalism and free trade," (p. 365). Halévy, *A History of the English People*, Vol. V.

[2] William Clark, 'The Industrial Basis of Socialism,' *Fabian Essays* (London: Allen & Unwin, 1948), pp. 73-77. Clarke's views were little different from the main current of European socialism and Liberal internationalism. W. C. Wilbur, Jr., in his 'The Origins and De- velopment of Fabian Socialism to 1890' (an unpublished Columbia

E

Clarke as the only Fabian who had been seriously interested in such matters.[1] It is difficult to say whether the pressure of world events or tactical considerations was the more influential in turning the attention of the Fabians toward imperial questions. We do know that the Fabians had settled upon a policy of 'permeation,'—they could, they believed, most readily accomplish their goal of a socialist Britain by converting the leaders of the existing parties. From the early 'nineties onward, we also know, they turned toward certain statesmen who belonged to the imperialist wing of the Liberal party as the most likely potential executors of their domestic programme.

The retirement of William Gladstone in 1894 had revealed the rift within Liberal ranks, which we have noted, between the Radicals and the Liberal-Imperialists. This latter group was described by Beatrice Webb, in her diaries, as 'collectivists and imperialists'; Mrs. Webb saw them opposed by 'the laisser-faire and anti-imperialist' group.[2] The fact that the Liberal-Imperialists had united to their interest in the empire a desire for social reform was pleasing to the Fabians. The fact that Liberal-Imperialist sympathy for social reform was not supported by a well-thought out programme was an irresistible challenge. The Fabians felt it was their job to supply such a programme to the followers of Lord Rosebery.

The coming of the South African War in 1899 sharpened, as we have seen, the Liberal split. The Gladstonian wing of the party denounced the imperialistic war of the Conservative government and took up the cause of the Boers. The Liberal-Imperialists supported the government's conduct of the war. The South African struggle was punctuated by a struggle at

University doctoral dissertation, 1953), f.n. p. 380, quotes the well-known historian and Fabian, R. C. K. Ensor's statement that 'Clarke became definitely estranged from the Society when it began to attack the Liberal Party in 1893.' Wilbur adds that 'Clarke resigned from the *Daily Chronicle* when it supported the Boer War, and undoubtedly was further estranged from the Society by its manifesto, *Fabianism and the Empire*, issued in 1900.'

[1] Sidney Webb, in his 'Introduction' to the 1920 reprint of the *Fabian Essays*, pp. x-xi.

[2] Beatrice Webb, *Our Partnership* (London: Longmans, 1948), pp. 104-105.

home between these two branches of Liberalism, a struggle
which took the form of rival dinner parties, as one wit described
it, 'war to the knife and fork.' The Fabian leadership was faced
with the necessity of making a choice in this 'war.' R. B.
Haldane, who had become a close friend of the two chief leaders
of Fabianism, Sidney and Beatrice Webb, on one occasion
invited Webb to appear at a dinner given by the Liberal-
Imperialists. This posed 'a dilemma,' Beatrice wrote in her
diary. 'Sidney is pro-Boer in sentiment; he agrees with Asquith
and Haldane, by reason; but he has not thought out the question,
has paid little or no attention to it.' Webb attended the dinner.
In a subsequent diary entry, Beatrice quoted Bernard Shaw as
having advised the Webbs to 'plunge in with Rosebery as the
best chance of moulding home policy.'[1]

Even before this dinner invitation, however, the leading
Fabians had made their decision in favour of imperialism so that
Sidney Webb's 'dilemma' had been substantially resolved at the
time it faced him—and resolved in a fashion which makes it
appear that opportunist political tactics were reinforced by
imperialist convictions. As early as 1899, a group of Fabian
rank-and-filers, led by the future guild-socialist, S. G. Hobson,
and supported by a few members of the executive committee,
had unsuccessfully attempted to get the Fabian Executive to
issue a statement of opposition to the war against the Boers.
The majority of the Executive had refused—giving as their
reason that the Society ought not to speak out on foreign
affairs. When the pressure of the anti-imperialists increased,
the Executive finally decided to set a date for a debate of the war
issue by the general membership.[2] A couple of weeks before the
debate, on November 24, 1899, one of the members of the
Executive, Frederick Whelen, in a public lecture, proclaimed
the inevitability of the annexation of the two Boer states as a
result, as he put it, of a struggle between the seventeenth-
century ideals of the Boers and British nineteenth-century
demands. Whelen, further, urged the nationalization of the
South African gold and diamond mines after the end of the war.[3]

[1] Beatrice Webb, *op. cit.*, pp. 217-220.
[2] *Fabian News*, IX, No. 9, Nov. 1899, p. 34.
[3] *Fabian News* (hereafter referred to as *F.N.*), IX, No. 10, December,
1899, p. 39.

From subsequent events, it would appear that Whelen was expressing the views of the majority of the Fabian Executive Committee.

The members who attended the general debate on December 8, 1899, were faced with an anti-imperialist resolution, moved by S. G. Hobson, and an equivocal amendment to that resolution proposed by George Bernard Shaw and grounded upon the sentiments of the Whelen statement of the previous fortnight. Hobson condemned the 'Imperialist passion that has overrun this country of recent years' and announced that the 'Fabian Society therefore formally disassociates itself from the Imperialism of Capitalism and vain-glorious Nationalism.' Shaw's amendment on the other hand looked forward to a British victory. One section read:

'3. That the country is therefore entitled to expect that in the event of the war being carried to a successful issue, the Government will take steps to:—
>   (a) secure public rights in the valuable mines of the Rand by placing them in public hands. . . .
>   (b) insist on a stringent Mines Regulation Act for the protection of the miners.
4. That, failing the above Imperial precautions . . . a result would [be to] expose the British Government to the charge of being the dupes of these speculators, and of having spent the nation's blood and treasure, and outraged humanity by a cruel war, to serve the most sordid interests under the cloak of a lofty and public-spirited Imperialism.'

Shaw, then, urged Fabian support of a 'lofty and public-spirited Imperialism,' an imperialism which, as in the case of the Rand mines, would rebound to the public interest rather than to private interests.[1] If the 'nation's blood and treasure' were to be spent, the Fabians insisted that the entire nation profit thereby.

The December 8th meeting was inconclusive. A large gathering of Fabians defeated Shaw's amendments and then removed Hobson's resolution from further consideration by passing the previous question.[2] This lack of decision led the divided

[1] *Ibid.*, pp. 37-38; see S. G. Hobson, *Pilgrim to the Left; Memoirs of a Modern Revolutionist* (London: E. Arnold, 1938), pp. 63-65.
[2] *F.N.*, IX, No. 11, January 1900, p. 42.

executive to stage a referendum to poll the approximately 800
Fabians by mail. The issue, on the face of it, was whether the
membership wished the Society to issue a statement denouncing
'aggressive capitalism and militarism' in South Africa or whether
it opposed committing the Society to an anti-imperialist
position.[1] A circular which urged members to vote in favour of
such an anti-imperialist pronouncement was signed by four
members of the fifteen-member Fabian Executive. A rival
circular asking members to vote against such a pronouncement
was signed by an eight-man majority of the Executive including
the 'old gang,' Sidney Webb, Bernard Shaw, Hubert Bland
and Frederick Whelen.[2]

The real issue did not concern simply the desirability of an
anti-imperialist pronouncement. The issue was imperialism vs.
anti-imperialism[3] as Bernard Shaw made clear in an address on
'Imperialism' delivered on February 23, 1900, the day the
Fabian mail poll closed. There was something new in British
imperialism, Shaw proclaimed, and it was the Fabian Society,
which had preached 'the application of Socialism to current
politics,' which had added the new element. 'For good or evil,
it is we who have made England Imperialist,' Shaw insisted.
Now that Imperialism had led to war, it was no time for
socialists to desert it. It was inevitable that the world fall to the
empire-creating powers. Any attempt of Englishmen to shirk
this national responsibility could only result in 'the evil of the
Chartered Company.' Shaw concluded that 'a Fabian is necessarily an Imperialist in theory,' and they 'should so declare
themselves.'[4] The result of the poll was 259 votes for the
position of Shaw and Webb and Whelen and 217 votes for
anti-imperialism.[5]

Among those who resigned from the Fabian Society when the
result of the poll became known were J. Ramsay MacDonald,
at that time a member of the Fabian Executive Committee and

[1] F.N., IX, No. 12, February 1900, p. 46.
[2] F.N., X, No. 1, March 1900, p. 1.
[3] The supporters of Hobson were called the 'opponents of Imperialism' in The Eighteenth Annual Report on the Work of the Fabian Society
(London, 1901), pp. 3-4.
[4] F.N., X, No. 1, March 1900, pp. 2-3.
[5] Ibid., p. 1.

the future leader of the Labour Party; two influential trade union leaders, Pete Curran and G. N. Barnes (who was to serve as a member of Lloyd George's War Cabinet); Walter Crane, an artistic and political associate of William Morris, and the celebrated future suffragette, Mrs Pankhurst.[1]

In April, the result of the referendum was confirmed when the annual election to the Executive was held. Imperialism was again the central issue. The anti-imperialists ran five new candidates in an effort to obtain a majority on the Committee. Webb, Shaw, Whelen led the poll—not a single member of the eight-man majority which had opposed an anti-imperialist announcement lost his seat.[2] The new executive assigned to Bernard Shaw the task of preparing a tract describing the Fabian position on the war.

The result was *Fabianism and the Empire*, the first full-blown statement of the society concerning foreign and imperial matters. The tract was very favourably received by press and public and remained, in Fabian Secretary, E. R. Pease's words, 'the only authoritative expression' of Fabian views.[3] Although drafted by Shaw, it received and incorporated the detailed critical suggestions of some 150 Fabians, and can be regarded as the view of the Fabian majority, not simply that of Shaw.[4] The tract's draftsman boasted, many years later, that he had managed, by this tract, to pull the society through the Boer War with the loss of fewer than two dozen members.[5] On

---

[1] Edward R. Pease, *The History of the Fabian Society* (London: Allen & Unwin, 1925), p. 133. The story of the Fabians and the Boer War is told on pp. 128-138. The report for the fiscal year ending March, 1900 revealed a decline of 50 of the Society's membership. Membership had been steadily climbing in the previous years. See *The Seventeenth Annual Report on the Work of the Fabian Society, 31st March, 1900* (London, 1900), p. 7.

[2] *F.N.*, X, No. 3, May 1900, p. 9.

[3] *F.N.*, XII, No. 2, February 1902, p. 6.

[4] *F.N.*, X, No. 9, November 1900, p. 34; H. G. Wells, in his *Experiment in Autobiography* (London: Gollancz, 1934), p. 260, described the document as 'drafted by Shaw and evidently revised and patched a great deal by warier minds.'

[5] Bernard Shaw, 'Sixty Years of Fabianism,' appended to the Jubilee Edition (1948) of *Fabian Essays*, p. 210.

another occasion, Shaw took obvious pleasure in the fact that the tract had disappointed those who believed that Socialists 'must oppose the war as a war of Capitalism, and support the Boers as its victims.' He delighted in having taken the opposite view. 'The Society, already suspected of Toryism, now stood convicted of Jingoism,' Shaw observed impishly.[1]

The Fabian manifesto was directed against a favourite Fabian whipping boy—the Radicalism of Harcourt and Morley, that section of the Liberal party which 'still clings to the fixed-frontier ideals of individualist republicanism, non-interference, and nationalism, long since demonstrated both by experience and theory to be inapplicable to our present situation'; the world had developed 'far beyond the primitive political economy of the founders of the United States and the Anti-Corn Law League.' Imperialism was the new stage of international polity, the tract maintained—the only question was whether Great Britain would be the nucleus of one of the world-empires of the future or whether it would stupidly lose its colonies and be reduced to a tiny pair of islands in the North Sea.[2] Shaw presented as 'the best answer for the purpose of excusing the war' the view that small nations, like the Boer Republic, were anachronistic in the new world of the twentieth century. 'The fact remains,' he concluded, 'that a Great Power, consciously or unconsciously, must govern in the interests of civilization as a whole; and it is not to those interests that such mighty forces as goldfields, and the formidable armaments that can be built upon them, should be wielded irresponsibly by small communities of frontiersmen.'[3]

The Fabians were not, the manifesto continued, viewing the Empire from any narrow standpoint, from the standpoint of the working class or any other class in the national community. The Fabians were concerned with 'the effective social organization of the whole Empire, and its rescue from the strife of classes and private interest.'[4] From their platform of the national interest, they recognized the necessity of Great Britain maintaining her

[1] Bernard Shaw, *Fabianism* (London, 1930), Fabian Tract No. 233, p. 15.
[2] Bernard Shaw, ed., *Fabianism and the Empire* (London, 1900), pp. 3-4.
[3] *Ibid.*, pp. 23-24.   [4] *Ibid.*, p. 6.

empire. What ought Great Britain to do to keep the empire intact and prosperous? First of all, a thorough reform of the British consular system was needed to take full advantage of the trade doors opened by British arms.[1] Secondly, and most important, it was necessary to keep British military forces in a high state of readiness to defend the empire. The tract's author attacked the brutality and stupid inefficiency of barrack-life, military law, and the British professional soldiery with all the vehemence of a socialist pacifist. He declared the old idea of a standing army obsolete, but asserted that Great Britain had to have a well-trained army of fighting civilians, of citizen soldiers. *Fabianism and the Empire* therefore suggested that the Factory Acts be amended to extend the age for half-time employment to twenty-one; the thirty hours gained in this way could be spent in 'a combination of physical exercises, technical education, education in civil citizenship . . . and field training in the use of modern weapons.' 'No payment beyond a supper would be needed to make the drills popular,' the tract concluded in most patronizing and startlingly unsocialist fashion—this at a time when both Liberal and Conservative parties opposed all forms of compulsory military training.[2]

THE COEFFICIENTS

The following year—in September 1901—Sidney Webb continued to identify the Fabian Society with imperialism, and in particular with the Liberal-Imperialists, in an article for the *Nineteenth Century and After*, celebrating Lord Rosebery's sharp, formal, public disavowal, earlier in the year, of the Gladstone, Harcourt, Morley school of liberalism. Webb, in his 'Lord Rosebery's Escape from Houndsditch' took the occasion to make a similar disavowal of the socialists whose reaction to the Boer War, he felt, had proved that they had no effective foreign or imperial policy. 'Outside the two spheres of labour and local government the majority of the Socialist leaders proved to be, notably with regard to the British Empire,' Webb wrote, 'mere administrative Nihilists—that is to say . . . ultra-Gladstonian, old-Liberal to the finger tips.' 'They out-

[1] *Ibid.*, pp. 7-13, *passim.*   [2] *Ibid.*, pp. 39-41.

morleyed Mr Morley,' and as a result the Independent Labour Party was now 'as hopelessly out of the running as the Gladstonian Party.' On the issue of the Empire, Hyndman of the Social Democratic Federation and Keir Hardie of the I.L.P. 'find themselves, in fact, by honest conviction' sharing the same platform as the Liberal anti-imperialists.[1] This would never do for the new England, an England which understood the need for 'the deliberate organization of the Empire,' an England in which 'the shopkeeper or the manufacturer sees his prosperity wax or wane, his own industry and sagacity remaining the same, according to the good government of his city, the efficiency with which his nation is organized, and the influence which his Empire is able to exercise in the councils, and consequently in the commerce, of the world.'[2]

Lord Rosebery's disavowal of official Liberalism, Webb regarded as 'the first step towards the regeneration of the Opposition'—'a live Opposition.'[3] Webb, like Rosebery, called for the formation of a new party, a party of 'National Efficiency,' a party which would remove slums, destroy the sweated trades, eliminate inefficiency in government, recapture British commercial supremacy, support 'a "National Minimum" standard of life' to help gird industry for trade competition, advocate sanitary reform (at least 'the minimum necessary for breeding an even moderately Imperial race'), poor law reform, housing reform ('How, even, can we get an efficient army—out of the stunted, anaemic, demoralised denizens of the slum tenements of our great cities'), educational reform ('It is in the class-rooms . . . that the future battles of the Empire for commercial prosperity are being already lost'), and the reorganization of the war office.[4] The people wanted 'virility in government,' Webb proclaimed and looked toward Rosebery, toward Asquith, Haldane, and Grey to convince them that the Liberal-Imperialists really desired to introduce 'the principle of National Efficiency' into government. The people already knew that the Liberal-Imperialists meant well by the Empire. The working class now wanted to know 'what steps' the followers of Rosebery would 'take to insure the rearing of an Imperial race.'

[1] Sidney Webb, 'Lord Rosebery's Escape From Houndsditch,' *Nineteenth Century And After*, No. CCXCV, September 1901, p. 374.
[2] *Ibid.*, p. 369.   [3] *Ibid.*, p. 366.   [4] *Ibid.*, pp. 375-385.

Worried lest the Liberal-Imperialists create their new party of national efficiency without Fabian aid, Webb concluded his article by reminding Rosebery that 'such a campaign' as he had undertaken was no one-man task. 'It involves,' the Fabian leader asserted, 'the close co-operation of a group of men of diverse temperaments and varied talents, imbued with a common faith and a common purpose, and eager to work out, and severally to expound, how each department of national life can be raised to its highest possible efficiency.'[1] A little over a year after the publication of these words, Sidney and Beatrice Webb decided to call together such a group of men of 'varied talents' but 'common faith' and 'common purpose' to plan, in the words of one of the members of the group, the 'aims and methods of Imperial policy.'[2]

We have noted that one of the watchwords of British social-imperialism was efficiency; its principal enemy was the Liberal spirit of 'muddling through,' as a consequence of which, the social-imperialists believed, the British Empire was approaching irrevocable disaster. Benjamin Kidd had called for social-efficiency, so had Karl Pearson. The Boer War had revealed the seemingly boundless depths of ineffectiveness which both bureaucracy and armed services could reach, and had revealed as well a Great Britain virtually friendless in a jealous world and therefore requiring a greater degree of readiness for combat than at any time since the defeat of Napoleon. Rosebery had made 'efficiency' his watchword during the course of the Boer War. Joseph Chamberlain was to take up the cry a few years later. Sidney and Beatrice Webb determined to form a new political grouping—perhaps a 'brains trust' for a new political party—which would be dedicated to the cause of efficiency in all areas. Hence the name of the group—one coined by Beatrice Webb—the Coefficients.

One of the Unionist members of the Coefficients has described the Webbs' motives in establishing the group in this fashion. 'That indefatigable pair, Sidney and Beatrice Webb,' he has recently written in his memoirs, 'were much more concerned with getting their ideas of the welfare state put into practice

[1] *Ibid.*, pp. 385-386.

[2] W. A. S. Hewins, *The Apologia of An Imperialist* (London, 1929), I, p. 65.

by any one who might be prepared to help, even on the most modest scale, than with the early triumph of an avowedly Socialist Party.'[1] Not only Grey and Haldane, among the Liberal-Imperialists, but the Unionist Prime Minister, Arthur Balfour, had indicated sympathy with the Webbs' programme, and the Webbs cultivated all these persons. The ostensible purpose of the Coefficients was to discuss the 'aims and methods of Imperial policy.' 'There was, after all,' this same observer has pointed out, 'nothing so very unnatural, as Chamberlain's own career had shown, in a combination of Imperialism in external affairs with municipal socialism or semi-socialism at home.' But if such a combined programme— and it was, as we shall see, essentially a social-imperialist programme—was to eventuate, it had to be thought out by a carefully selected body of men, 'a Brains Trust or General Staff.'[2]

It was early in November 1902 that Sidney and Beatrice Webb invited a group of their 'friends' to their already famous home at 41 Grosvenor Road to join the small dining club to be called the Coefficients. Each of the men was to be an 'expert' in a special field, and the Webbs had decided that no more than a dozen persons ought to be invited. The dozen assembled for their first regular meeting on December 8, 1902, at the home of the Liberal-Imperialist barrister and a close friend of the Webbs, Richard Burdon Haldane, who was to be the club's expert on the law. (Later meetings were held in the Ship Tavern in Whitehall and at St Ermin's Hotel.) Other 'experts' were Sir Edward Grey for foreign policy; the economist and Liberal-Imperialist politician, regarded by many as 'a coming man' in the Liberal party, H. J. Mackinder, then a Reader in geography at Oxford who 'represented' Liberal-Imperialism; Sir Clinton Dawkins, a gentleman who had held government offices in all parts of the empire and who was at that time a partner in the financial house of J. S. Morgan and Company, represented finance; W. A. S. Hewins, the Director of the London School of Economics, founded by the Fabians, represented economics; Bertrand Russell, a grandson of the great nineteenth-century

[1] L. S. Amery, *My Political Life* (London: Hutchinson, 1953), I, p. 223.

[2] *Ibid.*, p. 223.

British prime minister, was the expert in science; the editor of the *National Review*, Leopold Maxse, represented journalism; a recently retired naval officer who had begun to write on naval questions for the press, Carlyon Bellairs, was the club's naval expert; L. S. Amery, *The Times'* chief Boer War correspondent who was a keen advocate of army reform, was the club's military expert; Sidney Webb—a long-time member of the London County Council—was of course present as the expert on municipal affairs; W. Pember Reeves, the Agent General in London for the New Zealand Government, spoke for the colonies; and H. G. Wells, already one of the more famous of the contemporary novelists, represented literature. The count revealed that about half-a-dozen of the Coefficients were attached to the Liberal-Imperialist group, two to the Fabian Society, and the others were Conservatives dedicated to forsaking traditional methods in the interest of efficiency.[1]

H. G. Wells has discussed the Coefficients at some length in his autobiography and the group appears as the 'Pentagram Circle' in the novel, *The New Machiavelli*. In his autobiography, Wells has related how foreign the extreme imperialism of certain members of the group had seemed both to him and to Bertrand Russell. At one of the dinner meetings, Russell, after listening to a series of fanatical statements about the empire, had insisted that there were many things he valued above the empire, that for example 'he would rather wreck the Empire than sacrifice freedom.' Russell realized that some of the other members of the club strongly disapproved of his position and he felt obliged to resign. Wells himself had not been present at this exchange. When the incident was reported to him at the subsequent meeting, Wells asserted that he agreed with Russell. 'The Empire,' he added, 'was a convenience and not a God.' This is what Wells reported followed his statement: 'Hewins in protest was almost lyrical. He loved the Empire. He could no more say why he loved the Empire than a man could say why he loved his wife. I ought to resign.' Wells, characteristically, refused to leave unless he were thrown out. He was not.[2]

---

[1] *Ibid.*, p. 224; H. G. Wells, *Autobiography*, pp. 761-2.

[2] See H. G. Wells, *Autobiography*, p. 765; also Bertrand Russell, *Portraits from Memory and Other Essays* (London: Allen & Unwin, 1956), pp. 76-77.

He was at that time too much of an imperialist to have merited such treatment.[1]

In *The New Machiavelli*, Wells described other matters which concerned the 'Pentagram Circle.' First, there was democracy; a typical Coefficient view of democracy was that of Oscar Bailey (Sidney Webb) who declared it a sham behind which civil servants ruled. Then there was the club's estimate of the international situation. The members of the Pentagram Circle were convinced that 'a day of reckoning with Germany' was in the offing. The Germans were ahead of the English because they were more efficient: 'Germany is beating England in every matter upon which competition is possible, because she attended sedulously to her collective mind for sixty pregnant years, because in spite of tremendous defects she is still far more anxious for quality in achievement than we are.' Inevitably, the Pentagram members were 'very keen on military organization' and, Wells added, 'with a curious little martinet twist in their minds that boded ill for that side of public liberty.' On the other hand, 'they were disposed to spend money much more generously on education and research of all sorts than our formless host of Liberals seemed likely to do.'[2]

Speaking of real-life Coefficients, Russell confirmed Wells' description of anticipation, 'without too much apprehension,' of war with Germany. Russell has also told us that at one meeting of the club, Sir Edward Grey, then of course not yet in office, had advocated an *entente* with France and Russia, a policy 'which was adopted by the Conservative Government some two years later, and solidified by Sir Edward Grey when he became Foreign Secretary.'[3] In addition, we know that members of the Coefficients, Amery in particular, were strong supporters of Earl Roberts' National Service League and that Haldane was one of the chief advocates of the view that the British educational system ought to be more efficiently organized, organized in fact like that of Germany.

[1] See Edward Mead Earle, 'H. G. Wells, British Patriot in Search of a World State,' in Edward Mead Earle, ed., *Nationalism and Internationalism* (London: Oxford University Press, 1950), pp. 79-121.

[2] H. G. Wells, *The New Machiavelli* (London: Collins, 1911), pp. 352-3, 338-9.

[3] Russell, *op. cit.*, p. 77.

Perhaps we ought to take a closer look at some of the men who were the original members of the Coefficients. One of the most curious was Leopold James Maxse. After Harrow and King's College, Cambridge, where he took a second in the historical tripos of 1886 but never his degree, and where he was president of the union, Maxse had spent a year travelling through the British Empire—India, Australia, New Zealand, Canada. He had returned home a fervent imperialist. His ambition had been the bar and parliament, but when a serious illness made these goals impossible, his father, Admiral Frederick Augustus Maxse, purchased the *National Review* for his son so as to provide for him a career fitted to his impaired health. The politics of the journal were grounded upon the politics of Admiral Maxse, a remarkable gentleman who served as George Meredith's model for the hero of *Beauchamp's Career*. The Admiral had been a disappointed Liberal parliamentary aspirant, a close friend of Joseph Chamberlain who had joined Chamberlain in withdrawing from the Liberal party on the issue of Home Rule. It would appear that as early as the 'seventies, the Admiral had spoken with Chamberlain concerning the possibility of forming an English National Party.[1] Was his son now to help realize this goal through the Coefficients?

The admiral and his son made the *National Review* a faithful advocate of Chamberlain and his policies. In a famous article, 'Judas,' in 1893, in which he lauded Chamberlain, the Admiral presented the crucial elements of both the imperialist and social-imperial creeds.[2] For over a decade before Chamberlain's espousal of Tariff Reform, the *Review* was publishing articles advocating protection.[3] Nor was the *National Review* remiss in warning England of its foreign enemies, particularly Germany.[4]

[1] Viscountess Milner, 'Mr. Chamberlain's Letters to Admiral Maxse, 1872-1889,' in *National Review*, February 1933, C., pp. 248-255.

[2] Admiral Maxse, 'Judas,' *National Review*, September 1893, XXII, pp. 104-114.

[3] See, for example, F. N. Maude, 'Imperial Insurance,' *National Review*, January 1894, XXII, pp. 601-611; C. E. Howard Vincent, 'The Colonies and the Empire,' *National Review*, September 1894, XXIV, pp. 23-28.

[4] See Leopold J. Maxse, *'Germany on the Brain'* ; *or, The Obsession of 'A Crank'; Gleanings from the National Review, 1899-1914* (London, 1915).

When Sir Alfred Milner, in 1899, offered Leopold the editor-
ship of South Africa's *Cape Times*, young Maxse had replied:
'I must stay in England to warn people of the German danger.'[1]
Leopold—the Admiral died in 1900—devoted himself steadfastly
to this goal until 1914. Many in England tended to dismiss
Maxse as a crank, referred to him as 'that lunatic Leo', and
suggested that he had 'Germany on the brain.' Certain aspects of
his behaviour did indeed resemble lunacy. A friend, Lord
Newton, in an obituary article, has described, for example, how
Maxse, a frequent guest, persisted in believing that a mild
German lady employed in Newton's home as a governess, was
in reality a dangerous spy! The columns of the *National Review*
advocated the construction of an alliance with France and Russia
from the very beginning of the century.[2]

Another Coefficient was Leopold Amery. Amery had had
charge of *The Times* correspondence during the Boer War in
1899-1900 and was, in 1902, engaged in editing *The Times
History of the War in South Africa*. Born in India, educated at
Harrow and Balliol, Amery had, while at Oxford, been thought
a socialist—he had even helped in founding an Oxford branch
of the Fabian Society. But what was persistent in his political
attitudes was not socialism but his opposition to *laissez-faire*.
Out of Oxford, he became political private secretary to Beatrice
Webb's brother-in-law, the Radical Leonard Courtney. After
his return from the war in South Africa, Amery set out to secure
reform, much needed reform, of the army which he had seen in
battle. He wrote a series of articles in *The Times* on the problem,
articles which attracted the approving attention of Colonial
Secretary Chamberlain himself.[3] During the next several years,
Amery was to do a good deal of speaking and writing on behalf
of Lord Roberts' National Service League as well as to make
several attempts to enter parliament as a supporter of Chamberlain's policies.

[1] See Viscount Milner's article on Maxse in *D.N.B.*, *1931-1940*,
p. 607.
[2] See H. W. Wilson, 'L. J. Maxse As Editor,' and Lord Newton,
'L. J. Maxse As I Knew Him,' in *National Review*, February, 1933,
C, pp. 175-187.
[3] See Amery, *op. cit.*, I, *passim* and L. C. M. S. Amery, *The Problem
of the Army* (London, 1903).

Sir Clinton Dawkins—the Coefficients' financial expert—was an ex-bureaucrat born into a family of bureaucrats. His father had served in the foreign office. He himself, after Cheltenham College and Balliol, had entered the India Office in 1884 and had risen to become Private Secretary to the Secretary of State for India two years later. In 1889, he had served in a similar capacity to Chancellor of the Exchequer Goschen, then he went to Egypt in 1895 as Under-Secretary of State for Finance, was Financial Member of the Council of the Governor-General of India in 1899, and became the chairman of the Committee on War Office Reorganization in 1901. In 1900, the imperial bureaucrat—and a leading Liberal-Imperialist—had been made a partner in the financial house of J. S. Morgan & Co.

Carlyon Bellairs—the group's naval expert—was a son of a lieutenant-general in the army who nonetheless made his own career in the navy. He had entered the Royal Navy in 1884, at the age of thirteen, studied at the Royal Naval College, and retired as a Torpedo Lieutenant in 1902. The Navy remained his overwhelming interest. During the years immediately after his retirement, during the years he attended the meetings of the Coefficients, he acted as a special correspondent on naval manoeuvres for *The Times*. In addition, he served as the Vice-chairman of the Navy League and as the founder of the Parliamentary Navy Committee. He was an active Liberal-Imperialist. In 1906, Bellairs was to be elected Liberal M.P. from Kings Lynn. As early as 1902, however, he seemed to Bertrand Russell 'half-way on the journey from the old party to the new one,'[1] the Unionist party, which he joined in 1909, very much like the hero in Wells' *New Machiavelli*. Also among the original twelve Coefficients was William Pember Reeves, a socialist and a member of the Fabian Society. Born in New Zealand, he had been sent by its socialist government to be Agent-General in London. There he became associated with the Webbs and was to succeed two of his fellow Coefficients— Hewins and Mackinder—as Director of the London School of Economics.

During the years that followed, the Coefficients continued to meet fairly regularly, once each month, up until 1908. New

---

[1] Russell, *op. cit.*, p. 76.

members were added to the group. The most prominent of
these, perhaps, was Viscount Milner who joined the Coefficients
soon after his return from South Africa. Milner, in many ways,
was a hero to all segments of the Coefficients and, as we shall
note, a well-nigh perfect expression of social-imperialism. In
1904, Henry Newbolt, the poet-editor of *Monthly Review*
—it survived by only a few months his admission to the
Coefficients—joined the Liberal-Imperialists within the group.
Newbolt was to be the collaborator in the writing of the official
History of the Great War: Naval Operations of still another
Coefficient, the naval historian and celebrator of the exploits of
Drake and Nelson, Julian Corbett. Frederick Scott Oliver, the
biographer of the father of the American national system,
Alexander Hamilton, was invited to dine with the Coefficients in
1907, the year after his book on Hamilton had been published.
The journalist, perhaps the most famous one of his day, J. L.
Garvin, was a later addition to the club; so was the biographer
of Disraeli, W. F. Monypenny; the noted expert on Indian
economics, Theodore Morison; Amery's successor as the
military expert of *The Times*, Charles Reppington; the chairman
of the South Africa Company, Sir Henry Birchenough; and there
were others. During the last days of the Coefficients, a third
Fabian, Bernard Shaw, was admitted.[1]

An important question concerning the Coefficients remains to
be answered; why did not the Coefficients succeed in becoming
the brains trust of a new social-imperial political party as the
Webbs had hoped it would? Why had it remained simply a
dining club, composed of rather remarkable and influential
men, true, but still a dining club? There are no doubt many
reasons for the failure of the Webb design. The most obvious
one was Joseph Chamberlain's Tariff Reform campaign which
divided English social-imperialists and consequently split the
Coefficients. In his autobiography, W. A. S. Hewins has written
concerning the intrusion of the snake into Eden. Hewins had
been born a Roman Catholic but told friends that he had
substituted a faith in the British Empire for his faith in the
Church. He was absolutely convinced that Free Trade would be
the ruin of his beloved Empire. There are grounds for believing

[1] See Amery, *My Political Life*, pp. 225-226; Wells, *Autobiography*,
pp. 761-5.

F

that he, more than any other single individual, was responsible
for convincing Chamberlain to campaign for Tariff Reform in
May 1903.[1] At the third meeting of the Coefficients, January
1903, Hewins introduced the subject of preferential tariffs.
'Present divisions of opinion came out very clearly,' he noted,
'and Amery and Maxse were the only two who genuinely supported my views.'[2]

After Chamberlain made his crucial speech of May 15, 1903,
the issue became the most pressing one among the Coefficients.
The Coefficients remained united in their goal of an efficiently
organized empire, but how was that goal to be achieved? Amery
has related how he was at work in his *Times* office the day after
the Chamberlain speech when Leopold Maxse burst in, 'seizing
both my hands in his he waltzed me round the room as he
poured forth a paean of jubilation at the thought that, at last,
there was a cause to work for in politics.'[3] The Liberal-
Imperialists were torn between allegiance to their party's
traditional adherence to free trade and their desire for a
strengthened empire. Both Amery and Hewins testify to Sir
Edward Grey's wavering before choosing to remain faithful
to Liberalism. Halford Mackinder ruined a promising future
within the Liberal party when he allowed himself to be converted to Tariff Reform.[4] The Fabians appeared to be covertly
sympathetic to the new Chamberlain policy, but their ties to
socialism or, perhaps, to Liberal-Imperialism did not permit
actual acceptance. In his novel, Wells has noted that the members of the Pentagram Circle were nearly 'all mysteriously and
inexplicably advocates of Tariff Reform, as if it were the
principal instead of at best a secondary aspect of constructive
policy.'[5]

Since Tariff Reform was to be the leading political issue of the
next three elections, all chances of a unified political approach
for the original dozen Coefficients, with its few staunch Unionists, its Liberal-Imperialists, and their national socialist allies
were doomed to failure—and with it the dream of both Rosebery
and the Fabians for a party of national efficiency.

[1] Russell, *op. cit.*, p. 76.   [2] Hewins, *op. cit.*, I, pp. 65-66.
[3] Amery, *My Political Life*, I, pp. 237-238.
[4] *Ibid.*, p. 224; Hewins, *op. cit.*, I, p. 69.
[5] Wells, *New Machiavelli*, p. 338.

IV

JOSEPH CHAMBERLAIN'S 'SQUALID ARGUMENT'

The peace of shocked Foundations flew
Before his ribald questionings.
He broke the Oracles in two,
And bared the paltry wires and strings.
He headed desert-wanderings;
He led his soul, his cause, his clan
A little from the ruck of Things.
'Once on a time there was a Man.'

. . . A bolt is fallen from the blue.
A wakened realm full circle swings
Where Dothan's dreamer dreams anew
Of vast and farborne harvestings;
And unto him an Empire clings
That grips the purpose of his plan.
My Lords, how think you of these things?
Once—in our time—is there a Man?

> *Things and the Man,* (In Memoriam Joseph Chamberlain), by
> RUDYARD KIPLING

Asked by Mr Chamberlain whether it was his opinion that the wages of his hands would rise under such a system, Mr Baines looked a trifle puzzled, and confessed that he did not understand the drift of the question.

MR CHAMBERLAIN (smiling pleasantly): 'I will put my question in another form. Would you offer your employés a portion of the profit so acquired?'

MR BAINES (bewildered): 'Why should I?'

THE POSTMASTER GENERAL (Austen Chamberlain): 'Let me tackle him, father. . . . (To Mr Baines): 'I take it all your men have a vote? . . . Well, now, the question is this: if we give you £1 down for every ton of pig iron you shove on the market, and we make it a condition that you pay at least 5s. of it in extra wages, will you clinch?'

MR BAINES: 'Like a nut!'

The witness, who was complimented by Lord Landsdowne on the manly and straightforward way in which he gave his evidence, then stood down.

> HILAIRE BELLOC,
> *The Great Inquiry,* 1903

In 1902, the then Chancellor of the Exchequer, Sir Michael Hicks-Beach, had revived a 'registration' duty on corn as a revenue-producing device to help pay debts incurred during the late war in South Africa. The duty was nominal: 3d. per hundredweight on imported corn and 5d. per hundredweight on imported flour. In 1903, the new Chancellor, Ritchie, moved to repeal this duty—not because of any effect it might have upon the future price of bread but because, as a Free Trader, he thought it, on principle, a move in the wrong fiscal direction. Many imperialists, on the other hand, had long been convinced that such a duty ought to be imposed, and then remitted in the case of corn and flour imported from the colonies, this as a step toward promoting greater imperial unity. On May 15, 1903, Joseph Chamberlain, the Colonial Secretary, a long-time hero of these imperialists, publicly adopted this position, spoke out in favour of a full system of Tariff Reform and imperial preference, and began an energetic campaign to convert the nation to his position.

The protectionist movement had been agitating for tariffs for over twenty years before Chamberlain's public conversion. In 1881, the National Fair Trade League had been formed by manufacturers interested in tariff protection. During the 'eighties, the 'Fair Trade' idea had become popular within the Conservative party. Local party organizations and national party conferences passed resolution after resolution giving their support to Fair Trade. The leader of Tory Democracy, Randolph Churchill, had at one time acknowledged himself a Fair Trader. This earlier tide of protectionist sentiment within the Conservative party had been suppressed by the political leadership in the interest of overall party strategy. A chief issue in the 'eighties and 'nineties was the question of Home Rule for Ireland. A sizeable number of Liberals had been willing to lend their support to the Conservatives in order to maintain the Union with Ireland. The bulk of those 'Liberal-Unionists' and their chief leaders—Goschen, Chamberlain, and Hartington— were, at that time, convinced Free Traders who hesitated to give support to Salisbury for fear that the Conservatives were on the verge of adopting a Fair Trade programme. The Salisbury leadership, determined to conclude what ultimately became the Unionist alliance, willingly sacrificed rank-and-file

Conservative Fair Trade sentiment toward this 'higher' end.[1]

But in 1903, Chamberlain, who had been an enemy of protection, emerged its champion. How can this be explained?
Chamberlain, a Birmingham screw-manufacturer was responding
to the new needs of the industrial midlands, responding in loyal
fashion to the many honours which Birmingham had bestowed
upon him since his service as its Lord Mayor in the 'seventies.
A perceptive contemporary French observer, Victor Bérard, has
given us a picture of Joseph Chamberlain as the spokesman
for 'le radicalisme *brummagem*,' the special radicalism of
Birmingham, the radicalism of the industrial midlands, of 'black
country' England. Chamberlain, for Bérard, was no doctrinaire
Liberal, in the mode of Cobden or Bright, but a utilitarian, a
believer in the greatest good for the greatest number—of
Birmingham. Why had Chamberlain led his band of midland
Radicals from the Liberal to the Tory Party in the 'eighties?
Because Gladstone, by proposing Home Rule, had seemed to be
preparing the way for the loss to hard-pressed British manufacturers of still another market.[2] A Unionist platform of the
'nineties was to defend the Union in just these terms, the
Union 'without which there will be no longer any trade for the
employer nor wages for the employed.'[3] This, indeed, had for
some time been Chamberlain's attitude toward the entire
empire. As early as May 1888, he had said:

'Is there any man in his senses who believes that the crowded
population of these islands could exist for a single day if we were
to cut adrift from us the great dependencies which now look to
us for protection and assistance, and which are the natural
markets for our trade? . . . If tomorrow it were possible, as some
people apparently desire, to reduce by a stroke of the pen the
British Empire to the dimensions of the United Kingdom, half
at least of our population would be starved.'[4]

Not only the industrial midlands but cotton-manufacturing
Lancashire had united behind the Unionists in their effort to
keep the markets of Ireland.

[1] See Benjamin H. Brown, *The Tariff Reform Movement in Great
Britain, 1881-1895* (New York, 1943), pp. 58-84.

[2] See Bérard, *op. cit.*, pp. iii, 1-41, *passim*.

[3] Quoted in *Ibid.*, p. 32.   [4] Quoted in Langer, *op. cit.*, I, p. 77.

The midlands, however, were in a much more awkward position than Lancashire. Birmingham, formerly unrivalled as the iron and steel, the metal-goods centre of the world, was losing out to foreign, especially to German competition. Delegates of the Birmingham Chamber of Commerce told this story to a Commission of Inquiry into the causes of the decline of British commerce as early as 1885:

'We are being ruined. We work as hard now as ever but without profit. . . . In the past we supplied the entire world with arms. Governments and private individuals always used to apply to us. . . . To-day the greater proportion of these governments manufacture for themselves, and America has popularized her arms from Springfield and Winchester; in fact, America obtained the orders for the Carlist and Turkish Wars. . . . We used to enjoy a monopoly for screws and nails. Protective tariffs have closed the civilized markets to us. . . . Under the shelter of tariffs, Germany and America have developed their factories, and making their profit out of home sales, the Germans throw the surplus on our markets at absurdly low prices. Time was when the Asiatic and Oceanian East purchased our nails. To-day German nails actually compete here on our own market of Birmingham. Buttons, which we used to sell to the whole of Europe, now come to us from Germany instead. German iron wire is now sold in our Birmingham shops.'

Other midlands cities had similar stories to tell. What remedy was there? The answer to the Birmingham Chamber of Commerce in 1885 had been clear: 'Commercial union with our Colonies. A Customs Union comparable to the German Zollverein should be established between them and the home country.'[1]

Birmingham had looked to Chamberlain to maintain the integrity of the Empire against the threat of Home Rule and Chamberlain had not failed his city. Now Birmingham looked to Chamberlain to defend it against foreign competition. It was more difficult for the former Radical Mayor of Birmingham to espouse the protectionist heresy, a doctrine especially obnoxious to many, including the manufacturers of Lancashire,

---

[1] Quoted in Bérard, *op. cit.*, pp. 57-58.

who had supported him on Home Rule. The McKinley Tariff of 1891 hit the midlands especially hard and revived agitation for 'fair trade.' In 1896, Chamberlain hesitantly and most cautiously appeared to endorse the movement for protection but, doubtlessly feeling that the moment was not right, did not launch a campaign. By the end of the Boer War, Chamberlain had begun to feel that the moment had come, that enough Britons had come to feel the pinch of foreign competition for his proposal of an imperial *Zollverein* to receive a sympathetic hearing.

The economic 'facts' were drawn upon by both Free Traders and protectionists in the course of the debate which followed the initiation of Chamberlain's campaign. At the beginning of the twentieth century, Great Britain could have looked back over fifty years of commercial and industrial superiority under Free Trade. During the preceding half-century, the United Kingdom had led the globe in almost every area of production, and the City of London had been and still was the chief financial and commercial centre of the world. The parliament at Westminster governed the largest and most populous empire history had ever recorded. Britain's position appeared impregnable. It was a shock and surprise to many when the Secretary of State for the Colonies proclaimed that Great Britain could not hope to survive as a power of the first class unless she made drastic revisions in her trade policy. British exports had been declining because of foreign competition, Chamberlain asserted. Without a tariff to exclude foreign goods from the home market, without preference needed to hold and improve her position in colonial markets, Britain's economy and power would disintegrate. Wages would go down; many more thousands would be unemployed. However, Chamberlain's prophecy of impending doom was pitted against the determined opposition of a united Liberalism, a working class intent upon keeping the cheap loaf, and even Unionists who were doctrinaire Free Traders. The Free Traders replied to Chamberlain's challenge with the 'facts.' Board of Trade statistics revealed that, at the time of Chamberlain's pronouncement, British exports, although there had been a slump in years before, had been climbing steadily in value. In 1859, the level of value of exports had stood at £130,412,000 and they had continued to increase in value until 1872 when they reached £256,257,000. Then there had followed a rapid

decline. In 1879 the figure stood at £191,532,000. During the
'eighties and 'nineties there were considerable fluctuations; in
1890, the 1872 high was exceeded, only to decline once more.
The tide had definitely turned, however, during the period
1899 to 1905:

Year	British Exports (£)
1899	£264,492,000
1900	291,192,000
1901	280,022,000
1902	283,424,000
1903	290,800,000
1904	300,711,000
1905	329,817,000

After a period of some stagnation, trade was improving; this was
an important aspect of the Free Traders' argument. Trade,
indeed, continued to improve until the coming of the war, a
circumstance which no doubt played a part in Chamberlain's
ultimate defeat. In 1913, British exports reached a total of
£525,245,000 in value, an increase of 80% over 1900.[1]

During the last thirty years of the nineteenth century, however, a profound change *had* occurred in Britain's industrial and
trade position—and it was this which was central to Chamberlain's supporters. On the continent, Germany had begun the

[1] The material for these sections was gathered from a number of
sources. Among them were *Memoranda, Statistical Tables, and Charts
Prepared in the Board of Trade with Reference to Various Matters
Bearing on British and Foreign Trade and Industrial Conditions; 1903
Cd. 1761*—hereafter referred to as *Fiscal Blue Book for 1903*; A. D.
Webb, *New Dictionary of Statistics* (London: Routledge, 1911);
C. R. Fay, *Great Britain from Adam Smith to the Present Day* (London:
Longmans, 1948); J. H. Clapham, *An Economic History of Modern
Britain* (Cambridge University Press, 1930-38); Werner Schlote,
*Entwicklung und Strukturwandlungen des englischen Aussenhandels von
1700 bis zur Gegenwart* (Jena, 1938); W. W. Rostow, *British Economy
of the Nineteenth Century* (Oxford University Press, 1948); R. J. S.
Hoffman, *Great Britain and the German Trade Rivalry, 1875-1914*
(Oxford University Press, 1933); Halévy, *op. cit.*, Vols. V, VI, VII.;
G. P. Jones and A. G. Poole, *A Hundred Years of Economic Development
in Great Britain* (London: Duckworth, 1948).

construction of a huge industrial machine which was causing concern to certain British manufacturers by the end of the century. Across the Atlantic, the United States had emerged as a serious industrial competitor. Across the channel, the French Republic showed signs of industrial competence and of a desire to resume the centuries' old rivalry with her neighbour. All three had begun to reach out for colonies to supply raw materials for their factories and to buy the finished goods of the mother country. All three had set up high tariff walls to exclude the produce of rivals. The German tariff became frankly protectionist in 1879 and even more so in 1885; France dug in behind the tariff of 1882; the United States found itself well sheltered by the McKinley tariff of 1891 and the Dingley tariff of 1897. Other European nations—Italy, Austro-Hungary, Russia—followed the example of the protectionist powers. As a result of the growth of rival industrial powers sheltered behind tariff walls, Britain had suffered a decline in the rate of expansion of her foreign trade which seemed serious when it was compared with the booming expansion of German, American, and even French trade. The same observation could have been made in important fields of production such as steel manufacturing and in exports of British manufactured goods. Only in the export of raw materials did the rate of British expansion keep pace with the German, a sad fate for the 'workshop of the world.' British manufacturers were not only deprived of continental and American markets by tariffs, they were compelled to meet the competition of these industrial rivals in their colonies and in the open home market as well.

Although British exports were indeed increasing at a rapid rate during the first decade of the twentieth century, the pinch continued to be felt—as in the 'eighties—by the British iron and steel industry of the midlands. For iron and steel, the dumping of German goods in the home market and the attempts of the U.S. to purloin the Canadian market were not a potential but an immediate threat to profitable existence. As late as 1890, Great Britain had been the largest steel producer in Europe. Ten years later, in 1900, the results of the lag in Britain's rate of expansion were very visible: British production had increased, true, but German production, aided by the new Bessemer process, had nearly tripled, and Germany took over the European lead. By

1908, German steel production was double England's. In 1900, 283,075 tons of foreign steel had been imported into Britain; this figure doubled in 1902. The Birmingham metals industries suffered considerably. R. C. K. Ensor has noted that but for the Admiralty's insistence on British steel for naval ships, 'the plant and capacity to produce these great forgings might before 1914 have disappeared from Great Britain altogether.'[1] Similarly, the hardware, chemical, glass, pottery, and other midlands industries were hard hit by foreign competition, as were marginal producers in many fields of manufacturing.

These 'facts' of Britain's relative industrial decline—especially in the metals industries—were welded into a political argument—a finely wrapped social-imperial 'package' to be sold to the British electorate—by Birmingham's M.P., Joseph Chamberlain. Chamberlain was a sincere imperialist from his earliest years, even while Radical Mayor of Birmingham, as his biographer has told us, to the end of his days. In 1886, he had quarrelled with Gladstone over the question of Home Rule for Ireland and had led a group of Liberal-Unionists into the political merger with Salisbury's Conservatives—certainly proof of his attachment to imperialism. In 1895, he requested and received the post of Colonial Secretary in the Unionist government which took office that year. His many accomplishments in this post and his activities in South Africa before and during the Boer War are too well known to bear repetition.[2] Chamberlain, however, was more than an imperialist. He was a social reformer as well.[3] Before his break with the Liberals, he was regarded as the most dangerous of the Radical social reformers by the men of property. His programme of 'municipal socialism,' while he was Mayor of Birmingham, a programme of municipal ownership of the city's utilities and transportation facilities, had made the propertied tremble. Had he not, further, grimly suggested that the wealthy owed a 'ransom' to the poor

[1] Ensor, op. cit., p. 504.

[2] See J. L. Garvin, The Life of Joseph Chamberlain (London: Macmillan, 1932-34), 3 vols. Julian Amery has continued the life; volume IV appeared in 1951.

[3] See Elsie E. Gulley, Joseph Chamberlain and English Social Politics (New York, 1926). A different picture of Chamberlain as a social reformer than the one indicated here.

in return for which they would be permitted to retain their riches? Chamberlain's 'ransom' speech, in 1885, had shocked the propertied classes.

Chamberlain continued to display this strong interest in social reform even after his withdrawal from the Liberal party. When the idea of old-age pensions received intense public interest, on the occasion of Charles Booth's paper on the subject in 1891, Joseph Chamberlain became the first politician to adopt the proposal, and he presented a pension scheme the following year. Responding to Chamberlain's repeated urgings, the Unionist government had appointed a committee to investigate the question in 1896. Two years later, true, the committee had issued a report labelling the scheme impracticable, but another inquiry into the question had been instigated by Chamberlain in 1899. This time, the committee offered a plan by which five shillings a week would be distributed to the 'deserving poor' over sixty-five. The huge expenses of the South African War made it impossible to proceed further and little was heard of the subject until 1903 when Chamberlain returned to it during the tariff controversy. Chamberlain also interested himself in the question of workmen's compensation. There had been attempts to deal with this problem when H. H. Asquith, Home Secretary of the Rosebery Government of 1894 to 1895 had introduced an Employers' Liability Bill. However, House of Lords' amendments caused the Liberals to drop this bill. In 1897, the Unionists, spurred again by Chamberlain, did enact legislation to provide for payment by industry for all accidents, excluding from coverage only such categories of workers as seamen and agricultural labourers.[1]

After he left the Liberal party, Chamberlain tried to distinguish between his kind of social reform and the social reform ideas of his opponents. One scholar has recently declared that Chamberlain's municipal socialism and that of the Webbs, for example, were entirely different: the Webbs, W. A. Robson has pointed out, wished municipally-owned utilities to be self-supporting while Chamberlain wished them to earn a profit

[1] For Chamberlain's social reform activities during the 'nineties, see W. C. Mallalieu, 'Joseph Chamberlain and Workmen's Compensation,' in *Journal of Economic History*, May 1950, X, pp. 45-57.

which could be used to lower general municipal tax rates.[1] This anticipated his later views on tax policy. Chamberlain's social-imperialism of the future was anticipated in a speech before the Edgbaston Conservative Club in January, 1894, where he confessed his dislike of the Radicalism of the Harcourt wing of the Liberal party not only in the foreign but also in the domestic field:

'They have ceased to pursue the old object of Radicals—the greatest happiness of the greatest number. They are never satisfied with making anybody happy now unless at the same time they can make somebody else unhappy. . . . Their advocacy of compensation to workmen is tempered by their desire to do some injury to the employer. . . .'

Chamberlain, on this occasion, called for the formation of a National Party 'that will put country before the interests of any faction.' Only such a party, he had asserted, could deal with such social problems as 'the condition of the poor, the distribution of wealth, the relations between capital and labour' and yet still 'protect our interests in connexion with our foreign relations.'[2]

It was on May 15, 1903, that Chamberlain first proclaimed his adherence to the programme of Tariff Reform and imperial preference—and, perhaps, commenced his drive to construct such a national party. In a later speech he outlined his proposals in detail: a duty of 2s. a quarter upon all imported foreign grain except maize and a similar duty upon imported flour; a duty of 5% upon foreign meat and dairy products except imported bacon; an average duty of about 10% upon foreign manufactured articles. The products of the colonies were to be exempted from all these duties. The programme showed the combined influence of the imperialists, who wished to favour colonial food imports and bind the empire by means of a preferential system, and the manufacturers who wished to protect their products. The industrial protectionist aspects of the programme were a political necessity, it was felt, if widespread support were to be aroused, but Chamberlain preferred, at first, to regard his

[1] W. A. Robson, *Problems of Nationalized Industry* (London: Allen & Unwin, 1952), p. 336.
[2] Quoted in *National Review*, March 1894, XXIII, pp. 7-9.

proposals as exclusively imperial in scope. For almost six months, Chamberlain made no references to any 'social' issue in the course of his pronouncements on preference. He maintained the high tone of imperial idealism. It was first on October 6, 1903, at Glasgow, that he gingerly, almost apologetically, broached the social-imperial theme which was to dominate not only all his subsequent addresses but the whole Tariff Reform campaign.

'Your colonial trade,' Chamberlain began, 'as it stands at present with the prospective advantage of a preference against the foreigner means employment and fair wages for three-quarters of a million of workmen, and subsistence for nearly four millions of our population.' The leader of the Opposition would, he feared, describe this statement as 'a squalid argument.' 'A squalid argument,' Chamberlain retorted, 'I have appealed to your interests. . . . I have appealed to the employers and the employed alike in this great city. I have endeavoured to point out to them that their trade, their wages, all depend on the maintenance of this colonial trade, of which some of my opponents speak with such contempt.'[1]

Chamberlain had announced that the conversion of the working class to Tariff Reform was his prime political objective. Now he had his principal argument—one, we have seen, he had broached at least fifteen years earlier—the 'squalid argument.' At the time of the repeal of the corn laws, labour had not the vote with which to oppose the end of protection for the producer, Chamberlain declared. Now, however, the workers comprised the majority of the electorate. 'Unless I have the support of the working people,' he asserted, 'clearly my movement is already condemned and utterly a failure.'[2] It was as a self-styled representative of the working class that Chamberlain set out to undermine its confidence in Cobdenism; he was not a Labour representative, however, in a 'narrow and selfish sense': 'I represent Labour . . . which thinks not of itself as a class, opposed to any other class in the community, but as responsible

[1] Chamberlain, 'The Case for Tariff Reform,' Glasgow, October 6, 1903, in Charles W. Boyd, ed., *Mr. Chamberlain's Speeches* (New York, 1914), II, pp. 152-153.

[2] Chamberlain, 'Trade Unionism and Tariff Reform,' London, May 17, 1905, *Speeches*, II, p. 316.

for the obligations of the country and the Empire to which it belongs. . . .'[1]

During the previous half-century, Chamberlain warned labour, Free Trade had been destroying the British economy. It had already ruined agriculture. 'Sugar has gone; silk has gone; iron is threatened; wool is threatened; cotton will go! How long are you going to stand it?' he asked. 'At the present moment these industries, and the working men who depend upon them, are like sheep in a field. One by one they allow themselves to be led out to slaughter.' Chamberlain posed these questions: 'Do you think, if you belong at the present time to a prosperous industry, that your prosperity will be allowed to continue? Do you think that the same causes which have destroyed some of our industries, and which are in the course of destroying others, will not be equally applicable to you when your turn comes?'[2] Free Trade was good for the foreigner but was bad for the English workman. 'I admit that I am not cosmopolitan enough to wish to see the happiness, success, or prosperity of American workmen secured by the starvation and misery and suffering of British workmen.'[3]

British working men had combined into trade unions in order to 'secure full employment' and to raise their living standards, Chamberlain argued. 'My proposals have exactly the same object.' The trade unionists were producers first and, like their fellow producers, the manufacturers, they had never benefited from cheapness.[4] 'I ask you to say,' he declared, 'that the principle of trade unionism is the more generous principle, and, in the long run, better for the nation as a whole.'[5] 'Be Free Traders, if you like,' he told them, 'but you cannot be Free Traders in goods and not be Free Traders in labour.'[6] Just as British trade unions worked to prohibit sweat shops, to limit hours of work, to obtain some measure of security for the

[1] Chamberlain, 'A Demand for Inquiry,' Birmingham, May 15, 1903, Speeches, II, p. 125.
[2] Chamberlain, 'Retaliation,' Greenock, October 7, 1903, Speeches, II, p. 177.
[3] Ibid., p. 174.
[4] Chamberlain, 'Trade Unionism and Tariff Reform,' Speeches, II, pp. 317-318.
[5] Ibid., pp. 320.   [6] Ibid., p. 318.

working men within Great Britain, so must they see to it that
such conditions were not encouraged abroad. Permitting cheap
foreign goods to enter the British home market provided such
encouragement. But British working men ought also to bear in
mind that advances in labour standards added to the costs of
production, which, in turn, undermined the competitive position
of the British manufacturer, and inevitably, the economic
position of the working class.[1]

The industrial question was closely tied up with the imperial
one, Chamberlain insisted. The working man must make up his
mind whether he was to follow a policy beneficial to the foreigner
or one which would help colonials and consolidate the Empire.
'Remember,' declared Chamberlain, 'the colonial does a great
deal for you; the foreigner does nothing.' The foreigner, by
imposing high tariffs, shuts his door against British goods and
helps create British unemployment. For this he ought not be
blamed, since he must think first of his own working men. 'On
the other hand,' he argued, 'you have the colonial, who tries to
increase your trade.'[2] Chamberlain, of course, did not mention
that—like the foreigner—the colonies, too, had erected tariffs
against British goods. The colonial secretary expressed his
confidence that the choice between the foreigner and the
colonial was not going to be made on selfish grounds. He
thanked God that 'the working men are now, as they always
have been, patriots.' They were not concerned with a few
pennies in their pocket for they 'always put first in their creed
the welfare of the kingdom and the welfare of the Empire.'[3]
'England without an empire!' That was beyond conception.
'England in that case would not be the England we love.'[4]

Chamberlain employed the 'ransom' argument in reverse: if
you wish to maintain your jobs, he told the British working man,
you must be prepared to pay a 'ransom'—in the form of higher

[1] Chamberlain, 'Tariff Reform, Trade Unionism, and Shipping,'
Liverpool, October 27, 1903, *Speeches*, II, pp. 206-207.
[2] Chamberlain, 'Preference, The True Imperial Policy,' Gainsborough, February 1, 1905, *Speeches*, II, pp. 308-310.
[3] Chamberlain, 'Tariff Reform, Trade Unionism and Shipping,'
Speeches, II, pp. 200-201.
[4] Chamberlain, 'The Last Speech,' Bingley Hall, July 9, 1906,
Speeches, II, p. 367.

prices for bread, something the average working man dreaded.
But there would be many compensations. Chamberlain told of
conversations with foreign manufacturers in which he had been
assured that, immediately upon the acceptance of Tariff Reform,
they would move their factories to England. This would quite
obviously be of no advantage to British manufacturers who
would have to meet additional competition, but it would provide
greater employment.[1] By keeping out cheap foreign goods,
Tariff Reform would save British industry; by its preferential
aspects, Tariff Reform would save the British Empire; by both
these remarkable devices, the Chamberlain programme would
maintain high British labour standards and would save jobs for
British workmen.

What he aimed at, Chamberlain insisted, was the proper
distribution of Britain's growing national wealth. Returning to
the slogans of his early Radicalism, he spoke of the necessity of
Britain's 'advance toward a great laudable aspiration, the
greatest happiness of the greatest number.' This had always
been his goal, he declared. He had for many years spoken of a
great reform which would come in the future, a reform 'which
would do more for you than all these attempts at bettering your
condition—that was the reform which would secure for the
masses of the industrial population of this country constant
employment, at fair wages.' What he had had in mind during
those years, he asserted, had been Tariff Reform.[2]

In previous elections, Chamberlain had pledged the electorate
that he would secure old-age pensions for them. Chamberlain
confessed his previous inability to redeem this pledge because
such a programme would have required more money than was
available. The tariff revenues, he could now assure them, would
more than meet the necessary financial requirement. The
foreigner would be made to pay for British old-age pensions,
Chamberlain declared. Two years later, in 1905, Chamberlain
was compelled to withdraw this pledge of old-age pensions,
perhaps because it was logically difficult to explain how a
tariff which succeeded in protecting British industry could

[1] Chamberlain, 'Tariff Reform and the Cotton Trade,' Preston,
January 11, 1905, *Speeches*, II, pp. 286-287; and 'The Anti-Corn Law
Agitation,' Birmingham, November 4, 1903, *Speeches*, II, p. 251.
[2] Quoted in *The Times*, July 10, 1906, 11c.

successfully raise a huge revenue. Chamberlain's pension promise was replaced by a pledge that tariff levies upon imported flour would be balanced by reductions in the then existing duties upon coffee, tea and cocoa.

After his initial hesitations, Chamberlain used the social-imperial argument quite frequently. On the whole, however, he preferred to omit references to the 'squalid argument' and to keep the empire foremost in his addresses. There were others within the tariff movement to whom the primary responsibility for impressing the 'squalid argument' upon the British working class fell. Most prominent in this connection was the famous Tariff Reform League.

V

THE SOCIAL-IMPERIALISM OF THE TARIFF REFORM LEAGUE

The growth of trade unionism and the establishment of the Labour party were unhappy omens for the Tariff Reformers. The socialists of the Labour Party and the trade union leaders were firm believers in the gospel of internationalism shaped by both Cobdenite humanitarianism and socialist theory. They were anti-imperialist, anti-militarist, anti-protectionist. Their internationalism, furthermore, had the unpleasant bite of class antagonism: socialist doctrine, largely accepted by the Labour party, proclaimed that 'there is no cause for quarrel' between 'the workers of the world,' and asserted that the real enemies of the working class were the capitalists of each country.[1] The organized British working class regarded imperialism as 'inimical to social reform and disastrous to trade and commerce,'[2] considered it absurd to expect a government engaged in the destruction of the homes of others, as the British government had been during the Boer War, to execute a domestic housing programme.[3]

The Tariff Reformers feared that international socialism was making headway among the working classes. This is how Balfour, for one, interpreted the results of the election of 1906 in a letter to the King's private secretary in January of that year.[4] Faced with a growing socialist movement in Germany, Bismarck had compounded a system of protection, nationalism, and social reform to oppose it. The Tariff Reformers, in imitation of Bismarck, portrayed their system as a rival to that

---

[1] Labour Party, *Report of the Tenth Annual Conference of the Labour Party* (London, 1910), pp. 94-95.

[2] Labour Representation Committee, *Report of the First Annual Conference of the Labour Representation Committee* (London, 1901), p. 20.

[3] *Report of the Eighth Annual Conference of the Independent Labour Party* (London, 1900), pp. 3-4.

[4] Quoted in Halévy, *op. cit.*, VI, p. 92.

of the socialists. They attacked the socialist doctrine of class conflict with the Tariff Reform concept of the common interests of employer and employed and asserted that an imperial policy was the one best calculated to promote the prosperity of the working class.

The chairman of the Tariff Reform League—an organization which had been formed to support the Chamberlain proposals—Viscount Ridley, in 1906, spoke of 'two parties in the State' which 'knew their own mind,' and identified them as the Tariff Reform Party and the Independent Labour Party.[1] Arnold-Forster, one of the more important leaders of the tariff movement, declared that only a policy of imperialism could satisfy British needs and presented such a policy as an 'alternative' to socialism.[2] Edward Goulding, another Tariff League strategist, declared in the House of Commons in 1908 that 'the greatest obstacle that could be erected against the policy of the Labour Socialist Party was the policy of tariff reform linked with Imperialism. . . .'[3] One Tariff Reform League publication quoted a section from an I.L.P. pamphlet with evident approval: Tariff Reform, the I.L.P. had declared, 'would knit whole trades, master and man, together in support of the present (capitalist) system.' That goal, the League asserted, was a sound one.[4]

Consciousness of a common imperial patrimony, it was felt, would help to block antagonism between the classes. A Tariff Reform member of parliament addressed the House in these terms, on March 28, 1905:

'After all, the Empire belonged to the working classes just as much as to any class. Their grandsires spilt their blood to gain and keep it. Were they going to let their grandchildren say of them that, for a supposed mess of pottage, they deliberately

---

[1] Quoted in *The Times*, October 9, 1906, 7 f.

[2] H. O. Arnold-Forster, *English Socialism of Today* (London: Murray, 1908), pp. 190-191.

[3] *Parliamentary Debates*, Fourth Series, CLXXXVI, 1331, March 24, 1908.

[4] E. Ashton Bagley, *Question Time: Being a Series of Answers to Questions Asked at Indoor and Outdoor Tariff Reform and Unionist Meetings* (London, 1909), p. 39.

threw away the greatest inheritance that had ever been left to any people?'[1]

Fabian Ware, an influential Tariff Reform journalist, spoke of 'Imperial Democracy' which aimed at 'uniting all classes in the consolidation and defence of the Empire.' Imperial Democrats, although not socialists, wished, Ware added, to achieve 'national organization and unity,' and were 'determined to wipe out the greatest blot on the fame of England—the poverty which harbours vice and the distress which hovers on the verge of starvation.'[2]

THE TARIFF REFORM LEAGUE

It was the Tariff Reform League—as we have already indicated—which took the lead in the effort to wean the working class away from socialism. What was the nature of this organization? That shrewd statesman and long-lived observer of British politics, Winston Churchill, withdrew from the party of his father because of his disgust with the new imperial policies of Chamberlain. Churchill, a Free Trader, believed that the Tariff Reformers would destroy the Conservative Party as it was, 'with its religious convictions and constitutional principles.' The party which would take its place would be 'rich, materialist, and secular,' something like the Republican Party in the United States.[3] If the Tariff Reformers won, the Conservative party would become 'a party of great vested interests, banded together in a formidable confederation'; England would be reduced to dismal circumstances:

'corruption at home, aggression to cover it up abroad; the trickery of tariff juggles, the tyranny of a party machine; sentiment by the bucketful; patriotism by the imperial pint; the open hand at the public exchequer, the open door at the public-house; dear food for the million, cheap labour for the millionaire.'

[1] *Parliamentary Debates*, Fourth Series, CXLIII, 1490, March 28, 1905.
[2] Fabian Ware, 'Unionist Opportunism and Imperial Democracy,' in *Nineteenth Century*, 66 : 738-739, November 1909.
[3] *Parliamentary Debates*, Fourth Series, CXXIII, 194, May 28, 1903.

These would be the result of the victory of the policy of Birmingham. That policy, Churchill warned, must be vigorously opposed by the beneficent doctrines of Manchester.[1]

What had prompted Mr Churchill's prophecy were the early political activities of the Tariff Reform League. The League had been organized in 1903 'for the defence and development of the industrial interests of the British Empire,' by supporters of the fiscal programme advocated by the Secretary of State for Colonial Affairs. The first meeting of the League was held in London's Westminster Palace Hotel on July 21, 1903. Long-standing advocates of industrial protection like Claude Lowther and George Byng were present, as was the steadfast friend of agricultural protection, Henry Chaplin. The journalist and Coefficient L. S. Amery, Oliver Borthwick, the publisher of the *Morning Post*, and another Coefficient, the political economist and geographer H. J. Mackinder attended—Mackinder, indeed, newly converted to Tariff Reform, had at first been slated to direct the League—and were all elected members of the executive committee of the new organization. Conservative and Liberal-Unionist members of parliament like Griffith-Boscawen, Evelyn Cecil, and Sir Alexander Henderson likewise found themselves elected to membership on the T.R.L. executive. The usual assemblage of peers filled the lists of those elevated to office: the Duke of Sutherland was elected President of the League; the Duke of Westminster as Chairman of its Council, and Lord Willoughby de Eresby as a member of the executive. The aim of the new organization was to campaign in every constituency for the acceptance of Chamberlain's programme of imperial preference and Tariff Reform. The purpose of the group was underlined and its future methods forecast when Arthur Pearson, the proprietor of the *Daily Express*, was named to head the campaign to convert the nation.[2]

Almost immediately after its organization, the Tariff Reform League named a Tariff Commission composed of some of the nation's leading industrialists and economists to hear evidence and to conduct an inquiry concerning the state of the chief

[1] Liberal Publication Department, *Issues At Stake, A Speech Delivered by John Morley with One by Winston Churchill* (London, 1904), p. 19.
[2] *The Times*, July 22, 1903, 7e, f; also addendum to Tariff Reform League, *Tariff Reform By Pen and Pencil* (London, 1903 ?).

British industries. The Tariff Commissioners were carefully selected by the League. Among them were Arthur Pearson, the sociologist Charles Booth, who had already publicly endorsed the tariff programme, the economic historian and Coefficient, W. A. S. Hewins, who served as the Commission's secretary, and the author of *Social Evolution*, Benjamin Kidd.

Charles Allen, alphabetically the first member named to the Commission, a nephew of Bessemer, the great engineer and inventor, served as chairman of the firm of Henry Bessemer and Company and as managing director of Ebbw Vale Steel, Iron and Coal Company, Ltd. Sir Alfred Hickman, another Commissioner, was an ex-President of the British Iron Trade Association, Chairman of Alfred Hickman Ltd, and a member of the Council of the Iron and Steel Institute. Mr Arthur Keen was chairman of Guest, Keen, and Nettlefolds Ltd, and a vice-president of the Iron and Steel Institute. Sir W. T. Lewis, Bart., was a past president of the Mining Association of Great Britain and vice-president of the Iron and Steel Institute. These iron and steel men were joined by A. W. Maconochie, a large meat preserver and packer, and chairman of the Solderless Tin Company, Ltd; Sir Vincent Caillard, a director of Vickers, Sons and Maxim Ltd; J. J. Candlish, a Liberal glass manufacturer in Durham, who claimed still to maintain his Liberalism in all matters but the tariff; Hon Charles Parsons of the electrical and engraving firm of C. A. Parsons & Company; Mr J. Howard Colls, of Colls and Sons, builders and contractors; and Sir Charles Tennant, Bart., an octogenarian and former Gladstonian Liberal M.P. of the chemical manufacturing firm of Tennant & Sons. Iron and steel, tin, building materials, glass, and chemicals, all midlands products hard hit by German and American competition. These interests constituted the heart of the Commission and of the League itself.[1]

[1] *The Times*, December 18, 1903, 7e, f; *The Annual Register; A Review of Public Events at Home and Abroad for 1903; 234-235; Directory of Directors: A List of the Directors of the Joint Stock Companies of the United Kingdom, and the Companies in Which They Are Concerned* (London, 1907), XXVIII, *passim*. The business interests of the Commissioners were shared by many other important members of the League itself. The Duke of Sutherland, the president of the League, was also a director of the Florence Coal and Iron Company Ltd, and

Woollen goods and cotton goods had, it ought to be noted, no representation upon the Commission. The Liberals were quick to note two other important omissions from the roster of the Tariff Reform League's Commission. Mr John Ellis, M.P. (Nottinghamshire, Rushcliffe) asked in the House: 'Why was it that not a single banker of repute sat on the Tariff Commission.'[1] Mr Beckett, an M.P. for Whitby, in the North Riding of Yorkshire, chided Chamberlain in much the same fashion. 'Wide as the right hon Gentleman the Member for West Birmingham had spread his net, he had not been able to capture a single banker to serve on that committee of political blacksmiths who were engaged in forging fetters for British industry.'[2] Nor was there a workman on the Tariff Commission, a fact which allowed Lloyd George to exercise his parliamentary wit. 'Take this celebrated Tariff Commission. The right hon Gentleman the Member for West Birmingham would not put a workman on that Commission, because he could not afford to pay the expense.' Immediately there were cries of 'No, no!' from the majority benches. 'Was it wrong of him to quote the reason given by the right hon Gentleman the Member for West

the Stafford Coal and Iron Company. Sir Joseph Lawrence, an active League official, was chairman of the Dunderland Iron Ore Company, Ltd., chairman of the Edison Ore Milling Syndicate, Ltd., and chairman of Linotype and Machinery, Ltd. Pike Pease, MP, a prominent member, was a director of the Normanby Iron Works Company, Ltd., and Sir J. Randles, MP, another, was director of the Workington Iron Company, Ltd. Imperial interests—especially South African interests—were well represented: F. Rutherford Harris, a member of the first Executive Committee, was a director of Cape Electric Tramways Ltd., the Capetown Consolidated Tramways and Land Company Ltd., and The Monomotapa Development Company Ltd.; Sir Henry Kimber, MP, the Chairman of the Wandsworth branch of the Tariff Reform League, was the director of eleven companies—all in either Africa or India—and was the chairman of more than half of these; A. Fell, MP, an active League member, was director of six African, and two Canadian companies; Charles S. Goldman, a member of the Executive Committee of the League, was a director of twenty-three mining companies, mostly gold, and practically all in South Africa.

[1] *Parliamentary Debates*, Fourth Series, CXXIX, 822, February 9, 1904.
[2] *Ibid.*, p. 1241, February 12, 1904.

Birmingham,' Lloyd George snapped back. 'He was not criticising it.'[1]

If we turn to consider the supporters of the Tariff Reform League in parliament, we are faced with the opinion of one authority that by the end of the nineteenth century 'there was no appreciable economic difference between the two great government-forming parties in the House of Commons.' How, then, can we explain the fact that nearly every member of the Unionist party in the House of Commons was associated with the Tariff Reform League? By 1900 many of the differences of interests between the Liberal and Conservative Parties had indeed disappeared. But certain differences persisted. A most significant one was the number of landlords in each of the parties in the parliament of 1900: 150 landlords in the Conservative Party to but thirty in the Liberal Party.[2] C. R. Fay, in commenting on an analysis of the vote on Corn Law repeal in 1846, has explained the what might have seemed surprising adherence of the 'railway interests' to the protectionist cause by citing the strong representation of landowners on railway directorates. Landowners had a real interest in whether fiscal needs were to be met by increased taxes on land or by tariff revenues—witness the reaction of the House of Lords to the Lloyd George Budget.[3] One of the principal owners of booming London real estate was the Duke of Westminster, the Chairman of the Council of the Tariff Reform League. Another significant difference, this time principally of sentiment, was in the service representation: seventy army men in the Conservative party to ten Liberal army men; four Conservative naval men, where there were none among the Liberals.

Yet Unionist support for the Chamberlain programme was hardly unanimous. The leader of the Conservative party in the House of Commons, Arthur James Balfour, was planted midway between the all-out Tariff Reformers and the unreconstructed Free Traders; behind him was marshalled a sizeable portion of

[1] *Ibid.*, p. 954, February 10, 1904.
[2] J. A. Thomas, *The House of Commons, 1832-1901: A Study of Its Economic and Functional Character* (Oxford University Press, 1939), p. 20. We have used the tables which appeared upon pp. 14, 15, and 21.
[3] C. R. Fay, *The Corn Laws and Social England* (Cambridge University Press, 1932), p. 102.

party sentiment. The Tariff Reformers never considered Balfour as one of their own. Austen Chamberlain described him as sympathetic to the idea of Tariff Reform but not a 'full-blooded Protectionist.' Balfour, he insisted, was really a 'fiscal reformer,' only interested in having at hand a weapon for use in commercial negotiations.[1] The Free Traders, on the other hand, believed Balfour had been won over for protection and preference, but was not revealing his hand in the interest of party harmony. Shortly after the announcement of Chamberlain's 1903 proposals, Balfour exhibited himself in a position of neutrality by securing the resignations from the Cabinet of the leaders of both Free Trade and Tariff Reform sections of the party. Mrs Dugdale, Balfour's biographer and niece, has written of a conversation which took place between her and her uncle some years after the end of the tariff crusade:

'*A.J.B.*: ". . . Joe's was a *new* doctrine. Joe was becoming an Imperialist, and he saw that Imperialism was impossible on the bare naked Free Trade basis,—or at any rate that it would lose half its strength."
Myself: "And you agreed with that?"
A.J.B.: "Yes I *did*—I should say I did certainly".'

Balfour's many long hesitations, Mrs Dugdale has suggested, resulted from his not wishing to split the party. On one occasion, Balfour boasted that the continued unity of the Conservatives during this period was due to the success of his 'Fabian methods.'[2]

The Tariff Reform League, however, did not share Balfour's scruples over splitting the party. Balfour was disturbed by many of the techniques used by the League to convert the country, and by their efforts to convert the party. Hewins reported him 'unduly sensitive to inaccuracies of expression' in the Tariff League propaganda. He was particularly irritated by what became the chief Tariff League slogan: 'Tariff Reform Means Work for All.' He felt there was no real basis for this claim.[3]

[1] Austen Chamberlain, *Down the Years* (London: Cassell, 1935), pp. 211-212.
[2] Quoted in Blanche E. C. Dugdale, *Arthur James Balfour* (London: Hutchinson, 1936), I, pp. 344-345; II, p. 84.
[3] Hewins, *op. cit.*, I, p. 187.

Much to the discomfiture of the Unionist leader, the extreme Tariff Reformers even made attempts to purge the parliamentary party of those of its members who were at all opposed to the Chamberlain proposals. The most dramatic instance of such an effort to undercut Balfour's leadership of the party was the formation of 'the Confederacy.' In the words of one of the chief 'confederates,' the purpose of the group was 'to drive the enemies of tariff reform out of the Conservative Party.' The Confederacy was an intra-party conspiracy on the part of Tariff Reform League stalwarts designed to 'put the fear of the Confederacy into the hearts of all local Unionist Associations' so that no candidate who did not approve of the Chamberlain policy would be adopted. The members of the conspiracy were determined to fight constituencies in which such candidates were nominated even if this insured a Liberal victory. They preferred to have Liberal members seated rather than Free Trade Tories.[1] Austen Chamberlain has provided us with an example of the attempt of the Tariff Reformers to 'convert' Lord Robert Cecil. The Tariff Reformers told Cecil, a Tory Free Trader, in early February 1909, that he would be opposed in the forthcoming election unless he promised not to oppose the Chamberlain programme. If Cecil refused, 'then frankly,' Chamberlain asserted, 'I would sooner the seat were given to the Radicals or, if that could not be and we could not win, that Bob came in against us as an open foe.'[2]

But the most important job which the Tariff Reform League had set itself was not the 'purging' of the Unionist party, but the conversion of the British working classes.

PROTECTION AND THE WORKING MAN

The working class had received its education in economics from the writings of Harriet Martineau, the speeches of Richard Cobden, the pamphlets of the Anti-Corn Law League, and the parliamentary pronouncements of W. E. Gladstone. Free Trade had received the backing not only of nearly a century of Liberal statesmen, but even of Peel and Disraeli. To the British worker,

[1] Brigadier-General Lord Croft, *My Life of Strife* (London: Hutchinson, 1948), p. 43.
[2] Chamberlain, *Politics from Inside*, pp. 138-140, 181.

Free Trade meant the cheap loaf, the 'free breakfast table,' and the banishment of the possibility of return to the 'hungry forties.' The leaders of the organized working class supported Free Trade not only as good economics, but because it was set in the political context of internationalism and peace. The Trades Union Congresses passed Free Trade resolutions, and praise for Free Trade came from socialist leaders like Keir Hardie, Ramsay MacDonald, and Philip Snowden. The Tariff Reform League had undertaken no simple task when it set out to undermine the British worker's confidence in Cobdenism. Its efforts threw the nation into a gigantic economic debate comparable only to that which raged in the 'forties before the abolition of the corn laws. Every aspect of economic life was publicly dissected. At street-corner meetings, all of labour's grievances—unemployment, the decline of wages, bad working conditions—were explored by Tariff Reform speakers. The introduction of the Lloyd George budget of 1909 broadened and intensified the debate.

There had been no self-conscious working class in the so-called 'golden age' of Liberal Britain, between approximately 1850 and 1874. The trade unions of the period were wealthy friendly societies whose treasuries supported sick and burial funds and could not therefore be squandered in industrial strife. Inevitably they drew their members from the highly skilled, better-paid artisans. These unions identified their interests closely with those of their employers. The 'seventies and 'eighties saw the end of the idyll of master and man, arms linked. In the 'eighties, socialist societies were formed, and the Dock Strike of 1889 began the organization of the unskilled workmen. Socialist resolutions were passed by the Trades Union Congresses in the 'nineties, and the Labour Representation Committee, the forerunner of the Labour Party, was set up in 1900.

Still the working class had not arrived at a state which a socialist would describe as 'class-conscious.' They struck at the call of their union; they hated the blackleg worker; they might look for a union label on a purchased article. At the polls, however, only a small number had yielded to the persuasion of their leaders that there was a working class political pro- gramme, and most of the working class continued to vote either Liberal or Conservative. There was, furthermore, an imperviousness to principle among the rank-and-file workers. They were not troubled, for instance, when their representatives, their paid union officials, voted for socialist resolutions—of which they must have disapproved given their own contrary votes in parliamentary elections—at Labour Party Conferences. However, when a resolution proposing the raising of the school-leaving age to 14 was moved at the Labour Party Conference of 1912, the officials of the textile and miners' unions, who had previously voted for socialist resolutions without hesitation, understood that their constituents would not react kindly to their support of a proposal which would cut into family income. In spite of their admitted personal approval of the proposal, these union leaders voted against it, perceiving the primary importance to their worker-constituents of the regularity and size of the pay envelope.[1] The propagandists of the Tariff Reform League also understood what matters the English working man regarded as most important.

Between 1881 and 1891, the National Fair Trade League had worked to convert the nation to protection. (The use of the term 'fair trade,' like the subsequent use of 'Tariff Reform', indicated how odious was the word 'protection'—especially to the working classes.) Like their successors at the Tariff Reform League, the Fair Trade Leaguers had fixed their sights upon the working classes. Their tactics, however, were most unsuited to the task. The workmen whom the League employed were frequently corrupt and dishonest, and the fact of their receiving substantial sums to do their jobs became known and seriously limited their effectiveness among the working classes. The Fair Traders employed the most questionable of tactics. For example, they hoped to intimidate believers in trade orthodoxy by inciting mobs of workers to violence, and they actually provoked and led street riots. They alienated the bulk of the organized working class by an attempt to 'pack' the Trades Union Congress with their cohorts. There was, however, much in the Fair Trade agitation which appealed to the working class. For example, the efforts of the 'sugar men'— both British refiners and West Indian planters—to impose

---

[1] *Labour Party Conference* (1912), p. 105.

duties to offset the effect of bounties paid foreign sugar producers recommended themselves to part of the working
class because of several thousand unemployed sugar refinery
workers.

Many of the Trades Councils, during the 'eighties, including
the London Trades Council, gave active support to this anti-
bounty campaign. The Secretary of the London Trades Council,
George Shipton, was a leader of the anti-bounty forces. Still,
even these anti-bounty workers insisted that they were not
protectionists. An important limitation of Fair Trade efforts to
convert the working class was unofficial talk among Fair Trade
leaders of the need for increasing the hours of work and de-
creasing wages simultaneously with securing tariff protection.
This could not be regarded as too auspicious by labour. The
socialist union leader H. H. Champion believed that the
workers could not hope for an eight-hour day 'without conceding
to the *principle* of Fair Trade.' However, he insisted that the
first step the Fair Traders must take must be to reduce the
hours of labour. 'If you will do that,' Champion went on, 'and
can thus persuade the workman that your real object is to
improve *his* condition, and not to save the landlord's rent, the
mine-owner's royalty, and the capitalist's interest, you will
infallibly sweep the constituencies.'[1]

Joseph Chamberlain and the Tariff Reform League tried to
avoid some of the errors of their Fair Trade predecessors. For
one thing, they linked protectionist proposals with the popular
cause of imperialism, although this had a built-in stumbling
block, for as devoted as the working man was to the empire, he
was much more concerned with the 'cheap loaf.' Tariff Reform
attempts to convince the working man that protection and
preference was the 'poor man's programme,' were, furthermore,
undermined by the hostility generated by the Taff Vale decision
and the Tariff Reformers' position on the 1909 Budget, situa-
tions which were used by the Liberals to convince the working
class of Tariff Reformer interest in 'the landlord's rent,' and
'the mine-owner's royalty.' But, on the whole, the campaign of
the Tariff Reformers to convert the working man to protection
was directed more intelligently than that of the Fair Traders.

[1] Quoted in Brown, *op. cit.*, p. 30. See also pp. 29-39.

It was also more intensive. Many millions of leaflets were distributed. Many thousands of meetings—from those on street corners to those in Albert Hall—were held. The press blared daily the same terse message: 'Tariff Reform Means Work for All.' Local Tariff Reform Associations were formed in hundreds of constituencies to enlist the rank-and-file behind the Chamberlain programme. Tariff Reform teas were held and Tariff Reform pageants and plays were presented. Music hall ditties were composed on the subject. Finally, the Trade Unionist Tariff Reform Association, with hundreds of local affiliates, was formed to enlist the working man to the cause.

Chamberlain tried to model the strategy of his campaign upon that of the Anti-Corn Law League. In a letter written late in 1903, he stated that 'at present my work is in the towns—as Cobden's was in the first instance.'[1] And to the towns he went preaching the gospel of 'imperial-democracy.' If the strategy was to be that of the Anti-Corn Law League, the tactics were those of the high-pressure 'penny-journalist' Arthur Pearson, publisher of the *Daily Express* and chief mentor of the T.R.L. Chamberlain referred to Pearson as a 'hustler,' and the description was an apt one. Pearson introduced American political methods and tactics into the Tariff campaign and did so shrewdly. Every device was employed to bring the Tariff message to the electors. The gramophone was used to bring Chamberlain's voice to smaller audiences;[2] the music halls

[1] Quoted in Lady St Helier, *Memories of Fifty Years* (London, 1910), p. 288.

[2] Sidney Dark, *The Life of Sir Arthur Pearson* (London, 1922?), pp. 106-107. Pearson's biographer quotes a letter written by the publisher to Chamberlain on October 13, 1903:

Will you speak a twenty minutes' or half-an-hour's speech on the gramophone so that we can make its repetition a feature of our meetings. . . . A loud-speaking gramophone can be heard in quite a large hall, and your very clear enunciation would be all in favour of a good reproduction. . . . If you will fall in with this suggestion it will enable us to present a tremendous attraction to small audiences all over the country and will secure bumper attendances at all our meetings. Grover Cleveland made great use of the gramophone in its then still imperfect state of development during his last successful campaign.

sounded to sprightly Tariff tunes;[1] the muse of political doggerels was invoked.[2] But most important were the big guns of the penny-press. The largest Tariff Reform paper was Pearson's own *Daily Express*. Even before the opening of the Chamberlain campaign, the *Daily Express* had proved its mettle by engaging Ernest Williams, a former Fabian and the author of *Made in Germany*, to write protectionist articles for it. Articles on the necessity of an Imperial *Zollverein* were also appearing regularly in the *Express* before 1903. Nevertheless, when Chamberlain made his proposals, Pearson, like his colleague Northcliffe of the *Daily Mail*, did hesitate. Northcliffe never fully supported preference; he feared and disapproved of the tax on food, the so-called 'stomach-tax.' Pearson had similar reservations but was won over by the manoeuvres of Tariff Reform enthusiasts like Ralph Blumenfeld and J. B. Wilson of the *Express* staff and by the powerful charm of Chamberlain himself. The *Express* became the first London paper to back the Chamberlain proposals.[3]

[1] One example of music-hall Chamberlainia is this bit from 'The John Bull Store' quoted in Alexander Mackintosh, *Joseph Chamberlain: An Honest Biography* (London, 1906), p. 330:

> Our Joe is straight and square, and he's always played us fair
>   When we've trusted him with jobs before,
> So we'll help him all we can, and we'll find that Joey's plan
>   Is the saving of the John Bull Store.

[2] The movement had the services of 'poetess' Eva Bright, who dashed off such lyrics as:

> When wealth and mirth refill the earth,
> Let each man tell his neighbour,
> All this we owe to Chamberlain!
> Hurrah! Hurrah! Hurrah!

and

> With potent words he'll plead our great FRATERNAL cause,
> See written in a people's heart, 'REFORM OUR FISCAL LAWS';
> Restore our waning Commerce, dispel a Nation's gloom.
> One cheer, my lads!—Joe Chamberlain! He'll *gain* that mighty boon!
> *That's* the glad day coming, lads—the glad day coming soon!
>   (*Tariff Reform League Leaflet No. 63*).

[3] Dark, *op. cit.*, p. 100; Ralph Blumenfeld, *R. D. B.'s Diary, 1887-1914* (London, 1930), pp. 194-196; Blumenfeld, *R. D. B.'s Procession* (New York, 1935), pp. 197-198.

Ralph Blumenfeld, who had served his apprenticeship as a journalist on the sensational press of New York, directed the Tariff Reform campaign of the *Express*. Writing years afterward, Blumenfeld discussed the difficulties he had faced and described the solution. The Tariff Reformers—in mid-1903—were met by a solidly hostile press. The Liberal newspapers had 'almost hypnotised a large section of the public into the belief that if tariffs were imposed on any kind of foreign goods, the British working man would starve.' Blumenfeld met the situation by hammering steadily and repeatedly at the same line. He described its formulation and execution as follows:

'We who believed in Tariff Reform produced, by means of constant iteration and reiteration, mass thinking on our side. Joseph Chamberlain said to me one day: "If you can only make working men understand that tariffs will give them more work, you will have done the trick." I then invented the famous slogan, "Tariff Reform Means Work for All." We flaunted it day after day, week and week on the front page of the *Daily Express*. It was assailed as if it were a deadly plague. It focussed opinion, more than all the political speeches, on the point at issue.'[1]

The slogan 'Tariff Reform Means Work for All' was the heart of the campaign to convert the working class. 'Work for All' was a slogan the British workman could well appreciate, and the Tariff Reformers played repeatedly upon this theme with numberless variations. Press support for Chamberlain increased rapidly. In 1904 the Conservative but Free Trade *Standard* was bought by Pearson and under the editorship of H. A. Gwynne, it became a leading Tariff Reform stalwart. By the time of Pearson's acquisition of the *Standard*, 15 of the 21 London daily and evening papers supported Chamberlain and only six opposed him. The publications of Pearson alone wielded immense influence and included not only the *Standard* and *Express* but also the *Evening Standard*, *St James Gazette*, *Birmingham Daily Gazette*, *Birmingham Evening Dispatch*, *Leicester Evening News*, *North Mail*, *Midland Express*, *Newcastle Weekly Leader*.[2]

[1] Ralph Blumenfeld, *The Press in My Time* (London, 1933), pp. 48-49.
[2] Dark, *op. cit.*, pp. 113-119, 123.

The press was not the only weapon of attack. The British worker was assailed from all sides with leaflets, pamphlets, posters, diagrams, cartoons, and sheets of statistics. Upholding Cobdenism in the leaflet war were the Cobden Club, the Free Trade Union, and the Liberal party. Pressing the attack for Chamberlain were the Tariff Reform Leagues of London and Birmingham. The battle of the pamphlets continued throughout the period between 1903 and 1910, gaining momentum until it reached its peak of intensity with the two elections of 1910. After 1910, the activities of both the Tariff Reformers and the Free Traders took a sharp drop. The record of the activities of the Tariff Reform League of London indicates the size of the struggle. It published not only leaflets and pamphlets but monthly notes for members of the movement, notes for speakers, editor's news sheets, and a *Tariff Reformer's Pocket Book*; all were issued in large editions. In 1906, 1,603,000 leaflets, pamphlets, and posters were issued by the League; by 1907 the previous year's total had doubled, reaching 3,225,000; this last total almost doubled again when it reached 6,034,900 in 1908; between January 1909 and the end of the first election of 1910, the Tariff Reform League had distributed 53,169,716 leaflets, pamphlets and posters.[1]

To help sell Tariff Reform to the working class, the T.R.L. organized a Trade Union branch. In the 'eighties, the Fair Traders had also made use of the services of members of the working class. The value of the protectionist agitators of the 'eighties was, however, as has been mentioned, severely undermined by their questionable character and by disclosures of large sums of money which they were paid. By the time of the Chamberlain crusade, the use of obvious renegades was unnecessary; many 'bona-fide trade unionists' were sincere advocates of the new fiscal policy. The term 'bona-fide trade unionist' appeared again and again in reports concerning the Trade Union Branch to emphasize the genuineness of the working class character of the organization, to stress that if the branch members did not, indeed, represent, in any official sense, trade union organizations, they themselves were at least members of trade unions.

[1] Austen Chamberlain, *Politics From Inside*, p. 156; T. J. Mac-Namara, *Tariff Reform and the Working Man* (London, 1910), p. 19.

The Trade Union Branch of the Tariff Reform League, later called the Trade Unionist Reform Association, aped the activities of the parent body on a much reduced scale. Branches of the Association were formed throughout Great Britain; a Scottish, a Yorkshire, and a Lancashire District Council were set up.[1] There seems to have been a rather large number of branches throughout the country; however, the number of members each branch possessed is more uncertain. At times the Association, in announcing to the press the formation of a new branch, would cite with satisfaction the number of members who had already joined. These figures ranged from the 'between 30 and 40' who joined the branch established at Merthyr Tydfil to the '100 trade unionists' who had become members of a newly organized branch at Redheugh.[2] The Trade Unionist Tariff Reform Association was entirely dependent upon the Tariff Reform League for published material, publishing nothing of its own. Its function was to hold meetings in working class districts and to supply trade unionist speakers when requested. A large number of meetings was held under its auspices. In May 1909 the Association claimed it was holding an average, each month, of 200 meetings and that all the speakers at those meetings were 'bona-fide' trade unionists.[3] During the intensive election campaign of January 1910, the Association announced its intention of holding two or three meetings a day at Wolverhampton and thirty to forty a week in London.[4]

The president of the Association was F. Hastings Medhurst. The general secretary was Alderman G. K. Naylor of the London County Council, a member of the Electrotypers Union; the Association's central office was under Naylor's control. It cannot be said that any of the other members of the Trade Union Branch were at all prominent within the Labour movement. Some were officials in smaller amalgamated societies, others were officers in branches of the more important trade unions. At one of the conventions of the Trade Union Tariff Reform Association, those delegates who had also served as delegates to the Trades Union Congress were listed. These

[1] The Times, September 26, 1907, 2e; June 21, 1906, 13f; October 4, 1909, 12d.
[2] Ibid., May 29, 1907, 14a.   [3] Ibid., May 25, 1909, 16d.
[4] Ibid., December 10, 1909, 10b.

were, perhaps, the most prominent members of the Tariff League branch. They included W. Dyson of the Amalgamated Society of Papermakers; A. R. Jephcott, JP, of the Amalgamated Society of Engineers; S. Longville, vice-president of the Cardiff Typographical Association; W. Queen, general secretary of the Edinburgh and Leith Carters' Association; R. Wilson, general secretary of the Amalgamated Society of Slaters and Tilers; H. T. Pollard of the Carpenters; J. Reid of the Engineers; and the League's general secretary, G. K. Naylor of the Electrotypers.[1]

In spite of fairly energetic activities, it is doubtful that the Association was very effective in converting trade unionists to Tariff Reform. Its resources, both in finance and personnel, were too severely limited. Headed by a powerful trade union orator, it might have compensated for its lack of numbers and funds. Unfortunately, its general secretary, G. K. Naylor, had a bloated, boring, awkward style, unnecessarily complex for any audience.[2] Even if its secretary was not very effective in the field, the Branch still maintained its value as a demonstration of the existence of trade unionist Tariff Reformers, as 'proof' that the support given by the Trades Union Congress to Free Trade did not represent the unanimous opinion of the British working class.[3] The Trade Union Branch worked hard to secure 'official' recognition as a 'bona-fide' trade union organization but its claims were consistently turned down by the Trades Union Congress.[4]

[1] *Ibid.*, September 8, 1906, 7f; Imperial Tariff Committee, *Monthly Notes on Tariff Reform* (Birmingham, 1907), August 1907, p. 49.

[2] In a meeting at Limehouse in December 1904, Naylor fumbled in this manner:

> I would tell the trade unionists of this country that they are fighting their battle of principle with the proverbial millstone of free imports tied round their necks, absolutely precluding them from many movements for reform in other directions.
>
> How can trade unionists view with worse than practical indifference the dumping of goods into the home market, made under conditions that in their effect are equivalent in every respect to the introduction of cheap labour into this country?

(Applause). Quoted in *Ibid.*, January 1905, p. 7.

[3] See *Ibid.*, December 1905, p. 197; November 1904, pp. 162-193; *The Times*, January 1, 1906, 15f.

[4] *Report of Proceedings at the Thirty-Eighth Annual Trades Union Congress* (London, 1905), pp. 98-100.

THE TARIFF REFORM 'GOSPEL'
FOR THE WORKING CLASS

The Tariff Reform League appealed to workers both as a class and in their position as producers with interests in particular trades. The technique was pretty much the same as that used at an open-air Tariff Reform meeting described by the Liberal M.P., T. J. MacNamara:

'My lads! You see those Works over yonder—closed, dilapidated, and fallen into decay. When you were boys, £200,000 a year wages was earned in those Works. What killed them? Foreign competition! What ought you to do? Keep the foreigner out; and once again happiness, prosperity, employment, and—£200,000 a year wages!'[1]

If 'those Works over yonder' were still open, they were described as being in great peril. Imposing statistical proof was offered. Virtually all British trades were considered by League publications. Special leaflets were prepared for railway workers, cotton operatives, agriculturists, agricultural labourers, as well as workers in the book trade, leather workers, glove makers, dock workers, woollen workers, small gardeners and market gardeners, fishermen, coal miners, grape growers, glass workers, pottery workers, iron and steel workers, wood workers, silk workers, lace workers, paper-makers, hat-makers, engineers, linen workers, slate workers, clerks, potato growers, the building trade, carpenters and joiners, dry goodsmen, millers, and even piano makers.[2] All these leaflets described the benefits in wages and the new security of employment which would result from Tariff Reform and depicted in awful terms the disastrous consequences of the failure to adopt the Chamberlain programme.

Both the leaflets directed toward the problems of a particular trade and those dealing with more general themes stressed the

[1] T. J. MacNamara, *The Political Situation: Letters to a Working Man* (London, 1909), p. 7.

[2] Tariff Reform League Leaflets Nos. 26-28, 39, 40, 45, 46, 60, 69, 79, 81, 84, 105, 112, 115-117, 142, 143, 150-167, 170, 185, 190, 191, 199, 219, 221-226, 238, 243, 257, 267. In future notes, T.R.L.L. No. ——.

need of protection from the self-seeking, destructive foreigner. The foreigner assumed different shapes. Most often he was simply labelled the 'foreigner.'[1] At other times he appeared as a bloated 'Herr Dumper' who spoke in such unmistakable accents as 'hullo, mein freindt.'[2] At still other times the 'foreigner' took on a corporate shape: the American Beef Trust or the Chicago Meat Trust or the American Hop Trust. These American trusts were accused of conspiring to ruin British stock raisers and hop growers and to throw thousands of agricultural workmen out of their jobs.[3] The Tariff Reform League urged 'Fair Play for British Workers!'[4] and posed the alternative of 'Britisher or Foreigner? Free Trade means More Taxes and Less Wages— Tariff Reform means British Work for British Workers.'[5] One leaflet proclaimed that 'Every Vote for Free Trade Means Work *for the Foreigner and WANT for British Workmen.*'[6] Another inquired 'What is Retaliation?' and answered 'Justice for the British Worker.'[7] Foreign labour, German labour in particular, was said to work long hours for low wages: 'why allow goods made by blackleg labour to come into this country free of duty AND ROB BRITISH WORKERS OF EMPLOY-MENT & WAGES?'[8] A Tariff Leaflet spoke of the working class objection to the pauper alien because he accepted low wages and lowered living standards. 'You know this is bad for England, and your first duty is to your country,' it continued. 'But can you not see that it is worse to have him working against you abroad?' In England his labour at least helped to maintain the British Navy, 'in Germany it helps to build the German Navy, which we are really creating by our system of free imports.' 'Why not . . . make use of the Custom House officials to act as your pickets against the foreign blackleg?'[9]

The Imperial Tariff Committee of Birmingham produced a leaflet headlined 'Your Wages in Danger' which discussed the imminent possibility that the United States Steel and Iron Trusts would flood Great Britain with cheap iron and steel:

[1] T.R.L.L. No. 209.   [2] T.R.L.L. No. 212.
[3] de F. Pennefather, *The Hop Trust, the Beef Trust, and Their Free Trade Allies* (Hereford: 1903), p. 3, and T.R.L.L. No. 233.
[4] T.R.L.L. No. 217.
[5] T.R.L.L. No. 215.   [6] T.R.L.L. No. 211.   [7] T.R.L.L. No. 9.
[8] T.R.L.L. No. 217.   [9] T.R.L.L. No. 16.

'If the English iron and steel works shut down, there will be less demand for coal; and coal miners will have to be content with less wages; and the 100,000 men employed in iron and steel works will have to go elsewhere for their daily bread.

If you send steel made in England to America it has to pay a duty of 25s a ton. But the American can send his steel here for nothing and take away your bread. . . . Ask yourselves whether it is of any use to have cheap bread if you have no wages with which to buy the bread.'[1]

The German too was pictured as trying to deprive the British workman of his loaf. In belligerent tones one leaflet asked: 'British Workmen, how much longer are you going to allow German Workmen to take the Bread out of your Mouths by Dumping their Untaxed Goods into this Country below Cost Price?'[2] In sum the argument presented to the British workman was this: 'We are being unfairly beaten by the foreigner. Shall we take it lying down?'[3] It was a potent argument; it appealed to national pride, self-interest, and to canons of primitive justice. It undoubtedly had much success among the working class. A Free Trade journal discussed the Tariff Reform arguments in these hostile terms. 'The British workman,' it wrote, 'is essentially a bully, and nothing appeals more powerfully to him than the "hit-'em-back" and "take-it-lying-down" arguments.'[4]

Germany played a double role in the campaign of the Tariff Reformers. She was the enemy, the competitor who must be warded off British shores by a tariff, and she was the model, a nation in which the system advocated by Chamberlain was in effective and successful operation. It is not an infrequent occurrence in history that a nation prepares itself to meet its enemies by aping them. The Tariff Reformers pointed to the greatly expanded German industry and empire as proof of their contentions. The Free Traders placed their emphasis upon the

---

[1] Imperial Tariff Committee, *Trade and the Empire* (Birmingham, n.d.), Leaflet No. 15.

[2] Tariff Reform League, *Cartoon Series*, Leaflet D.

[3] T.R.L., *Tariff Reform by Pen and Pencil*, p. 28.

[4] A Student of Public Affairs, 'Mr Chamberlain's Future,' in *Fortnightly Review*, 81/75:451, March 1, 1904.

condition of the German working class and were quick to point out that the German socialist party was the largest in Europe.

The facts of the German domestic situation became an important part of English politics. The diet of the German worker, for example, was debated by the Free Traders, who insisted that he ate horseflesh and black bread, and the Tariff Reformers who felt compelled to deny categorically that the German working man ate bread made of anything but the fine kernel of the wheat and to assert that if he purchased horseflesh it was but to feed his dogs. Furthermore, the Tariff Reformers argued, both bread and horseflesh could be bought more cheaply in Germany than in England. In April 1908, the Secretary of the Tariff Reform League took the Liberal Publication Department to task for a pamphlet which listed the price for a 3 lb. loaf of black bread, in Germany, as 6d. The Tariff League insisted that a 4 lb. loaf of bread, one-sixth rye and five-sixths wheat, cost but 5¼d. The Secretary of the Liberal Publication Department replied in rebuttal, a week later, citing *The Economist*. It was a grand debate. British estimates of the range of prices for a 4 lb. rye loaf in Berlin in February 1908, ran from the Free Trade *Economist's* 8d, to the Board of Trade's 7½d, to the Tariff Reform League's 5¼d.[1]

Because of the difficulty of agreeing on figures, the Tariff Reform League arranged to transport English workmen to Germany where they could investigate German conditions for themselves. The 'tariff-trippers,' as these Tariff Reform workmen were called, returned to England full of information concerning the happy state of the German working class. They often reported the German situation with greater enthusiasm than accuracy and the results were sometimes embarrassing to the sponsors of their voyages. At a dinner at the Hotel Cecil, for instance, on April 14, 1910, Councillor Wilkinson, a recently returned 'tariff-tripper,' told the sixty-four working men luncheon guests of Viscount Ridley that in Germany black bread was baked only for horses, a fact which came as quite a shock to the attending Tariff Reform members of parliament who had just succeeded in introducing rye-bread at the House of Commons restaurant.[2] In sum, the British working man was told

[1] *Liberal Magazine*, June 1908, XVI, pp. 318-319; July 1908, p. 401.
[2] *Liberal Magazine*, May 1910, XVIII, p. 241.

by his travelling co-workers that 'in our "Free Trade" country glaring evidences of misery and poverty are to be met with on all sides, but in German towns things are different.'[1] German workers were paid better wages and had more favourable conditions of employment. Free Trade, on the other hand, meant low wages and dear food: 'Your Cobdenism is costing you more.'[2] Working class and socialist leaders regarded the 'tariff-trippers' as traitors and renegades, men bought by their enemies, men 'worse than a woman who has sold her virtue,' as 'judases' 'canonised for having accepted five guineas a week.'[3]

At the meetings of the Trade Union Branch, the social-imperial argument was dispensed in liberal draughts. At one meeting, for instance, the full gamut was run. The chairman of the branch, Medhurst, was the principal speaker; his subject was the eight-hour day. The Trades Union Congress, he declared, was in favour of an eight-hour day; so was the Trade Union Branch of the Tariff Reform League. 'If,' however, 'they wished to have an eight hours' day adopted, they would have to exclude from competition with our countrymen, who would work eight hours, the hand-work of foreigners who worked longer hours for less wages.' The remainder of the meeting consisted of bestowing praise upon the T.U.C. for having declared itself against the hiring of foreign fitters and joiners while their British counterparts were unemployed; a contention that the Labour Representation Committee 'was unconsciously on the way to tariff reform'; a citation of the colonial offer 'to give us trade and commercial advantages which would bring to us more profit and more money'; a motion by W. Dyson to end unemployment by revising the tariff system; and a declaration by a visiting Tariff Reform shipowner, J. H. Welsford, that 'there should be co-operation between capital and labour' and that, in view of the high rate of interest for capital abroad, 'industry must see that capital [at home] was made as productive and secure as it was abroad.'[4]

The leaders of the Branch made every effort to prove that on the important questions 'they were at one with . . . the other

[1] Tariff Reform League, *'Free Traders' and Germany* (London, 1910), p. 6.

[2] *Ibid.*, p. 48.   [3] *Socialist Review*, V, 243–244, June 1910.

[4] *The Times*, September 8, 1906, 7f.

trade union leaders.[1] They were at times wonderfully shrewd in their statements and took care not to step too heavily on labour toes. One of their manifestoes on socialism and Tariff Reform read:

'Trade Unionists, and others out of employment through foreign competition, are offered by certain of their leaders an academic remedy in the shape of nationalization of the means of production, distribution, and exchange, as to the merits of which we offer no opinion. We firmly believe, however, that neither we nor our fellow workers can afford to wait for the millennium, and we have no alternative but to support the business-like fiscal policy which has been brought forward by Mr. Chamberlain. This policy will, firstly, safeguard our industries from illegitimate and an unfair foreign competition; secondly, safeguard the workers of this country from having to compete with the products of sweated labour abroad; and lastly, by a reasonable businesslike arrangement with our comrades throughout the British Empire, secure British markets for British workmen.'[2]

THE TARIFF REFORM LEAGUE AND THE EMPIRE

The Tariff Reformers found it a most difficult task to 'sell' taxation of food to the working classes. The Tariff men were forced to admit that under their programme some items of food would most probably go up in price. This was the imperial side of Tariff Reform, the so-called 'idealistic' side. The British workman might be convinced that protection would save his trade from extinction, but the imperialists who dominated the tariff movement had decreed that a tax against German steel must go hand in hand with a tax against Argentinian wheat. The workman must therefore be sold not only on protection but on the empire. Preference and consolidation of the British Empire must be shown to be in the best interests of the weekly pay-envelope. Appeals to imperial sentiment were not entirely omitted; they were simply subordinated to matters commercial.

[1] *Ibid.*, May 16, 1906, 12e.
[2] *Monthly Notes on Tariff Reform* (Birmingham), December 1905, p. 97.

The Tariff League circulated widely a speech by Balfour which warned that if Britain did not move to effect the consolidation of the empire, its impending dissolution would cause a fatal injury to the great manufacturing industries of England.[1] The League also circulated the text of a speech Lord Milner had delivered in Montreal in 1908:

'By buying its wheat, so far as possible, from Canada rather than from the Argentine, the United Kingdom will be helping to build up the prosperity of the Dominion. By buying china and earthenware, or glass-ware, or cutlery, from the United Kingdom rather than from Germany or Belgium, Canada is giving employment to British instead of to foreign hands. Needless to argue that development and employment in any part of the Empire is more important than an equivalent amount of development or employment in some foreign country.'[2]

This was the general shape which the Tariff Reform argument on the Empire took.

'Now is your Opportunity!' urged one leaflet. 'Support Tariff Reform and Imperial Preference and Keep your Canadian Trade.'[3] 'Shall Yorkshire or America Have the Canadian Market?' asked another. 'If this trade goes to the Americans, Yorkshire Loses Work and Wages.'[4] A third leaflet posed the same question concerning Lancashire and not too surprisingly arrived at the same conclusion.[5] Still another described the meaning of Preference to the British worker: 'If Canada concluded a commercial treaty with, say, the United States of America, Yankee Workers would be the gainers and you British Workers the Losers!'[6] A fifth described the Australian preferential system under the title 'How Australia Helps the British Working Man.'[7]

A pamphlet published by the Rural Labourers League asked the British worker to consider who were his customers and who his competitors. 'He will see that it is *the British Possessions and*

---

[1] A. J. Balfour, *Mr Balfour on Imperial Preference* (London, 1910), pp. 16, 21.

[2] Lord Milner, *Our Imperial Heritage* (London, 1910), pp. 16-17.

[3] T.R.L.L. No. 270.   [4] T.R.L.L. No. 272.

[5] T.R.L.L. No. 274.   [6] T.R.L.L. No. 277.   [7] T.R.L.L. No. 131.

the neutral markets that are our salvation; and that if it had not been for these we should . . . have been bankrupt by now.'[1] A leaflet of the Imperial Tariff Committee warned that, because of world trade conditions, there was definite danger of losing the colonial markets. '*Colonial* Preference offers to the British Workman an advantage over Foreigners in the markets of British Possessions,' it added. 'If you reject Tariff Reform now, you are throwing away what may be the *last chance* of restoring the industry on which you depend for a living.'[2] A leaflet of the Tariff Reform League made the same grave warning and called for the forming of 'A National Trades Union' and 'an Imperial Trades Union.' 'A preferential tariff with the Colonies,' it added, 'will secure us the Imperial market, which is already the best market we have, but which will grow enormously under the influence of freer trade within the Empire.'[3]

The United Empire Trade League, in the late 'nineties, had warned Britain, as had the imperial-socialist Robert Blatchford, of the danger of starvation in case of war. It had urged Britain to return to agriculture, 'to provide British Food for Britons.' If not enough arable land was available in Great Britain, it counselled Englishmen to 'Look at Your Daughter Lands— Canada, Australasia, South Africa, India.'[4] The Tariff Reform League took up this cry. One leaflet proclaimed 'No Duty on Empire Wheat,' adding 'Support Tariff Reform and Preference Which Means A Big Imperial Loaf!'[5] The hope of a cheap Imperial loaf was held out, too, by another leaflet which maintained that 'Preferential Tariffs Will Develop the Vast Resources of the Colonies and Lower the Price of Food.'[6] The dream of 'A Big Imperial Loaf,' however, was not one of the staples offered by the Tariff Reformers. More often they discounted the petty matter of a small increase in the price of wheat by stressing the enormous trade advantages which

[1] Rural Labourers League, *Manufactured Goods: Whence They Come and Where They Go* (London, 1909?), p. 1.
[2] Imperial Tariff Committee, *Trade and Empire*, No. 114.
[3] T.R.L.L. No. 24, pp. 2-3.
[4] *United Empire Trade League Publications, New Series,* (London, 1897?).
[5] T.R.L.L. No. 220.
[6] T.R.L., *Cartoon Series,* No. G.

would be enjoyed as a result of preference and the disastrous results of failure to adopt preferential trade.

The doctrine of the Tariff Reform League presented to the British working man resembled that of contemporary protectionists elsewhere. Emphasis was placed upon the identity of interest of employer and employee; evidence was presented that their mutual interests were threatened by the foreigner; the conclusion was reached that only by a tariff could these interests be protected. What distinguished their 'gospel' from that of, say, German or American protectionists was the need to justify an increase in food prices as a means of cementing imperial ties. This posed a great difficulty and was generally presented not as a sacrifice to be made for the sake of the Empire—which was the argument many imperialists would have preferred to adopt— but, as we have noted, as an advantage to the English working man in the long run, citing that colonial markets for British goods would expand and the possibility of a cheaper imperial loaf in the future. It is very clear, however, that the protectionists of the Tariff Reform League did not feel too comfortable in the imperial clothes which they felt compelled to don at Chamberlain's insistence. They were cramping, indeed, and imperial questions were not usually emphasized in League publications.

'Doctrinal' differences concerning domestic protection and imperial preference (the first has been called the 'bread and butter' side and the second the 'sentimental' or 'imperial' side of Tariff Reform) divided the members of the Tariff Reform League increasingly as the years passed. Joseph Chamberlain had begun the tariff campaign as one for preference and imperial consolidation. The manufacturers of the Tariff Reform League, although more interested in domestic protection, had accepted the imperial programme as well. Protection, however, was fairly popular with many sections of the British electorate. Many hard-pressed capitalists and their employees could be persuaded to protect British industry. But imperial preference meant an increase in the price of food, and the Liberals had won many elections on the cry of a free breakfast table. In the last years of the campaign, many protectionists argued that preference be eliminated from the Tariff programme so that protection might triumph.

The 'sentimental' side, the imperial side of the movement, was not without its friends. The chief leaders of the Tariff Reform League were convinced imperialists who refused to compromise on imperial preference. Viscount Ridley, a Chairman of the Tariff Reform League, was a leading imperialist. In a speech at the Constitution Club in March of 1909, Ridley expressed his pleasure that 'Tariff Reform was not to come from the Radicals, who would have given a policy of pure Protection without any Imperial aspect.' He himself 'would not have touched the movement but for its imperial interest,' and he felt that his colleagues of the Tariff Reform League had acted similarly.[1] On another occasion, while discussing the comparative prosperity of the German and American workman as a result of tariffs, Ridley had suggested that the prosperity of the workman, 'important as it was, compared with the development of the Empire, was comparatively a side issue.'[2] Since the great theme of the Tariff Reform League campaign was that Tariff Reform was not primarily an imperial question, or a rich man's question, but a working man's question, Ridley's remark gave much good ammunition to the critics of the League's programme.

As the campaign progressed, however, despite all that Ridley and Chamberlain could do, imperial questions became a matter for perorations only. Many of the adherents of imperial consolidation became concerned lest the victory of Tariff Reform not bring with it imperial preference.[3] The question arose at the annual meeting of the Tariff Reform League held in 1908, when this resolution was presented:

'This conference is of opinion that the immediate interests of the working classes in this country would best be served if the proposed reform in Imperial taxation was limited for the present to a transference of a portion of the existing food taxes to imported manufactured articles.'

The intent of the resolution was clear: protection without preference. The Chairman immediately declared that the entire

[1] Quoted in *Liberal Magazine*, April 1909, XVII, p. 199.
[2] Quoted in *Ibid.*, December 1905, XIII, p. 682; see also issue of January 1908, XV, pp. 728-729.
[3] See *Ibid.*, August 1908, XVI, p. 467.

executive body would resign if the resolution were passed, and, with two or three dissenters, the motion was declared out of order. The debate was concluded by Medhurst, the chairman of the Trade Union Branch of the T.R.L., who declared that 'they must not run away from a single item of their policy.'[1]

Two narrow Liberal victories in 1910 separated the lambs from the wolves, the sincere imperialists from the industrial protectionists. During the period between the 1910 polls, much of the Tory press insisted that the Conservative party drop food duties. Succumbing to considerable party pressure, Balfour, in November of 1910, in a speech at Albert Hall, promised to submit a Tariff Reform budget to an electoral referendum should the Unionists be returned. The Tariff Reformers felt miserable and betrayed, but the party still had not deserted preference.[2] After the second defeat of 1910, party resentment turned against its weak and hesitant leader. Disgusted with Balfour's vacillating tactics, the Tariff Reformers began a campaign to force him out. 'B.M.G.', 'Balfour Must Go,' was their slogan. In November of 1911, Balfour resigned to be replaced as Leader of the Unionist opposition by an active Tariff Reformer, Andrew Bonar Law.

Subsequent events make it apparent that it had not really been Balfour's lukewarm position which had caused difficulty for the Tariff Reformers. After the defeat of 1910, contributions to the Tariff Reform League dwindled to almost nothing. Great pressure was brought to bear upon Bonar Law by local Unionist associations and by the mass-circulation party press to drop the highly unpopular food taxes. Finally, in January 1913, Bonar Law felt compelled to give way to these demands. The preferential aspects of Tariff Reform were unceremoniously abandoned. The Unionist party now stood on a programme of protection without preference. The imperialists were routed. In a moving letter to his stepmother, Austen Chamberlain, who had continued the fight initiated by his father after the imperialist leader had suffered a stroke, wrote:

'I have prepared you and Father for what this letter has to tell, yet I find it a very difficult one to write. I have done my best,

[1] *The Times*, February 8, 1908, 6c.
[2] Chamberlain, *Politics from Inside, passim*, pp. 298-312.

but the game is up. We are beaten and the cause for which Father sacrificed more than life itself is abandoned! It is a bitter confession to make and it is difficult for me to speak calmly about it.'[1]

[1] *Ibid.*, p. 508.

VI

FABIANISM AND LIBERAL-IMPERIALISM,
1903-1914

Because of the issue of protection versus Free Trade, the Coefficients' Club, composed of the leaders of the social-imperialist wings of the Liberal, the Tory, and the Socialist parties, was fated to remain a dining club rather than become the nucleus of a new National Party, a party of 'efficiency' as the Fabians had intended it to be. The Chamberlain campaign had revealed that social-imperialism was not a single programme but a policy by means of which different imperialist interests were determined to persuade a democratic—and largely working class—electorate that the economic policies most essential to them would in the long run promote the interest of the working class. In the course of the first decade of the twentieth century, there emerged two different social-imperialisms, one which held that a programme of protection and imperial preference was necessary to the prosperity of the working class and another which attempted to prove that social advance might be obtained under the system of Free Trade, but more of this later. The Liberal-Imperialists—along with the organized working class and the international socialists of the Labour party—retained their confidence in Free Trade. The leaders of Fabianism, on the other hand, were divided between a sympathy for the Chamberlain programme and a desire not to fully lose touch with the Liberal-Imperialists upon whom the Fabian leaders had previously pinned their hopes for influencing domestic legislation. In good political fashion, the Fabians jockeyed to see who would win—and were destined to obtain little for their pains as they attempted to align 'principle' with what they felt to be political necessities.

THE FABIANS

In 'Lord Rosebery Escapes From Houndsditch,' Sidney Webb had, in 1901, described the Conservatives then in power as a

caretaker government. For him, it was hardly an ideal administration—but at least it would have no truck with the imbecilities
of Radical dogma. The nation, however, was awaiting the
coming of the party of national efficiency. In 1901, Webb had
believed Rosebery would head this party. In 1904, the year
after Chamberlain began his crusade for Tariff Reform, a
Fabian tract, entitled *Fabianism and the Fiscal Question*, said
this about the Birmingham tariff crusader:

'If the next Cabinet be the usual Conservative Cabinet with
Mr Chamberlain at the head of it, then it is hard to say whether
Mr Chamberlain or the nation will be the more to be pitied. If,
however, it be a Chamberlain Cabinet, meaning a Cabinet of
younger men of Mr Chamberlain's own stamp, then—well,
then we shall see what we shall see.'[1]

Had the Fabians now found their statesman of the party of
national efficiency in the tariff imperialist, Joseph Chamberlain?
    The Fabian leadership was badly divided over the Chamber-
lain proposals. The anti-imperialists who had remained in the
Society of course remained faithful to Free Trade. This time,
however, they had the support of Sidney Webb who cast his
lot with Rosebery, Asquith, Grey and Haldane, all of whom had
determined to stand by Free Trade. In a public meeting, on
June 26, 1903, Webb declared that what was needed was not
Tariff Reform but social reforms which would make the British
people 'ever more efficient, mentally and physically.'[2] It was
clear, however, that certain other Fabians did not share Webb's
view. Cecil Chesterton, a member of the Fabian Executive,
spoke to a meeting of the Society on November 11, 1904, of the
failure of 'the dream of permeating the Liberal-Imperialists.'
By supporting Free Trade, Chesterton declared, the Liberal-
Imperialists had displayed their true colours and now were
back in Houndsditch.[3] Two other members of the Executive—
Hubert Bland and G. R. S. Taylor also sympathized with Tariff
Reform.[4] Bernard Shaw, too, was ready to accept the Chamber-

---

[1] *Fabianism and the Fiscal Question; An Alternative Policy* (London,
1904), p. 26.
[2] *F.N.*, XIII, No. 7, July 1903, pp. 25, 26.
[3] *F.N.*, XIV, No. 12, December 1904, p. 46.
[4] *F.N.*, XIX, No. 4, March 1908, p. 26.

I

lain programme—most especially, perhaps, because he was
convinced Chamberlain would win.[1] He was again chosen to
write the tract setting forth Fabian policy and the tone in which
he wrote clearly revealed his friendliness to protection.

Just as Webb had disavowed the internationalism, the anti-
imperialism of the main body of British and European socialism
during the Boer War, the Fabian tract on the fiscal question
disavowed the traditional support given by British socialism to
international Free Trade.[2] There were socialist Free Traders
and socialist protectionists, the tract asserted. The socialist
protectionists were opposed to the Chamberlain programme
only because they 'dare not trust our present class Governments
and their lobbies with the power of manipulating tariffs.'[3] It
would be another matter entirely if the tariff were set in the
national interest and not in the interest of a private firm or
individual. The tract affirmed that in so far as Protection means
'the deliberate interference of the State with trade' in order to
effect 'the subordination of commercial enterprise to national
ends, Socialism has no quarrel with it.' In fact, Shaw continued,
in these matters Socialism was 'ultra-Protectionist.'[4] Even before
the announcement of the Chamberlain programme, the Society
had announced its conviction that Free Trade was leading Great
Britain to the fate of Rome, a parasite upon her colonies,
compelled to grant her idle people *panem and circenses* because
it would be cheaper to do so than 'to invest capital and organize
industry at home.'[5] One of Bernard Shaw's novels, written in
the 'eighties, had made the same point.[6] By 1904, this argument
had become standard among Tariff Reformers in their
controversy with the Free Traders, and Shaw repeated it in the
tract on the fiscal question: if Britain continued to live like a

[1] Pease, *op. cit.*, p. 160.
[2] The 'international' socialists of the Labour Party continued to
support Free Trade. See J. R. MacDonald, *The Zollverein and British
Industry* (London, 1903); also Philip Snowden, *The Chamberlain
Bubble, Facts About the Zollverein, with an Alternative Policy* (London,
1903).
[3] *Fabianism and the Fiscal Question*, p. 14.   [4] *Ibid.*, p. 3.
[5] *Fabianism and the Empire*, p. 53.
[6] Bernard Shaw, *An Unsocial Socialist* (London, Constable, 1932).
pp. 207–10.

'magnified Nice,' Shaw warned, she would 'go the way of Rome or Babylon.'[1]

The Fabians classed themselves with the 'sincere Imperialist enthusiasts' who were prevented from joining the tariff movement because it was dominated by tariff 'schemers.' The tract expressed disappointment with the lack of Labour representation in the tariff movement, yet it was prepared to be encouraging to the Chamberlain forces. The intelligent portion of the working class could still be brought to support protection, it told Chamberlain, if the Tariff Reformers took two pledges: the first would be to adopt a statutory minimum wage which would operate upon a sliding scale in relation to prices so that the working class might be protected against a tariff-caused price rise; the second was that the Tariff Reformers' promise that not one cent of the tariff revenues would be applied to the reduction of taxes on unearned income. Such a pledge, the Fabian tract concluded, 'would at once find out which are the sincere Imperialist enthusiasts, and which the schemers . . . advocating the tariff solely as a means of reducing their own Income Tax bills.'[2]

Graham Wallas, one of the original Fabian Essayists, resigned from the Society after an unsuccessful attempt, at a Fabian meeting on January 22, 1904, to prevent publication of Shaw's tract.[3] H. G. Wells, who had only recently joined the Fabians, was barely persuaded to withdraw his offer to resign, in March 1904, after its issuance.[4]

We see, then, that by a series of positive acts between 1899 and 1904, the Fabians had, contrary to the example of the main body of British socialism and the bulk of the organized working class, turned against the cosmopolitan anti-imperialism of Richard Cobden, John Bright, and W. E. Gladstone. They not only rejected the do-nothing domestic programme of Radicalism, they also rejected Radicalism's imperial and trade policies. In an address to the Society in 1904, Cecil Chesterton had pronounced Socialism to be anti-Liberal. Chesterton was

---

[1] *Fabianism and the Fiscal Question*, p. 13.   [2] *Ibid.*, p. 26.
[3] *F.N.*, XIV, No. 2, February 1904, p. 6.
[4] F. E. Loewenstein, 'The Shaw-Wells Controversy of 1904-1908: A Chapter of Fabian History,' *Fabian Quarterly*, No. 41, April 1944, pp. 15-20.

especially unhappy with the 'liberalism' of the Labour party, a
liberalism which, he felt, would doom Labour's chances for
success: 'The typical working man is more Tory than Liberal,'
Chesterton declared. 'Probably he is at heart a Protectionist,'
and 'certainly . . . a Jingo.' The working man was repelled by the
Liberalism and by the 'bias of anti-patriotism which he perceived'
in the Labour party. It was up to the Fabians, free as they were
from Liberal dogma, to shape a programme 'which would really
attract' the working man.[1]

The Fabians objected to the 'narrow insularity' of Radicalism
which kept Great Britain 'backing, "on principle," out of its
proper place in the comity of the world.' 'The same atomic
conception of society' which characterized Liberal policy at
home, Webb had written, 'lay at the root of much of the feeling
of nineteenth-century Liberalism with regard to foreign and
colonial policy.'[2] Writing in 1920, Sidney Webb declared 'we
had little sympathy with the ideal of a universal cosmopolitanism
which some Socialists and many Liberals more or less consciously
cherished, as an exaggeration, if not a perversion, of the teachings of Mazzini on the one hand, and Cobden on the other.'[3]
In an article in the newly established Fabian weekly, *The New
Statesman*, in 1913, Webb had insisted that Socialists were not
' "pacifists" or Quakers'[4] and Clifford Sharp, the editor of the
Fabian weekly, some years later, remarked in similar vein that
'Pacifism, like Prohibitionism and Free Trade . . . is a Liberal,
not a Labour doctrine—a product of philosophic Radicalism.'[5]
But the fact remains that although the Fabians pretended to
speak on behalf of 'socialism' or 'Labour,' the main body of
British socialism and labour supported the Radical wing of
Liberalism on all these points, not the imperialist followers of
Rosebery.

[1] *F.N.*, XIV, No. 12, December 1904, p. 47.
[2] Sidney Webb, *Twentieth Century Politics: A Policy of National
Efficiency* (London: Longmans, 1901), pp. 4–5.
[3] Sidney Webb, in his 'Introduction' to the 1920 reprint of the
Fabian Essays, page xxiv.
[4] Sidney and Beatrice Webb, 'What is Socialism' in *The New Statesman*, I, July 26, 1913, p. 493.
[5] Clifford Sharp, 'Si Vis Pacem, Para Pacem,' in *The New Statesman*,
XXII, February 23, 1924, p. 560.

What was the relationship, if any, of the Society's socialism to its imperialism? During its later years the Fabians preferred to describe their doctrine as 'collectivism' rather than 'socialism.' 'Socialism' was working class politics, a class-oriented politics which, inevitably, was based upon a measure of class antipathy. The chief aim of the Fabians, on the other hand, was the promotion of the national and imperial interest. The most efficient, the least wasteful means of advancing British interests, they were convinced, was the intelligent direction of the imperial economy by experts, such as they had gathered together at the dinners of the Coefficients, and this could only be effectively managed if the empire were collectively organized. Of course, they were convinced that the improvement of the condition of the most depressed classes of the community ought to be at the very head of their programme. It was, as we have noted, substantially because they wished to influence the future domestic programme of a Liberal-Imperialist led government that they had originally identified themselves so forcefully with imperialism. Chamberlain's entrance upon the scene made certain Fabian leaders—Shaw, in particular—feel that they might have backed the wrong horse, so they loosened their dependence on Free Trade imperialism without quite severing the tie to the Rosebery group. The Fabians remained loyal to imperialism—just uncertain as to which brand it was to their best interest to support.

THE LIBERAL-IMPERIALIST GOVERNMENT

Chamberlain's campaign for Tariff Reform had united a badly split Liberal party. The followers of Rosebery, who had supported the war policy of the Unionist government, had separated themselves from the main body of Liberalism when they founded the Liberal League in 1902. The rift between these Liberal-Imperialists and the pro-Boers—who constituted the bulk of the parliamentary party—had been a serious one; the pro-Boer leaders—Rosebery's former secretary for war, Henry Campbell-Bannerman, and David Lloyd George, a parliamentary newcomer from Wales—had stumped the country during the war denouncing their Liberal-Imperialist colleagues as well as British imperialism on the Rand. Although the defence of Free

Trade had given them a common platform, there continued to be some dissension between the two groups.

When the resignation of Balfour made the formation of a Liberal government necessary in late 1905, the Liberal-Imperialists plotted to compel Campbell-Bannerman's elevation to the House of Lords and thus to deprive him of the substance of his power as Prime Minister. Campbell-Bannerman refused to go along with the plan. Having lost on this point, the Liberal-Imperialists did succeed in securing those offices of state with which they were most concerned. Sir Edward Grey was sent to the Foreign Office; R. B. Haldane assumed control of the War Office. H. H. Asquith became second in command as the Chancellor of the Exchequer. Upon Campbell-Bannerman's death in 1908, Asquith became Prime Minister and Lloyd George, whose previous position at the Board of Trade was then assumed by another Radical, Winston Churchill, became Chancellor of the Exchequer. John Burns—a former trade union official—was made President of the Local Government Board. The union between the two wings was solidified as Radicals were placed in the chief domestic positions while the Liberal-Imperialists took charge of foreign and military policy.

The campaign of 1906 had been a violent one. There were appeals to remember the 'hungry 'forties' and paeans in behalf of the cheap loaf as well as shouts of 'Tariff Reform Means Work for All.' The Liberals united in condemning 'slavery under the British Flag' in opposition to Milner's importation of Chinese labour for work in South African mines. The non-conformists— who were to receive 180 of the Liberal seats in the new parliament—were concerned about the threatening effects of the Education Act of 1902. The trade unions supported Liberalism in an effort to obtain legislative redress of the Taff Vale decision of 1900, which had held unions financially responsible for strike-caused damages. Élie Halévy has written that just as the election of 1895 can be interpreted as a call for imperialism, so the election of 1906 can be seen 'at bottom a victory of the proletariat,' and a call for social reform.[1] It was difficult to know the wishes of the electorate where so many issues were involved. The construction of the Liberal government—and the political

[1] For factual detail in these sections, see Halévy, *op. cit.*, *passim*.

philosophies of its leaders—made it necessary that both policies, one of imperialism as well as one of the social reform, should be pursued.

The Foreign Office was a post which the Liberal-Imperialists insisted be theirs—certainly the Cobdenites could not be trusted to ready Britain for the struggle against Germany which many of the Coefficients had anticipated and even longed for. During the last years of Victoria's reign, Great Britain had begun to doubt the wisdom of Salisbury's 'splendid isolation.' Disturbed by French opposition to British moves in Africa and the threatening movements of Russia into China and the buffer states of the Indian frontier, Chamberlain, in the years before the Boer War, had tried to negotiate an Anglo-German alliance. Germany did not respond favourably to these British diplomatic advances, which led Britain to conclude her first alliance in many decades with Japan, in January of 1902. A community of interest was achieved as Britain's concern with Russian threats to her Chinese market and to India were matched by Japan's concern with Russian advances into Manchuria and Korea. Growing German power soon led Britain to seek continental European friends as well. Moves were under way in 1903 to settle the festering conflicts in North Africa which had been disturbing Anglo-French relations, and which in fact had almost resulted in war after the Fashoda incident of 1898. In 1904, an Anglo-French Entente was signed settling outstanding African problems—a most important provision gave Britain a free hand in Egypt, the French receiving the same in Morocco.

The Liberal government of 1906—with the Liberal-Imperialist Grey at the Foreign Office—continued the 'entente' policy of its predecessor, a policy Grey had espoused at meetings of the Coefficients even before the construction of the Anglo-French Entente. Grey even conducted military discussions with the French concerning common defence against possible German attack. German efforts to split the Entente at Algeciras in 1906 strengthened it instead and the Entente was further implemented by the signing of the Anglo-Russian Convention of 1907 which dealt with outstanding Asian questions affecting the two powers and provided a satisfactory solution to conflicts of interest in Persia. The 'ententes' between Great Britain and both France and Russia turned into virtual alliances as a result of shifty German intrigues and—of greater significance—increasing British, French, and Russian fears of German strength. The diplomatic efforts of the Liberal-Imperialists to prepare for war with Germany were successful.

Another of the Coefficients, R. B. Haldane, had received the War Office and he worked with diligence and also with success to ready Britain's army for the struggle ahead.[1] But it was the navy—not the army—which most Britons considered their first line of defence. The German intention to build a large navy—announced by their naval programme of 1898 and reinforced in 1900—could not help but alarm both the British Foreign Office and the Admiralty. Sir John Fisher, who had become First Sea Lord in 1904, had quite early concluded that Great Britain was the target of the German naval build-up and worked to re-organize and modernize the British navy. He began the construction of a new type of naval battleship, the Dread-nought—larger, speedier, armed with more powerful guns than the conventional ship. The first dreadnought was launched in 1906. German yards began to build superships as well. The coming into office of the anti-militarist Campbell-Bannerman resulted in downward revision of naval expenditures and a partial suspension in the building programme, much to the annoyance of the Liberal-Imperialists. Asquith resumed the programme upon his assumption of the office of Prime Minister in 1908.

A chief issue for the imperialists during the decade before the war—and their chief point of conflict with their Radical colleagues—was in the field of armaments policy. Both Lloyd George and Winston Churchill—who had charge of constructing and securing the passage of the Liberal programme of social reform—continued to oppose the large service expenditures desired by the Liberal-Imperialists. Like others in the Radical wing, the Cabinet Radicals wished fiscal emphasis to be placed upon social reform. In 1907, there was a sharp struggle within the Cabinet on the issue of social reform vs. dreadnoughts. A public, aroused by the press to the dangers of German naval expansion—in 1909 England was in the throes of a 'naval panic' —demanded a full effort, however. 'We Want Eight (Dread-

[1] See Chapter XII, *infra.*

noughts) and We Won't Wait,' it told those Radicals who wished only four and the head of the Admiralty who was holding out for six. In three years, the British navy had eighteen. The struggle between the Radicals and the naval expansionists resulted in victory for both—as the Lloyd George Budget of 1909 was able to raise revenue for dreadnoughts as well as for national insurance.[1]

The Liberal-Imperialist moves to meet the German challenge, although supported by the imperialists in the opposition parties, by men like the Germanophobe Leopold J. Maxse, the pro-Chamberlain editor of the *National Review*, and by Robert Blatchford, the socialist editor of the *Clarion*, met the determined opposition of the Radicals and Cobdenites within their own party. The Radicals insisted that there was no foundation to fears of German aggression and believed that the Foreign Office should act rather to alleviate German fears of a British-French-Russian alliance. This was the declared position of Earl Loreburn, a former pro-Boer and a Cabinet critic of Grey's foreign policy, in his introduction to a pamphlet on the 'German panic.' The pamphlet, by J. A. Hobson, described how first France, then Russia, and now Germany had been successively portrayed as Britain's 'natural enemy.' The current talk was the work of 'the Protectionist party,' Hobson declared. Germany and Great Britain were not 'competing trading firms' as the protectionists insisted; in orthodox Cobdenite fashion, Hobson asserted that 'some private English firms' were simply 'competing with some private German or American firms.' The 'panic' was a capitalist scheme 'to divert the force of popular demands for drastic social reforms.'[2]

The Liberal-Imperialists, as Beatrice Webb has told us in her diary, were 'at once collectivists and imperialists'; their 'imperialism,' once in office, has been outlined. What of their 'collectivism'? Once in power, the Liberal-Imperialist led government amply demonstrated its desire to enact the social reforms necessary for the breeding of an 'imperial-race,' and thus to prepare the working class for the threat of a coming war with Germany. The working class electorate was able to see a profound difference between the promises of the Tariff Reformers

[1] See Chapter VII, *infra*.
[2] J. A. Hobson, *The German Panic* (London, 1913), pp. 3-30.

and the performance of the Asquith government. The Tariff Reformers continued to promise steady employment at good wages—an offer which seemed idyllic at best and the sweetness of which was definitely decreased by the thought of the stomach-tax and the failure of similar Tory promises in the past. So far as specific proposals were concerned, the Tariff Reformers frequently—though not always—suggested that the money necessary for old-age pensions might possibly be derived from tariff revenues. The Liberals on the other hand *enacted* a social programme which revealed full awareness that something had to be done to raise the living standards of the poor—and did so by taxing the wealthy, a most important distinction which will later be elaborated upon.

The enactment of these reforms was overseen primarily by David Lloyd George, first as President of the Board of Trade and then as Chancellor of the Exchequer, and by Winston Churchill, Lloyd George's successor at the Board of Trade. The Fabians had guessed wrong as to who would actually formulate domestic reform legislation when Liberalism achieved power, so their advice was not sought during the great period of reform, 1906-14. The Liberal-Imperialists whom they had cultivated in the Coefficients Club were content to guide foreign and military policy and let the Radicals, not the Fabians, establish policy on social questions.[1]

In 1908, an eight-hour day was instituted, with much conflict and difficulty, in the mines—first in the mines, probably, in deference to the parliamentary strength, both Liberal and Labour, of miners' M.P.'s. In 1908, the Liberals presented a programme of old-age pensions without destroying the cheap loaf. The Tariff Reformers had pointed to the conditions in the sweated industries and had suggested that a tariff would eliminate sweating by protecting domestic industry from cheap foreign goods. The Liberals attacked the problem differently, using the minimum wage as a weapon. The Trade Boards Act of 1909 applied to four trades which were notorious for sweat-shop conditions: ready-made tailoring, paper box making, machine-made lace and net finishing, and chain making. A board was set up for these trades and was authorized to fix

[1] R. C. K. Ensor, 'Permeation,' in Margaret Cole, ed., *The Webbs and Their Work* (London: Muller, 1949), pp. 66-71.

minimum rates for time workers and general minimum rates for piece workers.

A move to give substance to the Liberal-Imperial aim of housing fit for an imperial race was made by the Housing and Town Planning Act of 1909. The act increased the powers of local authorities to close and demolish unfit houses and encouraged them to build new ones. In dealing with the problem of relief for the unemployed, the Liberals also gained ground over their opponents. In 1909-10, legislation setting up a national system of labour exchanges was passed, and, by February 1910, sixty-one exchanges were operating under the authority of the Board of Trade. Part II of the famous National Insurance Act of 1911, modelled largely upon the German law of 1889, presented a complex plan of unemployment insurance. The act was to apply to some 2,250,000 workers in trades in which fluctuation of employment was most likely: construction, engineering, shipbuilding, iron founding, saw-milling, and vehicle construction. Both employer and employee were to contribute to the fund, with the state adding one-third of their joint contribution. The same act set forth a system of what can be called 'health insurance.' Beneficiaries included all manual workers between the ages of 16 and 70 and all others earning under £160 a year, excluding public employees. In all 15,000,000 persons were covered.

Mere promises of national insurance from tariff revenues had been made on the street corner, political brochure level by the Tariff Reform League and by such prominent Chamberlain supporters as the Birmingham economist, William Ashley. It was the Liberals, however, who succeeded in presenting to the electorate Bismarckian social insurance—yet on a Free Trade base. In addition, the Liberals had dealt with 'sweated' industries, had satisfied labour's demands for an eight-hour day, and had taken important steps toward their own goal of housing fit for an 'imperial race.' Certainly the Asquith government could not have presented a more radical set of reforms if it had depended upon the socialistic Fabians rather than upon the left-wing of their own party for their formulation.

FABIAN 'IMPERIAL-SOCIALISM'

Indeed, the basic attitude of the Fabians toward the problems of empire and social reform was, for practical purposes, indistinguishable from that of the Asquith government. The Fabians, too, were concerned about the rearing of an 'imperial race' to help meet the German challenge. The controversy over Free Trade had revealed a differentiating element. While the Liberal-Imperialists were disposed to accept Free Trade as unalterable dogma, the Fabians were not. In the years ahead, the Fabians were disposed to look more and more favourably upon the imperialists who had *no* commitments to Liberalism.

They turned with special interest, for example, toward the victor of the South African War, Viscount Milner, a Coefficient. In 1913, the Fabian weekly *New Statesman* published an editorial article which praised Milner's 'high ideal of "Imperialism",' his conception of national life, and his repudiation of the self-seeking gospel of philosophic radicalism. The Fabian journal regretted that 'modern Conservatism is much more touchy about the integrity of property than concerned about the integrity of the Empire' but regarded Milner as an outstanding exception within the ranks of Toryism. 'In his desire for the integrity of the Empire,' the journal concluded, 'Lord Milner, like the Socialists, is really concerned about the breeding of "an Imperial race"; and necessarily finds himself demanding legislation essentially Socialist in character.'[1] The socialists of the Labour Party and of the Second International might have demurred from the so-called 'Socialist' goal of breeding an 'imperial race.'

[1] *The New Statesman*, I, May 17, 1913, pp. 167-168.

VII

THE TWO IMPERIALISMS

> Men, iron, money, and bread be the strength of war, but of these four, the first two be most necessary; because men and iron find money and bread; but bread and money find not men and iron.
>
> NICCOLO MACHIAVELLI,
> *The Art of War*, 1521

> In all ages there have been cities or countries surpassing others in manufactures, trade and navigation; but the world has never witnessed a supremacy to be compared with that existing in our time. In all ages states have aspired to domination, but no edifice of power has ever been constructed upon so broad a base. How miserable appears the ambition of those who attempted to establish universal domination upon the power of arms, in comparison with the great attempt of England to transform her whole territory into an immense manufacturing and commercial city, into an immense port, and to become to other nations what a vast city is to the country, the center of arts and knowledge, of an immense commerce, of opulence, of navigation, of naval and military power; a cosmopolitic country supplying all nations with manufactured products, and asking in return from each country its raw materials and commodities; the arsenal of extensive capital, the universal banker, regulating, if not controlling the circulating money of the whole world, and making all nations tributary to her by loans and the payment of interest.
>
> FRIEDRICH LIST, *National System of Political Economy*, 1841

The story is told of the blind men who wished to discover the nature of an elephant. One, feeling the animal's sturdy legs, declared that an elephant must be like a tree, while another, seizing hold of its trunk, insisted that, on the contrary, it resembled heavy rope. The economists, historians, and polemicists who have investigated or debated the problems to which modern imperialism has given rise have been in a similar position. Each has found himself describing, more or less accurately, a part of the phenomenon and has insisted that it was the whole. The Marxists—with their insistence that modern imperialism has resulted exclusively from the need to export capital—have been most guilty in this regard. But more and more social scientists are coming to understand the complexities of the problem of imperialism, to perceive that, like the elephant, it cannot be understood by examining one part and ignoring the others. Inevitably, the aspects of imperialism which a historian will emphasize will be determined by his subject. In this investigation, we are clearly dealing not with a unitary, mono-lithic imperialism, but with two kinds of imperialism, which are epitomized in the excerpts quoted above.

Achille Loria, a professor of political economy at the University of Turin, wrote an article, in 1907, called 'Les deux notions de l'impérialisme,' in which he drew portraits of what he called 'economic imperialism' and 'commercial imperialism.' The first he described as violent annexation on the part of old and well-populated states of thinly populated states which because of special conditions—tropical climate, for example—cannot be colonized. This was the imperialism of the Boer War which Hobson had described, Loria added, the imperialism of capital export. 'Commercial imperialism,' on the other hand, pertained to the strengthening of bonds between the mother country and its colonies—it might mean an all-out fiscal union or simply the granting of tariff preference. The method by which the first imperialism was carried out was war, the second by peaceful agreement. The two imperialisms might clash, Loria continued, because well-established colonial areas might believe they were endangering their security by ally-ing themselves with a bellicose mother-country, but usually there was a harmonious relationship between the two—with commercial imperialism being nourished by economic imperialism. After a lengthy and intelligent discussion of his two imperialisms, Loria abandoned his attempt to distinguish between them and concluded that commercial imperialism was really 'un phénomène dérivatif,' already contained in the idea of economic imperialism, and hence only economic imperialism deserved to be the object of scientific research, thereby agreeing, substantially, with the Marxists.[1]

More recently, two young economic historians have made a

[1] Achille Loria, 'Les deux notions de l'impérialisme,' *Révue économique internationale*, 1907, III, pp. 459-477.

more insightful attempt to distinguish between types of modern imperialism. Gallagher and Robinson have painted a picture of 'the imperialism of free trade' in their description of the extension of the British Empire through the course of the nineteenth century—even during the so-called anti-imperialist mid-century. The chief objective of this British imperialism was to make trade secure. In many instances, in Latin America for example, annexation was unnecessary to the expansion and security of British trade and investment. In other cases, along the Indian frontier, for example, wars and annexations were the rule even in mid-century. Different techniques were employed to suit different conditions, but there was continuous imperial expansion, both 'formal' and 'informal.' In the last part of the century, during the time of the partitioning of Africa, the use of more informal techniques was seriously undermined by foreign industrial and colonial competition. As a result there had to be greater reliance upon the policy of war and annexation, whence comes the view that imperialism replaced anti-imperialism during the 'eighties and 'nineties.[1] What was actually happening was that a neo-mercantilist imperialism was challenging a 'cosmopolitan' imperialism, a policy which sought commercial monopoly was battling a policy whose objective was the securing of free and safe access to markets, an imperialism of annexation and war was opposing the old imperialism of economic penetration and establishment of informal political controls. In political terms, the Tariff Reformers were challenging the imperialism of the Free Traders, the imperialism of Rosebery and the Liberal-Imperialists.

Although this view of two imperialisms is much more fruitful, it does not quite go far enough for our purposes. It tends too much to regard imperialism as all of one piece with the different imperialisms as responses to different conditions, one succeeding the other in almost mechanical fashion; when foreign competition made free trade imperialism difficult, neo-mercantile imperialism took over. The two imperialisms confront each other as alternate methods, one more appropriate to the time of British hegemony, the other to the time of keener international

[1] John Gallagher and Ronald Robinson, 'The Imperialism of Free Trade,' *The Economic History Review*, Second Series, Vol. VI, No. 1, August 1953, pp. 1-15.

rivalry. There is something to be said for this view especially when we look back on Edwardian England from the vantage point of the present. If, however, we scrutinize the ideas of the men of the time who called themselves imperialists, we will discover a period of overlapping conflict, a period when there was visible not merely two different methods of pursuing but a single objective, but two different objectives and two different ideologies corresponding to these objectives, and, more pertinent to the subject of this monograph, two different social-imperialisms corresponding to the two imperialisms.

There are a number of ways in which the two imperialisms can be distinguished. We can speak—as we have already—of the 'imperialism of protection' and the 'imperialism of free trade.' They might also, with some justice, be labelled the 'imperialism of finance' and the 'imperialism of industry.' At this point, the Marxist would object—Luxemburg, Hilferding, and Bukharin did so object—and suggest that such a distinction was nonsense, that during this period finance capital had taken over industrial capital, that the banks were the controlling forces in industry and the state. It is not our task to assess this analysis with respect to Germany or the United States—and the Marxists take most of their data from these countries. It is, however, possible to cite evidence which would indicate that such a development did not take place in England. Nikolai Bukharin, a prominent exponent of the Marxist view, in his *Imperialism and World Economy*, has concluded that 'only ignorance can at present refer to England as a representative of an entirely different economic type'—different, that is, from Germany and the United States. To prove his contention, Bukharin pointed to examples of British industrial concentration, however, not finance's control of industry.[1] Nor are the other Marxists more successful in proving the control of British industry by finance. Schumpeter, a non-Marxist economist, agreed with the Marxists that 'there has come into being a close alliance between high finance and the cartel magnates, often going as far as personal identity,' this 'although the relation between capitalists and entrepreneurs is one of the typical and fundamental *conflicts* of the capitalist economy.' 'Monopoly

[1] Nikolai Bukharin, *Imperialism and World Economy* (New York, 1929), p. 68 and *passim*.

capitalism,' Schumpeter asserted, 'has virtually fused the big banks and cartels into one.' But in an appendage worthy of emphasis, Schumpeter insisted that this had happened 'everywhere except, significantly, in England.'[1] In England the 'fundamental conflict' between capitalist and entrepreneur persisted.

The banks of England, luxuriating in the profits of England's position as the international clearing house, had no interest in going beyond the orthodox commercial banking policy of providing trade and other short-term credit. In many respects, this has remained to this day the position of a large segment of British finance. In England, it was possible for the banker to contemplate the decline of British industry with equanimity, feeling that his own interest was entirely unaffected. We have seen this attitude expressed by Halford Mackinder in his addresses to the Institute of Bankers. In England, then, if we follow Schumpeter, the typical and fundamental conflict of the capitalist economy—that between the capitalist (the rentier) and the entrepreneur—continued unabated. The financial interests were prospering under the system of Free Trade and felt that system essential to their successful operations. Naturally they and their political spokesmen, men such as Rosebery, Mackinder, and the other Liberal-Imperialists, supported Free Trade. Beatrice Webb, a shrewd contemporary observer, pronounced the Liberal-Imperialists as 'desperately in awe of the City.'[2] Elsewhere in her diaries she referred to Winston Churchill— who quit the Unionists and went over to the Liberals on the issue of Free Trade—as objecting 'to a self-contained Empire as he thinks it would destroy this cosmopolitan capitalism.'[3] The industrialist (the entrepreneur) on the other hand, opposed Free Trade as injurious to himself and demanded protection. In Schumpeter's view, in doing this, the entrepreneur had thrown away his capitalist birthright and had joined forces with the dark forces of the feudal past.

We have already noted that as early as the 'eighties two groups had appeared in the Imperial Federation League; one believed that closer imperial relations could be brought about only by preferential trade; the other believed that closer ties

[1] Schumpeter, *Imperialism*, pp. 106-107.
[2] Beatrice Webb, *op. cit.*, p. 219.   [3] *Ibid.*, p. 269.

K

were primarily a matter of sentiment—although they were interested in closer co-operation on matters of defence—and were convinced free traders. Howard Vincent, aided by the colonial spokesmen in the I.F.L., led the League's preference forces. The Liberal-Imperialist Rosebery was the chief spokesman for the Free Traders.[1] The debate over the Chamberlain programme between 1903-1914 continued this struggle.

THE 'INTERESTS'

Which were the economic interests devoted to Free Trade? British ship-builders, for one group, found their product still welcomed in protected continental markets, as well as, of course, in the home market. There was a good demand for British ships not only because of the skill of experienced British builders, but because their price was substantially lower than those of other ship-builders. Taking advantage of British Free Trade, German manufacturers 'dumped' steel at prices lower than German prices. The availability of cheap steel and ship-building skill helped to make it possible for Britain to reap full advantage of her position as an international entrepôt and facilitated the development of a huge mercantile navy which served as a common carrier for the trade of all nations. Not only the ship-builders, but the new class of ship-owners which had developed had an obvious stake in frustrating the design of the Tariff Reformers to turn inward and throw overboard the profits of the highly developed international common-carrier trade.[2]

Lancashire's cotton industry, too, ranged itself on the side of Free Trade. Not that Lancashire had not suffered from the competition of foreign textile mills sheltered behind protective tariff walls; Lancashire had suffered, and had opposed Home Rule for Ireland so as to maintain imperial markets. During the final quarter of the nineteenth century, the consumption of raw cotton by the textile mills of the United States and the Continent nearly tripled. Yet, despite the closing down of continental and American markets for British cotton piece-goods, Lancashire's

[1] Tyler, *op. cit.*, *passim*.
[2] See, for example, Charles Booth, Jr., *Fiscal Policy and British Shipping from the Free Trade Point of View* (Liverpool, 1909). This Booth was not the sociologist.

cotton exports continued to grow. The average annual export of British cotton piece-goods from 1870 to 1874 was 3,446 million yards; it had climbed to 4,975 million yards between 1890 and 1894 and jumped to 5,295 million yards between 1900 and 1904; it reached 6,673 million yards between 1910 and 1913. Lancashire was more and more finding its new markets in China, in India, and in the Near East and continued prosperous. To compete successfully, Lancashire required cheap food and cheap raw materials which it believed tariffs would endanger.

The 'capitalists'—those who depended on foreign investments —were largely committed to Free Trade. The nineteenth century had witnessed an increasing rate of British investment abroad—interrupted briefly in the 'seventies and again in the 'nineties. Between 1886 and 1889, 60 to 80 million pounds annually were invested overseas. A contemporary survey of investments made between July 1, 1908, and June 14, 1909, showed 169 millions invested abroad during this period. Of this sum, well over half was invested not in the colonies but in foreign countries, mostly in the non-British Western Hemisphere, Argentina in particular.[1] The British investor, at the height of the tariff controversy, it appeared, preferred the risk and return of foreign investment to turning inward upon imperial resources. Protection had nothing to offer these recipients of dividends from overseas—substantially non-imperial—investments. The 'City'—the British financial community—was largely Free Trade. Ship-building, shipping freights, and dividends from investments abroad were only part of the story. Britain built ships and sailed them and British insurance companies prospered by insuring their cargoes. England's position as an entrepôt made profits for her financial institutions as a result of world-wide banking and discount operations. These 'invisible exports' were vital to the British economy. The average annual value of imports from 1902 to 1906, for example, was 559 million pounds. Exports—other than these services—during this period amounted to 390 million pounds. But for the income from these financial activities—dividends, interest, premiums, commissions, salaries and pensions—there would have been an unbridgeable trade gap.

[1] Survey results reported in A. D. Webb, *New Dictionary of Statistics*.

The 'organized' working class—remembering the stories of the hungry 'forties and cherishing the cheap loaf—remained loyal to Free Trade. Perhaps the numbers of workers employed by Britain's chief industries partially accounted for working-class support of Free Trade. According to the 1901 Census, the number of workers in the iron and steel industry, the largest industrial grouping which desired protection, was roughly 100,000. The industries committed to Free Trade, on the other hand, contained the bulk of the working class: in the textile industries were 1,500,000 workers; there were 1,000,000 coal miners (British coal exports were most welcome even in protected marketing areas); 200,000 seamen; 1,000,000 engaged in ship-building; 1,250,000 in various transportation enterprises.

The metals 'entrepreneurs' of the midlands—whose situation we have already discussed—who had fought to retain the Union of 1801 and their Irish markets now saw their Canadian and Australian markets threatened and turned to protection and preference in order to preserve the imperial union. Their conception of the empire was that of a closely unified, harmoniously operating economic and political system, much like the German *Zollverein*. They were convinced that unless such a system were constructed, the empire would go to smash and their trade would be ruined. What they saw happening in the colonies gave them considerable cause for concern. For the proposals for a preferential system had originally come from the self-governing colonies which had already turned their backs on Free Trade. The Canadian tariff of 1859 had been based upon the protective principle. In the 'sixties, Victoria, too, had adopted a protective tariff and her example was followed by other parts of Australia. Both Canada and Australia had urged the mother country to inaugurate a preferential system. If England refused, would these dominions long remain in the empire? In Canada, the Liberals were the advocates of reciprocal trade with the United States, and when the election of 1896 placed them in office, there were imperial fears that Canada might soon be lost to the United States.

All the self-governing colonies appeared to be vitally concerned about preference. The second colonial conference at Ottawa in 1894 had passed resolutions calling for preference.

At the third colonial conference in London, 1897, presided over
by Joseph Chamberlain, a resolution was passed that the
principle of preferential tariffs, which Canada had put into
practice that same year by granting a 12½% preference upon
British goods, should be extended. A similar resolution
recommending the granting of unilateral preference to British
goods was passed by the 1902 conference. The following year,
1903, New Zealand and South Africa put the recommendation
into effect; Australia did the same in 1907. In 1907, Canada
increased its preference to British goods to about 28%. British
Free Trade, however, made it impossible to form a cohesive
preferential union or for Britain to act in defence of imperial
trade interests. When Germany, for example, angered at
Canada's grant of tariff advantages to Britain, retaliated against
Canadian goods, a Free Trade Britain was helpless to reply.
Incidents such as these caused advocates of preference to believe
the empire lost if Free Trade were not speedily abandoned.
While the Tariff Reformers exulted over colonial grants of
preference, Free Traders wondered why the colonies should
impose any tariff at all against British goods; the Chamberlain
programme was certainly hampered by the colonial refusal to
enter an imperial *Zollverein* of Free Trade between the various
parts of the empire.

Was it realistic to regard the colonial market as the means of
saving hard-pressed British manufacturers and restoring
employment to thousands, as Chamberlain had suggested?
The *Fiscal Blue Book of 1903* revealed that the bulk of British
exports was still destined for points outside the empire. During
the last part of the nineteenth century, however, the colonies
were absorbing an ever greater proportion of British exports.
During the short period between 1890 and 1902, the value of
British exports to the colonies increased by 21·2% at the same
time exports to foreign countries had declined by 12%. Where
in 1890 the colonies accounted for 34·6% of British exports, by
1902, their share was 42·1%.[1] The case of the advocates of
preference had a real basis in fact even if their opponents
believed their conclusions overly optimistic. But the interests
benefiting from Free Trade regarded the adoption of a tariff

[1] *Fiscal Blue Book 1903*, pp. 32–33.

and preferential system—the turning inward upon the empire—equivalent to giving up the great world trade of Great Britain for a mess of imperial pottage. The profits of international banking and discount operations; the interest on foreign loans; the dividends on foreign investments; the premiums of an international insurance network—all depended on the 'cosmopolitan capitalism' based upon Free Trade under which Britain had prospered for over half a century. These 'capitalists,' the ship-owners, prospering from an international common-carrying trade, and the Lancashire cotton industry, still thought and acted in terms of the traditional Free Trade imperialism of the nineteenth century, the imperialism of capital export described by J. A. Hobson and N. I. Lenin. It was inevitable that those who were still benefiting from this older imperialism should combat a policy predicated upon the premise that it and all its benefits were irrevocably dead.

NEO-MERCANTILISM

If we consider the basic conceptions underlying the policies of the mercantilist statesmen of the sixteenth through eighteenth centuries, we can appreciate the similarities between the doctrine of the Tariff Reformers and that of the older mercantilists. Gustav Schmoller, one of the leaders of the German school of economic history, has described mercantilism as an agent of unification, as a nation-creating force which operated against the medieval combination of universalism and particularism.[1] One of the leading British economic historians, William Cunningham, who was to become an adherent of the 'imperialism of protection,' thought of mercantilism primarily as a system of power.[2] Eli Heckscher, the historian of mercantilism, combined these concepts when he spoke of as twin mercantilist objectives the effort 'to secure the state's power *internally* against particularist institutions' and the strengthening of 'the *external* power of the state in relation to other states.'[3] Neo-mercantilism

[1] Gustav Schmoller, *The Mercantile System and its Historical Significance* (New York, 1910).
[2] See *infra*, Chapter X, *infra*.
[3] See Eli F. Heckscher, *Mercantilism* (London: Allen & Unwin, 1935), II, p. 15.

accepted both these objectives. Can it not be said that the 'neo-mercantilism' of the Tariff Reformers had for its goal the construction of a national and imperial economy in opposition to the Liberal, Cobdenite synthesis of cosmopolitanism and individualism? Furthermore, Tariff Reform aimed not only at building up state power against *laissez-faire* individualism but also—using the mercantilist instrument of a tariff—constructing a protective rampart against foreign economic invasion.

The mercantilist thought first of all about national power not necessarily about national wealth. Sir Francis Bacon has been quoted as asserting the necessity of 'bowing the ancient policy of this estate, from consideration of plenty to consideration of power.' Even Adam Smith was enough of a child of the mercantile age to say that 'defence is of much more importance than opulence.' In line with these ideas concerning power, the mercantilist had set the goal of self-sufficiency and hoped that a colonial empire might help the state in its attainment. Furthermore, for the mercantilist, once again quoting Heckscher, the 'well-being of the subject had the function of furnishing the necessary support for the power of the state.' The mercantilist considered a large and healthy population essential for the defence of the state. 'People,' Davenant had written in the seventeenth century, 'are the real Strength and Riches of a Country.' Early marriage and large families were encouraged. The mercantilists set up employment as a criterion of national well being and, believing unemployment largely a result of a surplus of goods, argued that only by outright prohibition of imports or by tariff restrictions could employment be set aright. In 1671, the mercantilist theorist Coke had concluded that 'the end of Trade is threefold, viz. Strength, Wealth, and Employment for all sorts of People.' Since employment was so important, the mercantilist favoured exports of manufactured goods rather than raw materials. The mercantilist thought primarily of the interest of the producer of goods not the consumer, espoused the so-called gospel of high price which Child, Cary, and Defoe extended into a gospel of high wages.[1]

Was all this not like the programme of the Tariff Reformers? The alliance between the imperialists—determined to respond

[1] The quotations cited from the writings of the mercantilist economists were derived from *Ibid.*, II, pp. 16, 20, 49, 159.

to colonial offers of a preferential system, especially in view of colonial hesitancy to enter into closer political and defensive ties—and the manufacturers, hard-pressed by foreign competition, produced a neo-mercantilist imperialism. It was an imperialism of a self-contained empire, sheltered by high tariff walls. The tariff would be used as a retaliatory battering-ram by the empire to enter protected markets; preference would guarantee markets within the empire. The Tariff Reformers regarded with cynicism the oft-quoted Board of Trade statistics which indicated growing British prosperity. They were convinced this 'prosperity' was being achieved at the expense of the national welfare and security. They subordinated wealth to considerations of power just as their mercantilist predecessors had. Their emphasis was not upon ephemeral profits but upon what they considered the more abiding features of national strength. The title of a pamphlet written by a leading Tariff Reformer—*Money-power and Man-power*[1]—described in Tariff Reform terms the difference of attitude between the opposing systems. The Tariff Reformers were populationists, concerned about the growing unemployment. Dividends from an Argentine railway, they felt, might add to the national income, as reported by the Board of Trade, but did not add one whit to the national welfare: the railway did not give employment to one of Britain's thousands of unemployed; its existence did not in any way make Britain more secure against its enemies; the men whom it employed would not serve in British armies. Such an investment they regarded as first-class evidence of the pursuit of profit regardless of the national interest.

The mercantilist goal of the Tariff Reformers was to secure a 'self-sustaining' Empire.[2] The Tariff Reformers spoke of the necessity of changing the character of British trade. Bonar Law, speaking at Newcastle in 1907, referred to the need that 'a larger and larger proportion of our imports should consist of raw materials, to be worked up at home, and that a larger and larger proportion of our exports should consist of manufactured goods which have given employment to our own workmen.'

[1] H. J. Mackinder, *Money-Power and Man-Power: The Underlying Principles, Rather Than the Statistics of Tariff Reform* (London, 1906).

[2] See, for example, *Blackwoods Edinburgh Magazine*, CLXXIV, July 1903, pp. 145-164.

In discussing British exports of coal with this Newcastle audience, Bonar Law warned that 'coal is capital, and when once it has been removed it cannot be replaced.'[1]

The Tariff Reform view of international trade—like that of the mercantilists—was derived from their view of the world, a world in which all nations selfishly and ruthlessly applied their power to further their national interests. Free Trade had assumed an international division of labour and was cosmopolitan in outlook. For the Tariff Reformer, as for the mercantilist, a nation's welfare could only be purchased at the expense of her rivals—and the neo-mercantilist could base his economics upon 'scientific' Social-Darwinism! The Tariff Reformer regarded trade as war, not the war of cannon and sabre perhaps, although this might at times be necessary in the interests of trade, but an unending duel for raw materials and markets. Armies and navies and the threat of the use of force inherent in them were instruments in this war. So were tariffs and reciprocity and preferential arrangements. The very vocabulary of the Tariff Reformers demonstrated these modes of thought. An article in the *Fortnightly Review* which discussed this subject spoke of Tariff Reformers who stood 'entrenched behind their tariff walls and bombarded each other with exports. . . . Markets are "invaded," "captured," "held," etc., the "killing power of capital" shows itself in the dead and dying industries,' and so on.[2]

ON 'TERTIARY' INDUSTRY AND NEO-MERCANTILISM

One of the leading themes in the history of economic thought concerns *productive* and *unproductive* factors in an economy. The founders of modern political economy, the Physiocrats, began the debate by their assertion that only work on the land was genuinely productive, all other activities drew their parasitic sustenance from the land. David Ricardo placed the 'unproductive' label upon the landowner and Henry George was later to use the Ricardian law of rent as his argument for the expropriation of the landed property. Karl Marx regarded the

[1] Bonar Law, *The Fiscal Question* (London, 1908), pp. 37-38.
[2] W. M. Lightbody, 'The Protectionist Ideal of Foreign Trade,' in *Fortnightly Review*, February 1, 1904, 81/75:308-309.

worker as productive and the capitalist as unproductively fattening off the surplus value produced by labour. Theorists of protection have consistently vaunted the manufacturer as the productive element in economic life and have looked with the greatest suspicion upon those engaged in commerce.

Perhaps the most complete indictment of the merchant class was presented by the founder of the school of 'national,' protectionist economics, Friedrich List. List grounded his theory upon his rejection of the views of the classical economists, which he regarded as a mere theory of exchange values instead of one of productive powers. He was convinced that 'the power of creating wealth' was 'vastly more important than wealth itself.'[1] His *National System of Political Economy* lauded manufacturing and opposed 'that insane doctrine which sacrifices the interests of agriculture and manufacturing industry to the pretensions of commerce—to the claims of absolute free trade'; this was 'the natural offspring of a theory too fully preoccupied with values, and too little with productive power, and which regards the whole world as simply a republic of merchants, one and indivisible.'[2]

List was a Swabian bureaucrat turned professor of political economy at the University of Tübingen whose experiences in Germany and then in the United States of the early part of the nineteenth century had convinced him that Free Trade, although it might be good national policy for England, was bad policy for less industrially advanced countries which were thereby held in perpetual bondage to Britain. In his work on the 'national system,' he placed the element of nationality back into economics from which it had been expelled by the classical school. The classical school had confused the notions of private and public economy—they were, List maintained, entirely different. Classical doctrine was based on a 'chimerical cosmopolitanism' which had 'no regard for national interests, upon 'a disorganizing *individualism*,' upon 'a dead materialism,' which thought entirely of the profits of the moment and which took account 'neither of the moral nor of the political interests' of the future 'nor of the productive power of the nation.'[3]

[1] Friedrich List, *National System of Political Economy* (Philadelphia, 1856), p. 208.

[2] *Ibid.*, p. 341.   [3] *Ibid.*, p. 262.

Classical doctrine was formulated in the interests of the merchant, List had asserted. The political economists evidently did not perceive

'that the merchants can attain their object, which is wealth, by profits upon the commodities which pass through their hands even at the expense of agriculture and manufactures, at the expense of productive power, nay, even at the expense of national independence. They are under no necessity from the nature of their operations and purposes of regarding the effect which the goods they import or export have upon the morality, the prosperity, or the power of their country. They deal in poisons as readily as medicines.'

The merchants were not concerned with even so important a matter as national employment. The 'interests of the merchants' were consequently opposed to those of the nation.[1]

The Tariff Reformers were in many respects disciples of List, as can best be observed by their attitude toward what Colin Clark and other economists have described as 'tertiary industry.' Agriculture, the pastoral pursuits, forestry, hunting and fishing have been classified as primary industries; large-scale manufacturing as secondary industry; the term tertiary industry has been used to include not only the principal branches of commerce, but also finance, transportation, communication, the service industries, and small-scale manufacture. During the last part of the nineteenth century, Great Britain found herself in the midst of such a tertiary development, which profitable though it was, became the subject of Tariff Reform concern.

For the Free Trader the matter was quite simple. If Britain were faced with increasingly severe competition in the production of iron, steel, and woollens, she was certainly being amply compensated by her emergence as banker and common-carrier to the world and this was for the best. In accordance with the theory and ideal of the international division of labour, each nation would perform those functions for which it was best suited. If the immutable laws of economics had decreed that Great Britain could best function in the international economy as a centre of commerce and finance, the Free Traders welcomed

[1] *Ibid.*, p. 341.

the outcome, just as they had welcomed the previous decree banishing agriculture in favour of iron and cotton goods. In his study of *Imperialism*, Hobson presented this interesting brief in defence of tertiary industry:

'When a modern nation has attained a high level of development in those industrial arts which are engaged in supplying the first physical necessaries and conveniences of the population, an increasing proportion of her productive energies will begin to pass into higher kinds of industry, into the transport services, into distribution, and into professional, official, and personal services, which produce goods and services less adapted on the whole for international trade than those simpler goods which go to build the lower stages of a civilization. If this is true, it would appear that, whereas up to a certain point in the development of national life foreign trade will grow rapidly, after that point a decline, not in absolute size or growth but in relative size and growth, will take place.[1]

This coincided substantially with the attitude of the Liberal-Imperialists who also—witness Mackinder in 1900—were ready to see even an absolute decline in production while investments and 'services' bounded ahead.

The Tariff Reformers did not share this easy confidence. While the Free Trader saw Britain as a small production unit within an international, economic organism—say, a brain within a huge, sprawling body—the Tariff Reformer looked upon her as the organism entire, needing brain, and muscle, and senses. The British organism, the Tariff Reformer believed, was engaged in a struggle for survival with other national organisms, which were waiting to strike her down in a moment of weakness. The atrophying of any of her faculties would mean irrevocable disaster. In such a world Britain could not afford to be dependent upon any other nation and must constantly be in a position to wage successful defence against inevitable attack. In such a world the growing of corn and the making of steel could never be replaced by the manufacture of biscuits and lucrative foreign investments.

[1] Hobson, *Imperialism*, pp. 30-31; *see also* Colin Clark, *The Conditions of Economic Progress* (London: Macmillan, 1951), Chapters VII, IX, *passim.*

In the parliamentary session of 1903, Chamberlain launched an attack on the new tendencies of British economic development. He spoke of the ludicrousness of a 'great Empire' founded on 'jam and pickles.'[1] The cry of 'jam and pickles' was shouted from Tariff Reform platforms up and down the country. Sir Gilbert Parker, one of the more active speakers and writers for the Tariff Reform cause, made this appeal to the economic intuition of Britons: 'Do you think that a man who carried a load represents as much capital, represents as much to the country, as the man who fills his carriage with the load? Is it to be believed that a dividend upon a ship is equal to the dividend which represents the profit of the goods carried in that ship?' 'I don't think so,' was Sir Gilbert's answer.[2] Furthermore, the Tariff Reformers saw the great increase in the rate of overseas investments not only as a betrayal of national welfare and strength for thirty pieces of silver but as being 'earned' by artifice as compared with the 'natural profits' of manufacturing. Once more we turn to Sir Gilbert Parker:

'I don't believe that the interest upon a safe and sound investment in railway bonds or foreign loans, takes any place as an alternative against those natural profits which come from good investment in manufactures which give employment to the working man, which keep in the country, actively engaged, that energy, that paying energy, which is necessary for its progress and development.'[3]

A detailed criticism of tertiary economics was made in the House of Commons, January 30, 1908, by Austen Chamberlain, who had been Balfour's Chancellor from 1903-05. The British economy was faced with chronic unemployment, Chamberlain began. This was due not to intemperance, nor to the lack of education on the part of the workers, as some Radicals had claimed. The cause was more basic. Britons could be divided into those occupied in 'non-productive work and those who were engaged in the service of their fellows in one form or another.'

[1] Quoted in A. S. T. Griffith-Boscawen, *Fourteen Years of Parliament* (London: J. Murray, 1907), pp. 272-273.

[2] Sir Gilbert Parker, *A National Policy: Our Fiscal System and Imperial Reciprocity* (Gravesend, n.d.), p. 10.

[3] *Ibid.*, p. 110.

The 1901 Census had indicated an increase, over the Census of 1881, of 19% of those engaged in 'productive' work, and of 41·2% of those performing 'non-productive' work. 'I think it is a very grave feature of our existing system that so many of our people are led into unproductive instead of productive labour.' Unproductive labour was the unskilled labour of carmen and dockers as well as much of the labour in commerce and service fields—in a word, unproductive work was work in the tertiary industries:

'Here is a general movement which is turning off people from productive into distributing work; from manufacturing industries to trade distribution and service. I believe that that is responsible, in part . . . and a large part, for the fact that the unemployment has become chronic instead of merely spasmodic and seasonal; and if you want to go to the root of the matter you must increase the amount of productive labour for which the country can find occupation . . . one of the most essential reforms at which you must aim, if you are to deal with this growing question of unemployment, is that you ought to increase productive employment, then fiscal reform is the means by which you must do it.'[1]

Unemployment, the Tariff Reformers were convinced, was largely due to the working-out of the system of the 'cosmopolitan' capitalists and would be removed by the policy of the 'self-contained' empire.

The neo-mercantilists argued that their opponents were incapable of using the state to solve the problem of unemployment. The Liberals were accused of focusing attention on such political and social questions as Irish Home Rule, or Welsh disestablishment, or temperance reform, or non-sectarian education, as if these were crucial questions affecting the condition of the working class. The Liberals had refused even to recognize that unemployment was a result of economic conditions which could be altered by state action. The Tariff Reformers pointed to statements made by Liberals, like the following which had appeared in a 1909 publication of the Free Trade Union: 'The causes of unemployment are not so much

[1] *Parliamentary Debates*, Fourth Series, CLXXXIII, 276-278, January 30, 1908.

economic as social and they can no more be removed by a schedule of tariffs than can illness or immorality.'[1] This Liberal attitude was held up to ridicule in Tariff League publications: one cartoon pictured a ragged, patched, bearded workman, with cap and pipe, speaking to a top-hatted, cigar-holding Asquith:

'Mr. Asquith: "What you wanted, my man, was a better education."
Out-of-Work man: "What I want now, guv'nor, is more work".'[2]

It is difficult to chart the position of agriculture in the neo-mercantilist programme. Imperial not national self-sufficiency was the objective of the Tariff Reformers and, in spite of some talk to the contrary, the Chamberlain programme was designed to help colonial, not home, agriculture. This circumstance made some rural Conservatives turn against it as a policy which left British agriculture 'out in the cold.'[3] Jesse Collings, a long-time personal friend of Joseph Chamberlain, had made himself the advocate of what can be called 'peasant proprietorship.' He urged that the Tariff Reformers win the farm labourer's vote by giving 'some prospect of a fair number of them being restored to the land,' but no detailed programme toward this end was set forth.[4] Principally, the Tariff Reformers saw the land as a source of social stability. The unemployed, who might otherwise be troublesome, could go 'back to the land' which served as a towering 'barrier against chaos.' Furthermore, the land could be a chief source of men for the armies needed to maintain Britain's empire,[5] certainly good mercantilist doctrine. Many Free Trade imperialists, too, thought in terms of the land as a source of armies.[6]

[1] Free Trade Union, *The ABC Fiscal Handbook* (London, 1909), p. 114.
[2] Tariff Reform League, *Policy of Tariff Reform* (London, n.d.).
[3] J. A. Bridges, *Reminiscences of a County Politician* (London, 1906), pp. 255-256, 179.
[4] *The Times*, February 8, 1908, 6c.
[5] Sir Gilbert Parker, *The Land for the People; Small Ownership and Land Banks* (London, 1909?), pp. 9-10.
[6] The future postmaster general in the Asquith Cabinet, Herbert Samuel, was quoted in the report of a Radical land reform organization

THE TWO SOCIAL-IMPERIALISMS

We have already distinguished in various ways between the social-imperialisms of the Liberal-Imperialists and of the Tariff Reform League. There is one more vital distinction. Central to promises of social reform which came from both camps was the question of how the money to implement social legislation was to be raised. The alternatives proposed by the two imperialisms were derived, seemingly inevitably, from their chief tenets and, in certain instances, were made necessary by the political support of the interests affected. Certainly the rival 'budgets' were received differently by the working class, particularly the organized working class, and these conflicting financial programmes had an obvious influence in determining which of the rival programmes of social-imperialism the working class was to favour.

During the last years of the nineteenth century, the revenues collected from the conventional sources were proving insufficient for the greatly increased needs of Great Britain. This situation was not peculiar to Britain; it was duplicated in all the nations of Western Europe and in the United States. The expenditures of the British government which had been £70,000,000 in 1870 had reached a total of £90,000,000 in 1891 and had climbed to £100,000,000 four years later. The Boer War and the increasingly severe naval rivalry with Germany multiplied the rate at which these expenditures were growing as did parliamentary efforts to meet the strong demands for social reform. Where was the wherewithal necessary for increased naval expenditures and for the programme of social reform, promised by both parties, to come from? The Tariff Reform solution was that it should come from tariff revenues rather

in 1901 as stating that 'the reason for this scarcity of suitable men for the service was that we had not got the same proportion of healthy, sturdy, agricultural population as we formerly had.' Samuel described land reform groups interested in keeping 'a large population in the rural districts' as laying 'one of the truest foundations of imperial greatness.' Quoted in Ping-ti-Ho, 'Land and State in Great Britain, 1873-1910: A Study of Land Reform Movements and Land Policies,' (An unpublished Columbia University Ph.D. Thesis, 1950), p. 241, f.n.

than from increased direct taxation, which was the method generally favoured by the Liberals.

The Tariff Reformers opposed the taxation methods of liberalism on principle. The taxes on land, progressive taxation of income, super-taxes and the like were all 'direct' taxes. The Tariff Reformers insisted that new sources of revenue be derived from 'indirect' taxes. In the early part of the nineteenth century, indirect taxes—tariffs and excises—had constituted the prime source of government income. Liberal Chancellors of the Exchequer had aimed at producing budgets in which revenues came approximately equally from direct and indirect sources. Due to their efforts, the proportion of direct to indirect taxation was swiftly increasing. In 1871-72, the proportion of direct taxation to indirect stood as 27:73; in 1881-82, it was 40:60; in 1891-92, 44:56; in 1895, 48:52. By the turn of the century, direct taxes were supplying more revenue than indirect taxes, although as late as 1909 indirect levies still accounted for 45% of the total. In responding to needs for new revenue sources, Liberal Chancellors were wont to turn to direct taxation and Tory Chancellors to indirect. The financial requirements of increased governmental activity led to the introduction of death duties in the Liberal Harcourt Budget of 1894, for example, and the deficits growing out of the Boer War resulted in a small tax on imported corn under the Unionist Government in 1902.

In 1907, the budget of Liberal-Imperialist H. H. Asquith, the Chancellor of the Exchequer in the Government of Henry Campbell-Bannerman, began to differentiate, for tax purposes, between earned and unearned incomes—instead of simply taxing one shilling on the pound. A super-tax on estates over £1 million in value was also enacted. In 1909, Lloyd George, the Liberal Chancellor under Asquith, who had become Prime Minister after Campbell-Bannerman's death, presented his first budget. In that budget, the principle of progressive taxation was introduced; a super-tax was levied against incomes above £3,000; there was an increase in the liquor and tobacco excises; there was a substantial increase in death duties; a large duty on the unearned increment of land values, and another on the capital value of undeveloped lands were proposed. When this budget reached the House of Lords, the peers, in seeming violation of constitutional precedent, rejected it and provoked a

L

nation-wide debate on the issues of trade and tax policies, two general elections, and, as one result, the reform of the upper house.

It was primarily the taxes on land which had caused the peers to reject the Lloyd George budget of 1909. The Unionist party declared that the budget amounted to confiscation of wealth and its redistribution, that it was socialistic, that the Liberals, acting from a socialist philosophy of class antagonism, meant to expropriate the property of Englishmen.[1] The Unionists suggested that Tariff Reform, which would 'widen the basis of taxation,' would be the appropriate way of raising new revenues. In reply, Liberal election leaflets carried such slogans as 'The 1909 Budget is a good Budget because it places the Burden on the Right Back.' One huge black sheet with thick white lettering read: ' "Tariff Reform" would let off the RICH in order to TAX THE POOR.' Still another urged: 'Stick to Free Trade under which the nation makes both ends meet by putting the Biggest Burden on the Broadest Back.'[2]

That the land taxes which had aroused such a storm of Tory resentment were not a piece of personal demagoguery on the part of Lloyd George and that they were not solely designed as a trap for the Lords—as some historians have suggested—is the conclusion of a recent student of the problem who has demonstrated that they were the inevitable culmination of decades of agitation on the part of Radicals within the Liberal Party.[3] In the 'eighties and 'nineties, a large number of land reform societies flourished in Great Britain. The visit of Henry George to Great Britain in 1883 had initiated a widespread agitation among Radical elements to do something about the 'unearned' profits of the landlord. Anti-landlord sentiment had long been a part of the Radical tradition; Spence, Paine, Ricardo, and John Stuart Mill had all contributed to its formulation. George's visit, and writings, gave this sentiment a renewed impetus. These land reform groups espoused a wide variety of programmes, from the most moderate to one advocating land nationalization. In the early 'nineties, the most important of

[1] Austen Chamberlain, *Politics from Inside*, p. 182.
[2] *Liberal Publication Department Leaflets* No. 2347, 2331, 2332. (London, 1910).
[3] Ho, *op. cit.*

them united on a platform calling for taxation on the 'unearned increment' of the landed property. The 'unearned increment' was the increase of the value of the land due not to capital improvements on the part of the landlord but to general social development. From the 'eighties onward, there had been a tremendous expansion in the value of urban property resulting from British imperial, commercial, and industrial development. Here—the Radicals believed—was an obvious, and a just source of much needed revenues. The urban landlords in the House of Lords—generally supporters of Tariff Reform—howled with rage.

In a debate on the King's speech at the opening of the Liberal parliament of 1906, Joseph Chamberlain had expressed his doubts that the Chancellor of the Exchequer 'will ever find the money he requires for this policy of social reform, and especially for such a scheme as old-age pensions, unless he is able to widen very much more than I think he will be under the present system the basis of taxation.'[1] Chamberlain was right about the need to increase tax revenues and about the difficulties of widening the basis of taxation under Free Trade. The Liberals had chosen, however, not to widen the basis—this was the method of Tariff Reform—but to tax more heavily those already being taxed. That Tariff Reform was the only way to pay for social reform was an electioneering slogan. That Tariff Reform should be the way to pay for social reform, that any other method was socialist confiscation, was, for Chamberlain, a political principle.

In a letter to the Duke of Devonshire, August 25, 1903, Chamberlain had spoken of his belief that the social reforms 'which are certain to come in the future . . . ought in my opinion to be provided for by indirect, and not by an increase in direct taxation.'[2] In the House of Commons, some three months earlier, Chamberlain had announced that 'while it would be absolute confiscation to put the cost of social reform wholly on the shoulders of one class, and that the richer class, the minority, yet on the other hand it is fair and right that they should make a contribution in return for the indirect advantages they gain from the great prosperity and contentment of the country.' Three-fourths of the new food taxes would, he admitted, like all taxes

[1] *Parliamentary Debates*, Fourth Series, CLII, 163, February 19, 1906.
[2] Quoted in Bernard Holland, *Life of Spencer Compton, Eighth Duke of Devonshire* (London, 1911), Volume II, pp. 322-323.

on consumption, be paid by the 'poorer-classes'; one-fourth would be paid by the 'well-to-do.' 'That being so, according to my mind it is a matter of common justice that the working classes are entitled to every penny of the three-fourths; and I would give them without the slightest hesitation the other one-fourth as well.'[1]

There were many within the ranks of the Tariff Reformers who stood to gain by reliance on tariff revenues and who violently opposed further direct taxation. Some spoke rather openly of the benefits they would receive as a result of the increase of 'indirect taxation.' In an address to his fellow Tariff Reform League stalwarts, Sir Gilbert Parker spoke of the advantages to the working man of a return to the tariff and added, to the obvious delight of his listeners, that 'if we get revenue that way—well, we won't have to pay in other directions. (Hear, hear.) Your income tax will go down— (hear, hear)—and so will mine, I am glad to say—(laughter).'[2]

The social-imperial issue was clearly drawn. The answer given by the Free Trade imperialists to the question of how the money for social reform was to be raised was that it would be raised by increasing the 'ransom,' to use Chamberlain's earlier term, exacted from the profits, direct and indirect, of imperial activity. The Tariff Reformers, on the other hand, wanted the cost of social reform to be borne by the population as a whole, the major part of it by the poorer classes, a charge which, they asserted, working men might easily bear once employment was made more secure and more profitable by protection and imperial preference. This difference on financial questions had a considerable influence in determining the attitude of organized labour.

Even socialists sympathetic to Tariff Reform proposals, like the Fabians and Robert Blatchford, parted company with the Tariff Reformers on this question. The Fabians, in fact, made the issue of whether Tariff Reform should be tied to lowering income taxes the criterion by which to distinguish sincere from selfish Tariff Reformers.[3] The leaders of the working class were even more disturbed and provoked. The working-class leaders

[1] *Parliamentary Debates*, Fourth Series, CXXIII, 186, May 28, 1903.
[2] Parker, *A National Policy*, p. 18.
[3] See section on the Fabians, Chapter VI, *supra*.

agreed that there must be increased taxation to meet the cost of social reform but believed, in the words of Philip Snowden, that Tariff Reform in 'broadening' the basis of taxation was 'putting the cost of those so-called social reforms upon the people themselves by means of indirect taxation.' If, therefore, the cost of old age pensions were to be paid by the broad masses of the people, 'then there could not be in the aggregate any raising of the standard of comfort amongst the people.' A special Labour Conference on the Incidence of Taxation, which met on January 27, 1909, in conjunction with the Ninth Annual Conference of the Labour Party, called instead for 'a Super-tax on large Incomes; Special Taxation of State-conferred Monopolies; Increased Estate and Legacy Duties; and a really substantial beginning with the taxation of land values.'[1]

The Unionist attitude toward the Budget kept even trade union leaders sympathetic to protection on the Free Trade side. Class distrust of the Tories which resulted in Labour's support for the Liberals was deep and had revealed itself before the budget controversy. In an address to the Fourth Annual Conference of the Labour Party in 1904, John Hodge, of the Steel Smelters Union and Chairman of the Party, neatly compounded trade-unionist protectionist sentiment—of which there was a good deal—with trade union distrust of the Conservatives. If Chamberlain wished to help the British working man, Hodge argued, he could do so by 'giving our Trade Dispute Bill a helping hand.' Instead Chamberlain filled his Tariff Reform platform with barons and dukes and earls, and with Arthur Pearson, Hodge added, unable to restrain his protectionist impulses, a newspaper publisher 'whose "Xmas 'Xtra" was printed in Holland.' Hodge was no theoretical Free Trader; he simply could not support the party of Taff Vale and the 'Dukes.' 'If you watch a pot of treacle,' Hodge concluded, 'you won't find the flies far away.'[2] The gaps in the Cobdenite armour were filled with the hard putty of class hatred. The budget controversy confirmed these feelings to the great advantage of Liberalism.

[1] *Labour Party Report* (1909), pp. 104–106.
[2] *Labour Representation Committee Conference* (1904), p. 31.

VIII

SIR HALFORD MACKINDER: THEORIST OF IMPERIALISM

Halford John Mackinder, who has enjoyed considerable recognition as a founder of modern geographical study, achieved a widespread renown two decades ago as the pioneer of the 'science of geopolitics' of which Hitler had become a disciple.[1] His other accomplishments, however, have been rather neglected, especially his work as an economic theorist and politician. At the beginning of the century, Mackinder was a principal spokesman for the Liberal-Imperialists; he was, in fact, well on his way toward a cabinet post. As a Free Trade Imperialist, he described with unusual insight the imperialism of capital export, anticipating at some points the later analysis of Hobson and the neo-Marxists, Hilferding and Luxemburg. Then, after a remarkable and sudden conversion to the Chamberlain programme of protection, he demonstrated a similar grasp of the rival neo-mercantile imperialism, and became one of its leading public advocates.

Mackinder was born at Gainsborough in 1861. His father was a doctor and, his first interests being in the field of science, he accepted, in 1880, a junior studentship in physical science at Christ Church, Oxford, where he intended to specialize in biology. While at Oxford, Mackinder discovered how broad and varied were his interests and his talents. He read for two honours schools, natural science and modern history, and for the bar—he was called to the Inner Temple in 1886. More and more, however, he devoted himself to geography, a subject to whose acceptance as an academic discipline he was to make so signal a contribution. Applying his studies of science, economics, history, and law to geography, Mackinder developed a field he called historical geography. He established a national reputation as a result of his work with the Oxford extension movement when, between 1885 and 1903, he lectured on geography to adult

---

[1] See Robert Strausz-Hupé, *Geopolitics: The Struggle for Space and Power* (New York, 1942), pp. 53-9, 141-8, 154-9, 249-52.

audiences all over Great Britain. In 1887, he was appointed to the post of Reader in Geography at Oxford and in 1899 he was named Director of the first English school of geography, established at that university.[1]

For a long time, Mackinder had had an interest in politics. He had been President of the Oxford Union in 1883 and, according to report, was an excellent platform orator as well as university lecturer. During the 'nineties, he became attached to the Imperialist wing of the Liberal party, a group which revolved about the person of Lord Rosebery. The Liberal-Imperialists, as we know, opposed the party's Radical wing, the heirs of Gladstone; the Radicals maintained nineteenth-century Liberalism's traditional attitudes, which favoured *laissez-faire* and opposed imperialism and militarism. The Liberal-Imperialists were sympathetic to social reform and exponents of the Empire,[2] and Lord Rosebery, combining the two objectives, at one time asserted that 'an empire such as ours requires as its first condition an imperial race,' adding that 'in the rookeries and slums which still survive, an imperial race can not be reared.'[3] This was essentially Mackinder's position.

One platform on which both the Radical and Imperialist wings of Liberalism could unite was that of Free Trade. The Radicals regarded Free Trade as the keystone in the edifice of cosmopolitanism. For the followers of Rosebery, and for Mackinder, it was the economic basis of imperialism. Free Trade had become unassailable national orthodoxy during the 'sixties and 'seventies, the period when British industry remained unchallenged in the market places of the world. However, by the 'eighties, as we have noted, British industry—especially iron and steel, and the other metal trades of the midlands—had begun to feel the pinch of German and American competition and a 'Fair Trade' movement had been launched to

[1] For details concerning Mackinder's life, see E. W. Gilbert, 'The Right Honourable Sir Halford J. Mackinder, PC, 1861-1947,' *Geographical Journal*, CX, January 1948, pp. 94 ff.; and the same writer's 'Seven Lamps of Geography: An Appreciation of the Teaching of Sir Halford J. Mackinder,' *Geography*, XXXIV, March 1951, pp. 21-43.

[2] See Chapter III, *supra*.

[3] Rosebery, *Miscellanies*, II, p. 250.

convince England of the need for protection. The Imperial Federation League, an organization of prominent men interested in tightening the bonds of Empire, had been sharply divided, as early as the 'eighties, into two groups, one of which asserted that the Empire could only be maintained if Free Trade prevailed, and an ever more vociferous protectionist wing which felt that only an imperial *Zollverein* could prevent a crash of both British industry and the Empire. Lord Rosebery had maintained the Free Trade position within the League. For Rosebery, as for Mackinder, industry appeared to be of secondary importance to the preservation of the Empire—for the former Prime Minister the two greatest imperial assets were the navy and capital.[1] The followers of Lord Rosebery, however, never troubled to spell out the theoretical bases of their adherence to a Free Trade Empire; they were not economists but politicians. The job of providing such a theoretical framework was left to Halford Mackinder.

The Liberal-Imperialists were known to be closely connected with English financial interests, and it was fitting that Mackinder should have developed his insights into Free Trade imperialism in a series of lectures to the Institute of Bankers in London in 1899. In the course of these lectures, as noted previously, Mackinder carefully differentiated the interests of industry from those of finance. British industry, he asserted, was faced with the keenest foreign competition and soon British commerce might be in a similar position. This circumstance was a result of a tendency 'towards the dispersion and equalisation of the industrial and commercial activity throughout the world.' However, the more dispersed the world's industry and commerce might be, 'the greater will be the need of a controlling centre to it. Though in the human frame there are many muscles,' he continued, 'there is only one brain.' There may be many 'National Clearing Houses,' but there will be only one 'International Clearing House,' and, because of Britain's leading position in world commerce for two centuries, because of the vast and enormously profitable British carrying trade and the entrepôt system, because 'we have an enormous accumulation of wealth,' because 'we have a vast export of capital, and a great

[1] *The Times*, January 24, 1900, 7b, c. Mackinder agreed on this point; see his *Britain and the British Seas* (London: Heinemann, 1902), p. 346.

ownership of capital fixed in the outlying portions of the world,' and because the City was 'the most convenient market for capital, and therefore the most convenient settlement-place for loans, or debts,' London, he believed, was destined to remain the banking centre of the world. 'It appears, therefore, quite possible,' Mackinder suggested, most significantly, 'that the financial importance of the City of London may continue to increase, while the industry, at any rate, of Britain, becomes *relatively* less.'

What had this to do with imperialism? 'This gives the real key,' Mackinder proclaimed, 'to the struggle between our free trade policy and the protection of other countries—we are essentially the people with capital, and those who have capital always share the proceeds of the activity of brains and muscles of other countries. It is eternally true "that to him that hath shall be given".' Other powers felt a quite natural resentment and wished to prevent England from exporting capital (whether in the shape of rails, machinery, or monetary investment). 'It was a struggle,' Mackinder proclaimed in good Darwinist fashion, 'of nationality against nationality—it is a real struggle for Empire in the world.' To underscore his point, and in so doing anticipating J. A. Hobson's later analysis of imperialism, Mackinder suggested that 'it is for the maintenance of our position in the world, because we are the great lenders, that we have been driven to increase our empire.'[1]

In 1900, in the midst of the Boer War, a general election was called and Mackinder contested Warwick as a Liberal. He was in favour of the war, but the Radicals and the greater part of Liberal party organizations throughout the country were opposed to it. Mackinder was defeated. During the course of the war, to sum up what has been described earlier, the Liberal-Imperialists became more and more estranged from the main body of Liberalism and, in the middle of 1901, Rosebery made an address to the Liberal City Club which caused many to believe that the former Prime Minister was about to organize a new party, a party which he had indicated would make 'national efficiency' its objective. The leaders of Fabian socialism, Sidney

---

[1] Mackinder, 'The Great Trade Routes,' *Journal of the Institute of Bankers*, March 1900, pp. 154-5; May 1900, p. 271. See also *Britain and the British Seas*, pp. 343 ff.

and Beatrice Webb, and Bernard Shaw, had long been intimate with the leaders of Liberal-Imperialism, especially with Rosebery and Haldane. Interested in the possibility of a party of national efficiency, the Webbs and Shaw wished to join their collectivist programme to the imperialism of the followers of Rosebery. The Webbs decided to form a dining club—the Coefficients—which, they hoped, would serve as a 'brains trust' for the new political movement. They invited a dozen prominent individuals, representing both political parties, but having a common interest in a strong, effective Empire. Among the leaders of the Liberal-Imperial party, Sidney Webb asked Sir Edward Grey, R. B. Haldane, and Mackinder to join.

The very earliest meetings of the Coefficients were marked by dissension over trade policy. The chief advocate of protection within the group was W. A. S. Hewins, the rabidly imperialistic Director of the Fabian-founded London School of Economics. In January, 1903, at the third meeting of the Coefficients, there was a full-scale debate on the subject of preferential tariffs. Hewins has reported in his autobiography that 'present divisions of opinion came out very clearly and Amery and Maxse were the only two who genuinely supported my views.' The Liberal-Imperialists to a man had supported Free Trade. In May, 1903, as we know, Joseph Chamberlain, the Secretary of State for Colonies, after some years of toying with the idea, publicly took up the cudgels for protection and began a nation-wide campaign in favour of Tariff Reform and imperial preference. The issue was even more sharply debated at the dinners of the Coefficients. It became clear that two of the Liberal-Imperialists —Grey and Mackinder—were wavering in their adherence to Free Trade, and both Hewins and Amery applied every effort to convert them to Tariff Reform. Grey held firm. Mackinder, on the other hand, was persuaded by Amery that—to continue Mackinder's metaphor—if Great Britain were to remain a great power she required muscle as well as brain.[1]

Mackinder's conversion to protectionist imperialism was so complete that Amery and Maxse determined that he should help direct the campaign to convert the nation. They wished to elect him the organizing secretary of the newly formed Tariff

[1] See Chapter III, *supra*.

Reform League. Their plan miscarried.[1] When Hewins resigned his position as Director of the London School of Economics to accept, in 1903, appointment as Secretary to a tariff commission comprised of some of the nation's leading industrialists, the Webbs saw to it that Mackinder was appointed to succeed him. Mackinder's conversion to Tariff Reform, however, doomed his heretofore excellent chances of fulfilling his promise as a 'coming man' within the Liberal party. Amery has suggested in his memoirs that, but for his apostasy, Mackinder would probably have received a cabinet position in the Liberal Government of 1906.[2] In the coming years, from his post at the London School, Mackinder proceeded to supply a theoretical foundation for tariff imperialism just as, in the past, he had for Free Trade imperialism.

What had probably helped to convert Mackinder to Tariff Reform was a growing fear that, without such a programme, the Empire might disintegrate. The Oxford geographer had been convinced of the vital importance of the Empire to Britain's livelihood even while he was still a Free Trade Imperialist. 'Metropolitan England,' he wrote in 1902, 'owes much of its governmental and financial activity . . . to the imperial rank of London,' and 'would be poorer' but for 'imperial rule.' 'It would not be unfair,' he further asserted, 'to credit the imperial connection with nearly half the exports, most of the freight and interest, and—in view of the sum of sixty millions for re-export of colonial produce—with no small share of the commissions' included in the British trade balance.[3]

Mackinder was not Tariff Reform's only academic spokesman. W. J. Ashley of the University of Birmingham and William Cunningham, the economic historian, also contributed their energies to the Chamberlain campaign and both wrote considerably more than Mackinder. Ashley defended protectionism from the rather special standpoint of the German historical school, of which he can be accounted a disciple. Cunningham faithfully followed the Unionist party line in his polemics, but,

---

[1] Amery, *My Political Life*, I, p. 238.   [2] *Ibid.*, p. 224.
[3] Mackinder, *Britain and the British Seas*, pp. 352, 346, 348. For the importance Mackinder attached to imperial unity, 'to hold our own among the great Empires of the world,' see H. J. Mackinder, *The Modern British State* (London: G. Philip, 1914), pp. 252-265.

beneath the rhetoric, he rested his position on conservatism's conception of an organic, national community, a conception founded on Tudor and Stuart paternalism and mercantilism.[1] Mackinder, too, rested his argument on a mercantilist basis, but the emphasis in his writings was placed much more heavily on the need to augment British power in the new world of the twentieth century than on Cunningham's traditionalist prescriptions. In 1906, Mackinder published his *Money-Power and Man-Power: The Underlying Principles rather than the Statistics of Tariff Reform* in which he clearly took his cue from the writings of the early nineteenth-century German neo-mercantilist and 'national' economist, Friedrich List. Like List, Mackinder wished to proclaim the inadequacy of the accumulation of wealth when it was achieved at the expense of 'productive powers,' at the expense of Britain's physical capacity to defend her trade and her Empire.

Mackinder's contributions to the tariff campaign were forcefully presented and, in style, aimed at the formula-like completeness of the writings of the seventeenth century mercantilists. Mackinder had also adopted the mercantilist standard of power. 'More is at stake than a mere question of tariffs,' he wrote on the first page of his *Money-Power and Man-Power*. Citing examples from Britain's past, he demonstrated power as operative in times of peace as well as in times of war, concluding that 'we must regard the exercise of Power' in foreign affairs 'as a normal and peaceful function of the national life, to be steadily provided for, not as a spasmodic war-call to be insured against grudgingly.' Nor had power been wielded on these past occasions in behalf of some vague ideal of national honour or glory: 'our power has in almost every instance been exerted in connection with some substantial market of our commerce, where wages to the extent of millions of pounds annually were at stake.' British power had, for example, been applied to protect the Lancashire cotton industry and was thus 'employed to protect interests which are vital to our working classes.' Power, trade, wages, and labour were all arcs of the same circle and each was necessary to make it complete. 'Much power is needed to shelter a great trade,' he proclaimed. 'A

[1] See Chapters X and XI, *infra*.

great trade can alone supply much wages and support a great and efficient population. A great and efficient population is the only firm source of great power.'[1]

As a Liberal-Imperialist, Mackinder had welcomed the predominance of British finance in a cosmopolitan world at the expense, if this proved necessary, of British industry. Now he spoke in mercantilist terms of industry, of markets, of wages, of a great population as the enduring sources of power. What had changed Mackinder's view? We know that the Coefficients talked much of the coming day of reckoning with Germany, a day for which the Germans were steadily preparing. Mackinder had become convinced that the world of the twentieth century was not to be the peaceful world of the nineteenth. The Germans meant to do more than deprive England of industrial hegemony. What good would British capital be against German armed might? Could a nation living on foreign investments and broker's fees, deprived of the capacity to manufacture weapons, successfully defend herself against a well-trained, well-equipped nation of half again as many people? His famous article on 'The Geographical Pivot of History,' which was to form the basis of German geopolitics, was written shortly after his conversion to protection.[2] In it Mackinder described the threat which a great land-based power, whose strength was in its armies and its industry, posed for a sea-power on the periphery of the pivot, whose principal interest was peaceful trade. The moral was plain. In order to defend herself successfully against Germany, Great Britain had to be transformed.

Mackinder had become convinced of the essential soundness of mercantilist populationist theory for the conditions of the new century. He had become convinced that he, like the other Free Traders, had paid rather too much attention to money-power, the 'power of buying,' and too little to man-power, 'our power of doing.' Mackinder cited an example of an English capitalist who built a factory in a foreign land as a means of circumventing high foreign tariffs. The profits, the interest, the dividends which stemmed from such an investment were accounted a national gain by Free Trade economists. In reality, they were a

[1] Mackinder, *Money-Power and Man-Power*, pp. 1, 5, 7, 14.

[2] H. J. Mackinder, 'The Geographical Pivot of History,' *Geographical Journal*, XXIII, April, 1904.

national loss. The men who were employed by that capitalist would supply recruits for a foreign army—and the capitalist's earnings would be taxed to support that army. Overseas investments, which Mackinder had formerly championed as a 'share' in the 'proceeds' of the 'brains and muscles of other countries,' he now regarded as responsible for the ruin of many trades and the consequent emigration of thousands of un-employed British working men. Emigration, he now felt, was a blow at British power. 'The Tariff Reformer,' he concluded, 'aims at increasing the Man-power of the Empire.'[1]

Mackinder had not forgotten the emphasis of his former Liberal-Imperialist colleagues on the rearing of an imperial race. After his conversion, he continued to favour temperance legislation, to urge better housing for the working classes, and to suggest methods for improving public education—all favourite projects of the followers of Rosebery. Slums he described as 'the scrap-heaps of abandoned and disused portions of our national man-power.' Mackinder even supported the concept of a minimum wage, which the Fabians had made a chief item of their platform, and which Mackinder described as 'at the root of both trade unionism and Socialism' but, since it was 'inspired by the idea of economising man-power,' thoroughly acceptable. He condemned as wasteful of man-power 'irregularity of employment,' however caused, whether by strikes, foreign competition, or by 'failure of employers'; 'the Tariff Reformer's whole attitude makes him value the labourer and guard his wages.' 'The real strength of a nation,' Mackinder asserted, 'lies in its workers, its thinkers, its fighters, and its mothers.'[2] The last was a reference to his new view that an increased birth-rate was essential if Great Britain were to hold her own in the struggles for power of the twentieth century.

Mackinder resigned as Director of the London School of Economics in 1908—to be succeeded by a fellow Coefficient, Pember Reeves, the New Zealand Fabian—and devoted himself more fully to politics and to the cause of Tariff Reform. In 1909 he fought a by-election at Hawick Burghs, bearing his new party

[1] Mackinder, *Money-Power and Man-Power*, p. 21.

[2] *Ibid.*, pp. 21-24; also H. J. Mackinder, 'Man-Power as a Measure of National and Imperial Strength,' *National Review*, XLV, March 1905, pp. 142-143.

SIR HALFORD MACKINDER: THEORIST OF IMPERIALISM   175

colours of Unionist and Tariff Reformer, but once again he
went down to defeat. In the general election of January 1910, he
succeeded in securing election for the Camlachie division of
Glasgow. He carried the division by a scant majority of 434
votes, and retained his seat in the general election of December
1910, by only 26 votes. He is reported to have waged a most
persuasive campaign. He held his seat until he suffered defeat in
the general election of 1922.

In 1919, Mackinder published a volume entitled *Democratic
Ideals and Reality* in which he extracted the essences of both
Free Trade and tariff imperialism and proclaimed their inherent
sameness. The imperialists of both persuasions were
'organisers,' he explained; their enemies, the cosmopolitan
Liberals, the 'Cobdenites,' were 'idealists.' Among the
organizers, Mackinder cited 'three honoured voices': those of
Lord Rosebery, who had called for 'efficiency'; Joseph Chamberlain, who had called for 'economic defence'; and Lord Roberts,
who had devoted his last years to a campaign for military
training. These three, Mackinder lamented, had appealed 'to
our soverign people and were not heard.'[1] The idealists were
'internationalists' who were 'in futile revolt against all organisation,' while the organizers were patriots and nationalists.
The doctrine of the organizer is, for Mackinder, at the opposite
pole of democracy; the 'supreme rule of the organiser and of
blind efficiency' is 'the Nemesis of democratic idealism.' The
organizer, in the tradition of Hobbes, views 'men as existing
for the State,' and comes to regard 'his men as his tools.' While
'the democrat is thinking of the rights of man,' the organizer is
'thinking how to use men,' and has idealized the disciplined
state, the 'camp state.' Such a doctrine does not mean that the
organizer neglects human welfare within national society. 'On
the contrary,' Mackinder asserted, 'he regards that society as so
much man-power to be maintained in efficient condition.' This is
the case, he concluded, whether the organizer 'be militarist or
capitalist provided that he be far-sighted.'[2]

If, as Mackinder believed, imperialism and democracy were
based on antagonistic principles, which was likely to prevail in

[1] H. J. Mackinder, *Democratic Ideals and Reality: A Study in the
Politics of Reconstruction* (London: Constable, 1919), pp. 31-32.
[2] *Ibid.*, pp. 9-21.

England. This was, of course, one of the more important issues underlying British political life. Mackinder was convinced that, given the state of international economy, 'even democracies are compelled to annex empires.'[1] Were Britons, then, doomed to lose their freedom? The Oxford geographer had suggested, in 1902, that British democracy and imperialism could co-exist because of 'the intervening ocean.'[2] In 1924, he explained further how geography had enabled an imperial Britain to continue to enjoy democracy:

'The separation of the tropical Empire from the European island, although perhaps a source of weakness from a military point of view, has had this supreme advantage, that on the one hand imperial rule in the dependencies has not corrupted freedom at home, and on the other hand those who exercise that rule, go out generation after generation with the spirit of justice and trusteeship ever renewed from their free homes and schools.[3]

In 1919, the Coalition Government of Lloyd George appointed Mackinder British High Commissioner for South Russia—a part of the 'heartland' concerning which he had written some fifteen years earlier in his geopolitical articles. The failure to overthrow the Soviet government prompted his return in 1920, at which time he was knighted for his services and appointed Chairman of the Imperial Shipping Committee, a post he held until 1945. In 1926, the Government of Stanley Baldwin honoured him further by naming him a Privy Councillor and the Chairman of the Imperial Economic Committee. Mackinder's last years, then, were devoted to the continued service of that imperial ideal to which he had been drawn by the Chamberlain crusade. Before his death in 1947, he had witnessed two German wars, against which he had warned, as well as the final passing of the imperialism of Free Trade and the conversion of England to the protectionist position which he had adopted forty years earlier.

[1] Mackinder, *Britain and the British Seas*, p. 342.
[2] *Ibid.*, p. 349.
[3] Sir Halford Mackinder, *The World War and After* (London: G. Philip, 1924), p. 266.

IX

VISCOUNT MILNER:
SOCIAL-IMPERIAL IDEALIST

The Liberals regarded the campaign of Chamberlain and the Tariff Reform League to convert the working classes to protection as an appeal to the vilest instincts by entirely self-seeking interests. The Tariff Reformers, in Radical eyes, were selfish manufacturers determined to increase their profits even if this meant bringing back the 'dear loaf' and the 'hungry 'forties.' They were bloated landowners anxious that the increasing burden of taxation for defence and social reform should be placed upon the back of the working classes in the form of excises rather than upon their own huge unearned incomes. This Liberal analysis was in many respects an accurate one. The attempt to create a Bismarckian England revealed a play of motives that was no prettier than those involved in the creation of Bismarckian Germany or, for that matter, in the framing of an American tariff. Nevertheless, it would be wrong to assume that no larger ideals lay behind the movement for Tariff Reform and preference. The social-imperialism of Alfred Milner was, in many ways, a repository of this idealism. Although in basic agreement with the programme of the Unionist Party, Milner stubbornly chose to follow an independent course and held himself genuinely 'above party.' Obviously disinterested and guided by sincere and generous sentiments, he succeeded in winning the respect even of his political opponents.

Milner was born in Giesen, Hesse-Darmstadt, of English parentage, on March 23, 1854. His first four years were spent in Germany—his father was a teacher in a German university —his next eight in Chelsea, and the three following in a *Gymnasium* at Tübingen to whose university the elder Milner— a physician by profession—had returned as a Reader in English Literature. Unlike his social-imperial colleagues, therefore, Milner was not cut in any of the conventional English public school patterns. After a brilliant career at King's College,

M

London, he received a scholarship to Balliol College, Oxford, and subsequently a call to the bar from Inner Temple. After leaving school, he worked on the *Pall Mall Gazette*, first with the Cobdenite John Morley and then with the imperialist social reformer, W. T. Stead. He displayed an early interest in social reform and was a friend and a colleague of both Arnold Toynbee[1] and William Barnett. Milner served as joint secretary of the university extension movement for which, in 1882, he had delivered six lectures on socialism,[2] and was one of the founders of Toynbee Hall.

Milner's early politics were Liberal—he fought Harrow for the Liberals in 1885 and lost—but his Liberalism was never of the Cobdenite blend. He had, early in life, determined never to marry so that he might devote his life entirely to the state—itself a rejection of Cobdenite egoism. (He relented when he was sixty-seven years old). An enthusiastic imperialist, he followed Chamberlain in his break with Gladstonian Liberalism and served as private secretary to the Liberal-Unionist Goschen, Chancellor of the Exchequer in the Unionist cabinet of 1886. In 1887, he accepted the position of director-general of accounts in Egypt, thereby beginning his proconsular activities. He performed brilliantly in the position and was recalled in 1892 to become Chairman of the Board of Inland Revenue. While serving with the Board, he aided two chancellors, Harcourt and Hicks-Beach, in the preparation of their budgets; there is no way of knowing how great a role he played in placing death duties in the budget of the former, but there is no doubt that his influence was felt.

In 1897 Milner had been the choice of both parties to go to South Africa to try to solve the difficulties in British-Boer relations. His activities in South Africa before, during, and after the Boer War are well known. An advocate of the doctrine of the civilizing mission of the Europeans, of the 'white man's burden,' he could not tolerate the Boer's treatment of the native, an attitude, we are told, which played no small part in

[1] Milner has outlined the influence of Toynbee on both his imperial and social views in an admirable essay *Arnold Toynbee: A Reminiscence* (London 1901).

[2] Milner's six lectures on socialism were reprinted by the *National Review* in monthly issues from January through June 1931.

shaping his South African position.[1] Milner's return from South Africa was the occasion for both hoots and cheers. From that time onward, he was no longer judged as a man but as a symbol of British imperialism. One of the earliest acts of the Liberal parliament of 1906, for example, was a censure of Milner, by an overpowering vote of 355 to 135, for certain of his acts in South Africa. But to others he was a hero. He was welcomed into the Coefficients Club by his admirers. He became a mainstay of the Tariff Reform cause. He arrived home a peer, and, from that vantage point, he began to preach a 'higher' imperialism and a new concept of national life.

Milner, a target for the Liberals and the not-too-well understood hero of the imperialists, was never destined to be a popular figure. For one thing, he was not a good speaker: Austen Chamberlain's wife Ivy reported to her husband on one of Milner's speeches which was 'full of good stuff, but badly delivered, from vast sheaves of notes from which he read largely, losing himself at intervals';[2] W. A. S. Hewins described another speech of Milner's in behalf of Hewins' own parliamentary candidacy at Shipley, saying 'Yorkshire working men greatly appreciated the presence of so distinguished a person but wished they could understand what he said.'[3] His lack of concern with the purely pounds, shillings, and pence arguments of the Tariff Reformers served to alienate many Unionists. Hewins, the Secretary to the Tariff Commission and the technician of Tariff Reform, complained that Milner never 'wholeheartedly' supported Chamberlain's plan. Although Milner was a member of a Balfour-appointed tariff committee, Hewins could 'not remember that he ever made a single contribution to elucidating the technical tariff questions which we reviewed.'[4] In many ways, he was more a hero of the Fabians than any other political group.[5] He keenly felt his isolated

[1] Edward Crankshaw, *The Forsaken Idea: A Study of Viscount Milner* (London: Longmans, 1952). A recent work devoted to a presentation of Milner's ideas. Gives much attention to Milner's activities in South Africa. See also Cecil Headlam, ed., *The Milner Papers* (London, 1931-33), 2 Vols.

[2] Austen Chamberlain, *Politics from Inside*, p. 110.

[3] Hewins, *Apologia of An Imperialist*, I, pp. 39-40.

[4] *Ibid.*, p. 40.   [5] See Chapter VI, *supra*.

position. 'I am a free lance,' he declared, 'a sort of political Ishmaelite, who has found hospitality in the Unionist camp. It is certain that I could not have found it in any other.'[1]

The end of the nineteenth century had witnessed the resurrection of tribal ideals, of concepts of racial missions. These formed significant parts of both French and German social-imperialism. Among the British social-imperialists whose ideas we are discussing, Milner expressed this viewpoint most intensely. He asserted his conviction that 'the British race . . . stands for something distinctive and priceless in the onward march of humanity.'[2] Milner's imperial pride appeared in the full-blooded terms of the late nineteenth century:

'I have emphasised the importance of the racial bond. From my point of view this is fundamental. It is the British race which built the Empire, and it is the undivided British race which can alone uphold it . . . deeper, stronger, more primordial than these material ties is the bond of common blood, a common language, common history and traditions. But what do I mean by the British race? I mean all the peoples of the United Kingdom and their descendants in other countries under the British flag.'[3]

This was an unusual mode of expression, for British imperialism generally had a more pragmatic bent. In his view of 'racial' bonds and missions, Milner was joined in part by Chamberlain and by Cecil Rhodes, whose views on the subject were even more pointed,[4] and, of course, by the Social-Darwinist, Karl Pearson.

Like Pearson, Milner was an opponent of the 'divisive' brand of socialism, believing that, instead of encouraging organic development along national or racial lines, it threatened to subvert the state by promoting class hostility. Class conflict, he

[1] Lord Milner, 'A Political Ishmaelite,' Wolverhampton, December 17, 1906, *The Nation and the Empire*, p. 153. Second references will be to the title of the speech and the page of *The Nation and the Empire*. (*N and E*).

[2] Alfred Milner, 'The Two Nations,' East London, December 4, 1912, *N and E*, p. 496.

[3] *Ibid.*, xxxv.

[4] For Rhodes' views on race, see W. T. S. Stead, ed., *The Last Will and Testament of Cecil John Rhodes* (London, 1902), pp. 52, 58.

was convinced, posed the greatest danger to the British Empire. Milner elevated this observation into a firm political law: 'Among civilised peoples of more or less equal size,' he asserted, 'that one will be, as it will deserve to be, the strongest, which is most successful in removing the causes of class antagonism in its midst.'[1] The Unionist party, if it would be successful, must become a national party 'not a class party.' Milner suggested the running of Unionist Labour members. He had confidence in the patriotism and imperialism of the working class. He refused to believe that they were 'the unpatriotic, anti-national, down-with-the-army, up-with-the-foreigner, take-it-lying-down class of Little Englanders, that they are constantly represented to be.'[2] He had nothing but contempt for the doctrine of 'the solidarity of the workers of all nations' and affirmed his own belief in development 'on national lines,' in the 'mission of my country, of the British race.'[3]

When Chamberlain brought forth his programme, Milner gave it enthusiastic support. He dismissed the 'divisive' argument that the tariff would place an unequal burden on the poor. The programme of Tariff Reform, he declared, was framed in the interest of 'the nation as a whole—not of any one class.'[4] The Radical government was seeking funds for defence and for social reform by wholesale expropriation. It was 'stirring up class hatred or trying to rob Peter in order to pay Paul.'[5] Social reform and national defence were not matters that pertained to only one class; the nation as a whole was affected. All classes should pay, according to their ability, the expense involved. 'It is thoroughly vicious in principle,' Milner insisted, 'to divide the nation, as many of the Radical and Labour men want to divide it, into two sections—a majority which only calls the tune, and a minority which only pays the piper.'[6] The only

[1] Milner, 'The Two Nations,' *N and E*, p. 496.

[2] Milner, 'Unionists and Social Reform,' Rugby, November 19, 1907, *N and E*, p. 252.

[3] Milner, 'The Two Nations,' *N and E*, p. 496.

[4] Milner, 'Tariff Reform and National Policy,' Poole, November 16, 1909, *N and E*, p. 388.

[5] Milner, 'A Constructive Policy,' Guildford, October 29, 1907, *N and E*, pp. 214-215.

[6] *Ibid.*, p. 216.

method for raising the revenues necessary for a wide programme
of progressive social reform—the only method other than gross
expropriation—was Tariff Reform.[1] Tariff revenues would
supply funds for old-age pensions as well as support for the
military and naval services without draining the resources of the
well-to-do exclusively. Tariff Reform would be the ideal mechanism by which the sound revenue principle of 'Let all pay
according to their means' might best be applied.[2] Tariff Reform
would unite all classes and promote class harmony rather than
class conflict.

Milner regarded British industry as the 'national' industry
and therefore deserving of national protection. 'The point is,
that we should look at industry in a national spirit which aims
at the *maximum* of production and employment' he asserted,
'not in the purely commercial spirit which thinks of nothing but
cheapness.' The decline of any British industry must be set down
as 'a national loss.'[3] The Cobdenites had made a god of cheapness
and this deity was undermining the national welfare. 'It is surely
better to pay a little more for your goods, and keep thousands
of people in productive work, than to pay a little less for your
goods, and have ultimately to devote what you have saved in that
way to the relief of pauperism due to the loss of employment.'[4]

Milner was convinced that 'there can be no adequate
prosperity for the forty or fifty million people in these islands
without the Empire and all that it provides.'[5] British well-being
depended upon the continued allegiance of the great self-
governing nations of the commonwealth, the maintenance of
British control in the Empire's dependencies, and the capacity
of Great Britain to guard her interests in foreign countries
outside the empire. Should the empire be liquidated or should
Great Britain be unable to exert the force necessary to fulfill
her commitments or to induce other nations to fulfill theirs,
Britain would be reduced to a fifth-rate power. National
prosperity depended upon national power:

[1] Milner, 'Unionists and Social Reform,' *N and E*, pp. 244-245.
[2] *Ibid.*, p. 251.
[3] Milner, 'A Political Ishmaelite,' *N and E*, p. 162.
[4] *Ibid.*, p. 162.
[5] Milner, 'Tariff Reform,' Tunbridge Wells, October 24, 1907,
N and E, pp. 196-197.

'This country must remain a great Power or she will become a poor country; and those who in seeking, as they are most right to seek, social improvement are tempted to neglect national strength, are simply building their house upon the sand. . . . These islands by themselves cannot always remain a Power of the very first rank.'[1]

Milner was an imperialist; he believed that 'the maintenance and consolidation of what we call the British Empire should be the first and the highest of all political objects for every subject of the Crown.'[2] He was also a social reformer. He saw no contradiction between the two roles, believing imperialism and social reform entirely interdependent. If the Empire were to be consolidated and preserved, the strength of the entire nation was needed for the effort. If the nation was weak, unhealthy, impoverished—the very foundations of empire must crumble. He called upon the Unionist party not only to fight for the Empire but to join the struggle against 'irregular employment and unhealthy conditions of life.'[3] The Cobdenite believed in 'unfettered competition' and idealized 'cheapness.' Not so the Tariff Reformer: 'He does not believe that the mere blind struggle for individual gain is going to produce the most beneficent results. He does not believe in cheapness if it is the result of sweating or of underpaid labour.'[4] The social-imperialist understood that the community had an equity in the efficiency and well-being of all its members.[5] To those who were genuinely patriotic, 'to those, in whom that sentiment is really powerful, the existence of slums, of sweating, of health-destroying industries, and of all other conditions which lead to the degradation of great numbers of their fellow-countrymen, must appear an intolerable desecration of all that they hold most dear.'[6] A people's well-being consisted of having sufficient

[1] Milner, 'The Imperialist Creed,' Manchester, December 14, 1906, N and E, pp. 139-140.

[2] Ibid., p. 138.

[3] Milner, 'Unionists and Social Reform,' N and E, pp. 249-250.

[4] Milner, 'Unionists and the Empire,' Edinburgh, November 15, 1907, N and E, pp. 240-241.

[5] Milner, 'Sweated Industries,' Oxford, December 5, 1907, N and E, p. 260.

[6] Milner, N and E, p. xlvi.

'air, space, cleanliness, exercise, good houses, good food.' A sound imperialism was based upon a vigorous people, an 'imperial Race.' To sustain the empire 'you must have soundness at the core—health, intelligence, industry; and these cannot be general without a fair average standard of material well-being.' If one called himself an imperialist, Milner asserted, 'he must care that the heart of the Empire should beat with a sounder and less feverish pulse.'[1] 'Patriotism,' Milner warned, 'like all the ideal sides of life, can be choked, must be choked, in the squalor and degradation of the slums of our great cities.' If patriotism were extinguished, so would Imperialism, which 'is simply the highest development of patriotism,' be extinguished.[2]

Milner extended the old Conservative ideal of 'community,' to include the entire Empire, every land in which men of British blood and tradition lived:

'The conception which haunts me is the conception of the people of these islands as a great family, bound by indissoluble ties to kindred families in other parts of the world, and, within its own borders, striving after all that makes for productive power, for social harmony, and, as a result of these and as the necessary complement and shield of these, for its strength as a nation among the nations of the earth.'[3]

He regarded himself a 'collectivist' and could not condemn the goals and ideals of socialism. He disliked the socialism of the class struggle but himself preached the creed of a 'nobler Socialism' as an essential of a new 'national life.' 'I am unable to join in the hue and cry against Socialism' he wrote:

'There is a nobler Socialism, which so far from springing from "envy, hatred, and all uncharitableness," is born of genuine sympathy and a lofty and wise conception of what is meant by national life. It realises the fact that we are not merely so many millions of individuals, each struggling for himself, with the State to act as policeman, but literally one body-politic; that the

---

[1] Milner, 'The Imperialist Creed,' *N and E*, pp. 139-140; Milner, 'Imperialism and Social Reform,' Montreal, November 2, 1908, *N and E*, p. 352.

[2] *Ibid.*, p. 354.

[3] Milner, 'A Political Ishmaelite,' *N and E*, p. 163.

different classes and sections of the community are members of that body, and that when one member suffers all the members suffer. From this point of view the attempt to raise the well-being and efficiency of the more backward of our people—for this is what it all comes to—is not philanthropy: it is business.'[1]

Milner's 'nobler Socialism' was in conception little different from the 'collectivism' of the Fabians who considered the South African proconsul most worthy of their praise.

In one other sphere, Milner's social-imperialism stood out from the general body of British social-imperial theory—in his attitudes toward democracy and parliamentary institutions. Continental social-imperialists regarded these as corrupt and inefficient. Without accepting such an extreme position—as, we shall see, Blatchford did—and without making his position at all a crucial part of his doctrine, Milner, too, had reservations about what he called 'the system.' In a letter written during the course of the tariff controversy, Milner despaired of Chamberlain ever being able to do anything 'great' because of the 'system.' The 'system' left the 'ultimate powers on all matters, without appeal, with an *ignorant* people,' a people 'having no adequate appreciation of the supreme value of trained knowledge, or of the difference in *size* of the questions submitted to them, so that they are capable of the same levity with regard to the biggest things as with regard to trifles.' Under the system, party politics were a meaningless struggle between the ins and the outs, a struggle having little to do with principle. Government was in the hands of a 'huge, unwieldy Cabinet' dominated by 'second-rate men.' More important, there was no 'grading' of questions as to their importance. More often than not, important national questions were put aside in favour of 'local and *temporary*' ones.[2] Milner's views were not unusual among bureaucrats, experts, working in democratic government—and Milner was a bureaucrat for a good part of his life. Here, too, he was in substantial agreement with the Fabian position.

Throughout his career, Milner failed to make himself understood by the democracy. But his ability and integrity made him a necessary instrument for that democracy in its times of need. He was sent to South Africa as the choice of both parties to deal

[1] *Ibid.*, p. 161.   [2] Quoted in Crankshaw, *op. cit.*, pp. 135-136.

with a difficult situation; he was invited to join a five-man inner
war cabinet in 1916 by David Lloyd George, the war-time
Prime Minister, a leader of the Liberal forces which had
censured him in 1906. His qualities made him the idol of a group
of young men who had served with him in South Africa and who
went on to serve the nation in prominent places. Milner's famous
'kindergarten' included the journalist Leopold Amery, who rose
to the Cabinet rank in his later years; the historian Basil
Williams; Geoffrey Dawson, who was to become the editor of
The Times; John Buchan and Lionel Curtis. Under the editorship
of Curtis, the 'kindergarten' established *The Round Table* as a
periodical in which imperial problems could be reviewed.[1]

At Milner's death, in 1925, the editors of *The Round Table*
published an unsigned obituary which described the 'deep
affection and absolute confidence' which Milner inspired in
all who knew him. He was 'never self-seeking,' never the
demagogue; 'he could not be anything but straight.' His
imperialism was 'no more strongly held than was his determination to assist those whom he thought weak or downtrodden,
whether it were the Kaffir in South Africa or the working man
at home.' Milner was, in fact, almost alone among social-
imperialists and imperial-socialists in expressing concern for
the native peoples in the Empire. In matters of social policy, the
editors reported, he felt 'a sympathy with the Labour party.'
To the end he remained an imperialist, firmly believing that the
strengthening of the British Commonwealth of Nations was 'the
best means of securing and adding to the liberty, happiness and
progress of mankind.'[2]

Chamberlain's chief motivation, as noted, was the prevention
of the disintegration of the empire. His social-imperialism was
too obviously a mixture of nostalgic reminiscences of his
Radical past and sheer opportunism. Promises, made, revised,
withdrawn, presented again; this was his pattern and perhaps it
was an inevitable one for a political leader in a mass-democracy.
Chamberlain feared that his promises of employment and social-
reform would be regarded as a 'squalid argument' and would

[1] Vladimir Halpérin, *Lord Milner et l'évolution de l'impérialisme
britannique* (Paris, 1950), *passim*; pp. 189-213. A recent volume
devoted to Milner's activities and influence.
[2] 'Lord Milner,' *The Round Table*, No. 59, June 1925, pp. 427-430.

much have preferred an appeal solely on the patriotic platform of saving the empire. Chamberlain, a demagogue, guiltily half-believed his social-imperialism pure demagoguery. Milner, out of the public eye, offered no apologies for a social-imperial doctrine he fully believed. As concerned with the empire as was Chamberlain, Milner was convinced that its preservation was essential to the welfare of the working class and that the strength and health of the workers were essential to the empire. If we were to attempt to construct an 'ideal' social-imperialist— analagous to the 'ideal' gas of the physicists—Milner would come closest to fulfilling its properties. He was also an 'idealist' in the popular, non-metaphysical sense. He represented the noblest, least self-seeking side of Tariff Reform social-imperialism. For him, support of the social-imperial complex constituted —in his own words—the 'highest development of patriotism.'

X

WILLIAM CUNNINGHAM:
NATIONAL ECONOMIST

Professor H. S. Foxwell described Archdeacon William Cunningham, in an obituary article, as 'a great National Economist,' in the tradition of Thomas Mun and William Petty.[1] The description was most appropriate. As an economist, Cunningham made the preservation and strengthening of the nation-state his most weighty political and economic objective. As an Archdeacon of the Church of England, he sometimes spoke as if the nation-state were the loftiest expression of spiritual life as well. In his later years, he came to regard all of European development as a preparation for the emergence of the national state—and he considered this a worthy final goal of historical evolution.[2] He believed the breach with Rome in the time of Henry VIII to have been a declaration of self-sufficiency, evidence of England's recognition that Church and State were twin aspects of the same national community.[3] Since that time, he asserted, England had consciously moulded both her political and economic policy to provide for a sound and prosperous national life. Archdeacon Cunningham suggested that there had been but one break in this long tradition of concentration upon the national interest, one reversion to the cosmopolitanism of the pre-Reformation times, the one which had been engineered by the political economists who followed the Free Trade dogmas of Adam Smith, Richard Cobden, and John Bright. Both as economist and as clergyman, the good Archdeacon devoted his energies to battling this most recent cosmopolitan threat to the sacred national community, much as his Tudor ancestors had risen in opposition to the Church of Rome.

William Cunningham was born in the city of Edinburgh in

[1] H. S. Foxwell, and Lilian Knowles, 'Archdeacon Cunningham,' *Economic Journal*, September 1919, XXIX, pp. 384-385.

[2] William Cunningham, 'Economic Change,' in *Cambridge Modern History* (Cambridge, 1902), I, pp. 493 and 529, and *passim*.

[3] William Cunningham, *Christianity and Politics* (Boston, 1915), pp. 32-33.

1849. After studying at the Edinburgh Institution and the Academy, he attended the University of Edinburgh from 1865 until 1869, when he entered Caius College, Cambridge. His ambition during his early period of study at Edinburgh was to accept orders in the ministry of the Presbyterian Church. In 1868, however, he spent a fateful two months at the University of Tübingen. At the German university, he made the acquaintance of two American students who introduced him to the Anglican Book of Common Prayer. He was much affected by his reading of it. Anglicanism attracted him with its sense of historical continuity. Therefore, despite previous ambitions, he determined to become a clergyman of the Church of England and was so ordained in 1871. His study at Tübingen is also said to have 'influenced his conception of the State,' and to it, one of his later admirers asserted, 'may be traced his tendency to emphasize order and discipline in social life.'[1]

At Cambridge, Cunningham became one of the pioneer lecturers in the university extension movement. He began his extension lecturing in 1870, just a year after entering Caius College, although his full-scale extension activity did not begin till four years later. He lectured on political economy and economic history. In 1878, Cunningham was appointed an examiner in the historical tripos at Cambridge in which a paper in economic history had been assigned. There was no one to teach the subject, however, and not even a textbook in the field, so Cunningham undertook to provide such a text, thereby setting the groundwork for the study of British economic history in British universities. It was this book—*The Growth of English Industry and Commerce in Modern Times*—published in 1882, which established his reputation as an historian. After the appearance of its first edition, Cunningham held a number of academic positions. He was University Lecturer in History at Cambridge from 1884 to 1891. In 1891, he was appointed Tooke Professor of Economics at King's College, London, a post he held until 1897. In 1899, William Ashley, then Professor of Economic History at Harvard, invited Cunningham to join him at that university as Lecturer in the field. Cunningham's clerical duties were performed along with his academic ones

[1] W. R. Scott, 'William Cunningham, 1849-1919,' *Proceedings of the British Academy, 1919-1920* (London, 1920), p. 467.

during all this time. Nor were these neglected. As vicar of Great St Mary's from 1887 to 1908, he was reputed to know the names of all the children in the parish. For the last twelve years of his life, from 1908 to 1919, Cunningham served as Archdeacon of Ely.[1]

But it is Cunningham the national economist and the pioneer economic historian with whom we are concerned rather than Cunningham the clergyman or teacher. More specifically, our interest is in Cunningham's rebellion against the cosmopolitan canons of classical political economy. The principal conclusion of the 'economic law' of the political economists—and perhaps the chief practical reason for its existence—was the necessity and beneficence of international Free Trade. Great Britain had been the first nation to be converted to the new doctrine and British commercial supremacy, based upon Free Trade, served as the chief support for continental schools of political economy during the nineteenth century. On the continent, however, 'natural law' economics had been effectively opposed, by midcentury, by both politicians and academicians. It had been Friedrich List who had first led the fight against the political economists. His successors had been the famous German historical school of Roscher, Schmoller, Knies, Brentano, and Nasse, who set up their historical, statistical, and inductive method in opposition to the abstract deductive method of the political economists. No longer could *laissez-faire* be regarded as immutable economic principle, a necessary conclusion deduced by irrefutable logic from undeniable axioms. On the contrary, the new school of historical economists appeared more sympathetic to economic paternalism. The school of Roscher and Schmoller, in fact, quickly received the sobriquet of *Katheder-Sozialisten*, 'socialists of the chair.' Their emphasis was national not cosmopolitan. Their ideals were derived from the long centuries of Europe's economic past and owed more to medieval paternalism and seventeenth-century mercantilism than to the comparatively fleeting moment of nineteenth-century Cobdenism.[2]

[1] For information concerning Cunningham's life, see H. S. Foxwell and Lilian Knowles, *op. cit.*, pp. 382-393; Audrey Cunningham, *William Cunningham: Teacher and Priest* (London: S.P.C.K., 1950).

[2] See List, *op. cit.*; for the *Katheder-Sozialisten*, see Schumpeter, *History of Economic Analysis*, pp. 800-814.

It was William Cunningham, along with Arnold Toynbee, who was to become the leader of the modern English school of historical economics, and, as we have seen, Cunningham, like his German counterparts, was a nationalist. In his textbook of economic history, he had commended mercantilism as the means by which, during the sixteenth, seventeenth and eighteenth centuries, Great Britain had increased her national power. Thus, as an adherent of the historical and inductive method, he could not believe that the political economists were sound in suggesting that Free Trade was the sole method of furthering the national interest. Nevertheless—very much like List in the first half of the century—Cunningham was originally convinced that, if not uniformly excellent, Free Trade was at least the best policy for Great Britain to pursue.[1] Shortly before Joseph Chamberlain began his national campaign to persuade Englishmen that Free Trade was endangering Britain's future, however, William Cunningham underwent a change of opinion and began to see the end of Free Trade's usefulness as an instrument of national policy.

A study of Cunningham's writings reveals evidence of the conversion of the Archdeacon from a nineteenth-century Free Trader to a twentieth-century protectionist. We can date this conversion with some definiteness at about 1902, although it should be noted that the seeds of Cunningham's protectionism—a most un-Cobdenite nationalism and imperialism—were never absent even in Cunningham's 'free trade' writings. The 'fact' of conversion can be best observed by comparing the second edition of his *Growth of English Industry* and the fifth, the second edition appearing in 1892 and the fifth in 1910. Writing in 1892, Cunningham had seen the repeal of the Corn Laws as marking the end of the era in which the national economy was directed to the increase of national power and the beginning of a more blessed time when economic policy would be guided by considerations of plenty and of human welfare. Patriotism had been responsible for national bitternesses and hatreds, he had written. The new cosmopolitan order which had replaced that based upon economic nationalism was more appropriate in an

[1] William Cunningham, *The Growth of English Industry and Commerce in Modern Times* (Cambridge, 1892), *passim.*, and pp. 680-686. Second edition.

age in which the position of the working class was everywhere similar, an age in which, therefore, there was 'an international sympathy between the labourers of different races and languages.'[1]

The Cobdenite cant of the second edition was entirely absent in the fifth. In this later edition, that of 1910, Cunningham attributed the power-goal of national economics to all of English policy from the Elizabethans up to and including Adam Smith; the tendency 'to disparage the ambition for national power' was a nineteenth-century perversion which had found 'its fullest expression in Socialism.'[2] The Cobdenite dream of international Free Trade had not been realized, he asserted. It was vain fantasy. Cunningham therefore advocated ending British trade *laissez-faire* and erecting a tariff system which would secure to England an ample food supply, benefit commerce, stimulate trade, and widen the tax base.[3] A specific example of Cunningham's reversal was his changing attitude toward British investment abroad. As late as 1900, he had written:

'So long as moneyed Englishmen continue to prefer their own country and make it their home, it is a matter of comparative indifference to the Government, whether their capital is invested in India, or the colonies, or in this island; it still pays its quota of revenue to the Crown.'[4]

The standard here employed by Cunningham is the conventional one of nineteenth-century British capitalism—one which emphasized wealth. After his conversion, Cunningham displayed a quite different, if not precisely contradictory, view:

'While the transference to foreign parts of an industry, which might have been carried on in Great Britain, may be profitable to the capitalists . . . it brings no advantage to the British workman. A lace factory which is built and carried on in England

---

[1] *Ibid.*, p. 681.
[2] William Cunningham, *The Growth of English Industry and Commerce in Modern Times* (Cambridge University Press, 1910-1912), p. 877. Fifth edition.
[3] *Ibid.*, pp. 869-871.
[4] William Cunningham, *An Essay on Western Civilization in Its Economic Aspect* (Cambridge University Press, 1913), II, p. 253.

offers a larger direct demand for English labour than a lace mill which is built and carried on with English capital in Switzerland.[1]

The 'Cobdenite' had become a Tariff Reformer. The standard of Free Trade capitalism had been replaced by the mercantilist one of national employment. It is interesting to note, though, that even where Cunningham had adhered to Cobdenite theory, his examples of alternative areas for investments are all drawn from within the British Empire.

During the time of the tariff campaign, Cunningham was a loyal member of the Unionist party. H. S. Foxwell has pronounced his position as one of 'uncompromising support of the Tariff Reform party,' adding that he was a good party man and 'did not try to insist upon his own formulation of the precise issue.'[2] He was one of the founders of the Cambridge University Tariff Reform Association and was an active member of the Compatriots Club, whose membership included the leading Tariff Reformers. Through participation in Club activities he was brought into association with such leaders in the tariff movement as Chamberlain, Garvin, Amery, Fabian Ware, Ridley, and Milner. His expert knowledge was useful to the Unionist leadership on many occasions.[3] Cunningham was a most prolific writer. He revised his *Growth of English Industry and Commerce in Modern Times* several times. He contributed frequently both to the *Economic Review* and the *Economic Journal*. In the last three decades of his life he published a long succession of works in which he carefully set down his views upon all phases of British politics and described his ideal of a British national life.

Cunningham was to suggest that what had changed was not so much his ideals as his method of reaching them. For some time after his conversion, he continued to call himself a Free Trader, a loyal follower of Adam Smith. He preferred to regard the adoption of a tariff by Britain as a step toward the achievement of international Free Trade. The retaliatory blow of British protection would, he felt, send the unstable U.S. tariff

---

[1] William Cunningham, *The Causes of Labour Unrest and the Remedies For It* (London, 1912), p. 12.
[2] Foxwell and Knowles, *op. cit.*, p. 389.
[3] Audrey Cunningham, *op. cit.*, p. 104.

N

system, erected at the expense of the producers of raw materials,
reeling.[1] But we must carefully distinguish between words—
the Cobdenite cant of the second edition and his formal espousal
of the ideals of international Free Trade—and Cunningham's
genuine attitude. A clue to the distinction was that, more and
more, his ideals of cosmopolitanism were assuming an unearthly
glow. The Archdeacon began to draw a sharp dividing line
between this world and the next. The nation-state as the
supreme ideal was a thing of this world: 'It can have a certain
definiteness and concreteness, because the great States of the
world have left material records of their achievements.' While
it was 'only in religion, and in the acknowledgment of an
overruling God to whom every man is responsible, that we find
the condition which is most favourable to the creation of a
federation of the world.'[2]

It would appear that even in his 'free trade' period, the
Archdeacon had never really deviated from the nationalist
standard which he had accepted upon his conversion to Anglicanism. He had been a Free Trader because Free Trade seemed
sound national policy, a policy designed to increase British
strength. He ceased to be a Free Trader when he came to
believe that a tariff was necessary to the furthering of national
power. While still a Free Trader, the Archdeacon had already
attached some of the more unpleasant insignia of the nationalist
battle armour to his clerical garb. For example, in a volume on
alien immigrants, published in 1897, at a time when he was still
a 'Cobdenite' and, if logic prevailed, a believer in unrestricted
immigration, his views revealed a most un-cosmopolitan
xenophobia. After a discussion of the benefits that England had
reaped as a result of immigration through the past centuries,
Cunningham argued that England had already received all the
advantages that foreigners could confer. Certainly, Cunningham
wrote, 'we have not much to gain from imitating the institutions
of the Polish Jews.'[3]

[1] William Cunningham, 'The Failure of Free Traders to Attain
Their Ideal,' in *Economic Review*, January 1904, XIV, pp. 47-48.
[2] William Cunningham, *The Progress of Capitalism in England*
(Cambridge University Press, 1916), p. 135.
[3] William Cunningham, *Alien Immigrants to England* (London,
1897), p. 266, and *passim*, especially concluding chapter.

Nor had he adopted the anti-imperialism of the Radical Free Traders. His view during the 'nineties could be described as a 'cosmopolitan imperialism' much like that which Rosebery and Asquith were to maintain during the tariff controversy. In 1899, he wrote that Britain could not hope to survive without maintaining her imperial position. He insisted, however, that British imperialism was different from all others. England did not seek exclusive economic control over her colonies; the reason for her imperialist activities was 'not to pursue a nationalist policy of our own, but to keep neutral markets open to cosmopolitan trade and to give our own industry a fair chance.' In the eighteenth century, he suggested, British imperialism had been dominated by nationalism; in the nineteenth, Britain's cosmopolitan policy had made it possible for the entire world to reap an advantage from Britain's imperial activities.[1]

During his Free Trade period, Cunningham was a man divided. His briefs for cosmopolitanism, we have noted, were contradicted by his obvious sympathy for imperialism. His nationalism was affronted by Cobdenism's insistence on free immigration. His conversion to Tariff Reform resolved the conflict. He could now speak his mind without his previous inhibitions. The Cobdenites regarded the nation as evil and selfish, and patriotism as the cause of destructive wars, he asserted. 'Such disparagement of national life' was 'idle' and 'mischievous.' The hope for an international division of labour on a Cobdenite basis was illusory. He considered 'anti-patriotism' as self-centred, selfish, anarchical.[2] From nationalism flowed the virtues necessary for the construction of a society based upon social justice; 'consciousness of nationality,' Cunningham was convinced, was essential to the 'recognition of a Common Weal throughout a given territorial area.'[3]

After his rejection of Free Trade economics, there was a marked change of tone in his conception of imperialism.

[1] William Cunningham, 'English Imperialism' in *Atlantic Monthly*, July 1899, LXXXIV, pp. 1-7.

[2] William Cunningham, *Christianity and Economic Science* (London, 1914), pp. 56-57.

[3] William Cunningham, *The Common Weal* (Cambridge University Press, 1917), p. 6.

Cunningham now played the part of a battle chaplain sending the faithful on to conquest for the greater glory of king and country. To justify its existence, he wrote, England must cherish 'a high national ideal' and must train its people to live up to that ideal. 'It was the glory of the Elizabethan age,' he continued, 'that Englishmen awoke to a sense of a national mission to exercise an active influence for good on distant peoples.' In the eighteenth century, the British people were aroused 'to a new sense of collective responsibility for the millions of India, and began to endeavour to train and guide them so that they might attain their full development, and be able to contribute their own quota of thought to the life of the great world.' This was Britain's national mission. Racial differences were so deep that any talk of a personal sense of brotherhood was foolish and 'ineffective.' The welfare of mankind could be promoted only by the fulfilment of such a mission as was Britain's.[1] The entire history of Great Britain, her great national tradition of civic probity and integrity, made her especially 'qualified to take up the white man's burden among the uncivilised races of mankind.' This tradition and the British 'sense of imperial duty' transformed the nature of British imperialism, making it considerably more than the mere struggle for power and profit.[2]

Britons must keep in mind, he warned, the obligations that went hand-in-hand with their imperial mission. The Archdeacon had a short-way with the conscientious pacifist. They were 'bad citizens' who were 'anxious to enjoy all the advantages of life in a community, while at the same time they claim a right to act on their own judgment, and to defy the General Will.'[3] Since they had the duty of bringing and enforcing law and order among the peoples under their sway, the English must retain the military character of the state. An imperial nation could not afford to be pacifistic or cosmopolitan.[4]

[1] Cunningham, *Christianity and Economic Science*, pp. 96-99.

[2] William Cunningham, *The Case Against Free Trade* (London: J. Murray, 1911), pp. 10, 4-5.

[3] Cunningham, *The Common Weal*, p. 108.

[4] William Cunningham, 'The Economic Basis of Universal Peace— Cosmopolitan or International?' in *Economic Review*, January 1913, XXIII, p. 9.

Since England would undoubtedly have to call upon her sons to defend, and possibly to extend, the Empire, in pursuit of its imperial mission, Cunningham was convinced that certain steps would have to be taken at home so that all classes—most particularly the working class, whose loyalty seemed at times in doubt—would be both able and willing to fight. As a clergyman, Cunningham had given much thought to the moral and religious issues inherent in social problems. He regarded himself as a disciple of F. D. Maurice, the mid-nineteenth-century Christian Socialist.[1] Early Christianity had had a definite bias against wealth, and many latter-day Christians had come to 'socialism' as a result of study of Scripture. For Cunningham, however, despite his professed 'Socialism,' private property was 'sacred.' The propertied man was the steward of the Lord. 'It is not our place,' declared the Archdeacon, '. . . to judge His servants, or re-allot the charge He has given them.'[2] But, if the owner of property was the steward of the Lord, he must be expected to exercise thrift and prudence in caring for his charge and must devote his property to carrying out 'his Master's known wishes.' The man of wealth was urged to apply his property 'for the greatest good of others.'[3] Everyone, furthermore, had the duty to work—though Cunningham was a little uncertain as to whether this duty was owed God or to the Nation-State. The rich, too, although not compelled to work in order to live, must not be idle. They, too, must serve the national community —but they enjoyed the privilege of being able to choose how to be of service.[4] The selfishness of 'a large section' of the wealthy classes had led to an undiscriminating resentment of all the rich, 'whether they are doing the duties of their station or not.'[5] The socialists played upon this resentment in very destructive fashion, the economist-clergyman warned.

For Cunningham, socialism, that form at least which promoted class conflict, was the principal enemy of the nation-state. He was convinced that although the immediate interests of master and man might *seem* to be opposed to each other, their permanent

[1] F. R. Salter, 'Preface,' Audrey Cunningham, *op. cit.*, p. ix-x.
[2] William Cunningham, *The Church's Duty in Relation to the Sacredness of Property* (Cambridge, Mass., 1895), pp. 6-9.
[3] *Ibid.*, pp. 7-8.
[4] Cunningham, *Causes of Labour Unrest*, p. 28.   [5] *Ibid.*, p. 13.

interests were identical. The relationship between employer and employee must not be seen as a struggle, he urged, but as a co-partnership.[1] Cunningham's proposed solution for the social problem was the widespread adoption of Sir George Livesey's scheme for 'co-partnership' then in operation in the gas companies, a plan which had been designed to stem the rising tide of municipalization of such utilities. Such an arrangement brought 'to the front the interests which masters and men have in common.'[2] Of course, the 'co-partnership' principle and that of trade unionism were at variance, and, while proclaiming his desire to further the interests of the working classes—interests he believed to be identical with those of the nation—Cunningham struck out directly at the unions who, in their supposed pursuit of the 'working-class interest,' were, he declared, endangering the common good. 'The consideration of interests,' he warned the unions, 'can never be a substitute for a sense of national duty and of personal duty.'[3] All groups had understood this vital principle. Only the trade unions had failed to appreciate it and were constantly battling for petty immediate gains at the expense of the national welfare. Cunningham was quite concerned when the Liberal parliament of 1906 passed the Trade Disputes Act which removed certain restrictions from trade union activity. He believed the new law placed the unions in a position of 'irresponsible power.'[4]

Despite his often proclaimed allegiance to the 'ultimate' realization of international Free Trade, Cunningham's references to the doctrine became more and more bitter as the years passed. Free Trade, he asserted, had been 'generated with a vein of class-hatred' which like socialism and trade unionism could easily become a threat to society. The Cobdenites' constant maligning of the capitalists and the landowners was proof of their affinity for 'the destructive side of Socialism.' 'From inculcating on the elector carelessness about maintenance of the existing order so long as his needs are

[1] William Cunningham, *Politics and Economics; An Essay on the Nature of the Principles of Political Economy, Together with a Survey of Recent Legislation* (London, 1885), p. 238.

[2] Cunningham, *Causes of Labour Unrest*, p. 18.

[3] Cunningham, *Christianity and Politics*, pp. 208-216.

[4] Cunningham, *Causes of Labour Unrest*, p. 21.

satisfied,' he believed, 'there is but a step to encouraging him
to destroy that order with the view of satisfying more of his
needs.'[1]

How then was happiness to be brought to the discontented
if the socialist, the Liberal, and the trade union solutions were
to be ruled out as unpatriotic and un-Christian? Discontent was
largely a 'personal' matter, Cunningham insisted. It was the
duty of Christianity, the duty of the Church, to eliminate such
discontent 'by striving to awaken and maintain a stronger
sense of duty in all the members of the community.'[2] The
national Church was to be the hand-maiden of the Nation-
State.

Yet despite his middle-class Victorian suspicion of working
men and trade unions, Cunningham, in neo-mercantilist fashion,
was concerned about the welfare of the working classes. Like
Viscount Milner, Cunningham was much upset by 'sweating' and
regarded it as 'a standing warning against the dangers which
are inherent in unregulated competition.'[3] Like all his colleagues
of Tariff Reform persuasion, he was an advocate of a producer-
oriented economics: 'the mere consumer appears to be an idle
person battening on the labour of other people.'[4] More
important than these matters, and constituting a most significant
link with the thought of fellow mercantilist economists like
H. J. Mackinder, was Cunningham's adoption of the sufficiency
or insufficiency of employment as a principal criterion of a sound
national life. Like Mackinder, he feared England's following the
tragic course of imperial Rome which had failed to find
productive employment for its population and was forced to live
in parasitic fashion upon the sinews of its colonies. He wished
his countrymen to be employed producing goods and not simply
playing the part of middle-man, however prosperous. Before
the political economists had adopted the practice of surveying
trade balances to measure the prosperity of the country, the
older economists, he asserted, had set up a wiser standard. For

[1] Cunningham, *Case Against Free Trade*, pp. 115-116.
[2] Cunningham, *Causes of Labour Unrest*, p. 26.
[3] William Cunningham, *Christianity and Social Questions* (London: Duckworth 1910), p. 123.
[4] William Cunningham, *The Rise and Decline of the Free Trade Movement* (Cambridge, 1905), pp. 9-10.

them 'a vigorous population' was the most important condition
for the material progress of the nation. Now again, Cunningham
noted with approval, 'the question of the effectiveness of our
population for industrial or military pursuits is once more
attracting the attention it deserves.'[1]

Cunningham's ideas on social reform and imperialism placed
him with those Liberal-Imperialists who were interested in the
breeding of an 'imperial race,' as well as with the Tariff
Reformers who felt that the working class owed its prosperity
to the empire and ought to make sacrifices to maintain it if they
expected to have good jobs at good pay. Imperial needs were of
course paramount, but Cunningham emphasized that a programme of social reform was in its own way essential to the
maintenance of the empire. 'It should be our ideal,' he wrote,
'to render the rising generation, in all classes of our population,
fit for work, and for responsibility, in some part of the Empire
overseas.' Vigorous, healthy British manhood was needed to
replenish the population of the self-governing dominions and
must be made fit to take up 'the white man's burden in the
dependencies.'[2] The Tariff Reformers, Cunningham believed,
had these higher goals in view. The Cobdenite political economists were, on the other hand, only concerned with the profits
of the moment, entirely unmindful of the ideal of a better
national life or of their debt to posterity. The aim of the national
economists, on the other hand, was the husbanding of the
nation's resources so as *to sustain and prolong our national
life.*[3]

This Apostle of the National Life hammered constantly at the
themes of national mission, national duty, and national
prosperity. His enemies, the little satans and beelzebubs in his
nationalist and imperialist theology—the pro-Boer pacifists,
the City of London cosmopolitans, the nation-splitting socialists
and trade unionists—seemed determined to undermine the
centuries-long work of creating the British national community.
His study of history had proved to Cunningham the strength,
the endurance, and the beauty of national ideals. His study of the
word of God had proved that the Lord meant men to live within

---

[1] Cunningham, *Politics and Economics*, p. 159.
[2] Cunningham, *Case Against Free Trade*, pp. 136-137.
[3] Cunningham, *Politics and Economics*, pp. 273-275.

Nation-States. The Cobdenites, by refusing to understand the will of God and the lesson of History and by maintaining their allegiance to the false idol of cosmopolitanism, would, he feared, bring about the destruction of the British people.

XI

SIR WILLIAM ASHLEY
AS 'SOCIALIST OF THE CHAIR'

William James Ashley was one of a small band of pioneer scholars—William Cunningham, W. A. S. Hewins, H. S. Foxwell, and H. J. Mackinder were others—who constituted the English 'school' of economic history at the turn of this century. The efforts of this group were overshadowed by those of the German historical school which, first under the leadership of Wilhelm Roscher and then of Gustav Schmoller, devoted more attention to theoretical problems and questions of methodology, was more far-ranging in acquiring and utilizing other departments of knowledge, was considerably more prolific, and had even become a force in German political life. The English school cannot, however, be set down as a mere offshoot of the German; it was of native growth and worked independently, turning its attention to a rather different type of problem. Ashley, alone of the leading English economic historians, belonged not only to the school of Adam Smith, Thorold Rogers, and Arnold Toynbee, but also to the German school of historical economists whose historical, statistical, and inductive method had been brought to England in the 'seventies and 'eighties by Cliffe Leslie and J. K. Ingram and posited against the abstract, deductive method of the followers of Ricardo and Say.

Ashley began his career at Oxford, as a history scholar of Balliol, in 1878. There his interests were formed under the influence of Toynbee, Stubbs, and Maine. He took a first in History in 1881 and remained at Oxford for several years as a private tutor. In 1888, he was invited to occupy the chair of political economy and constitutional history at Toronto where he did much to stimulate the work in economic history which has since been associated with that university. In 1892, Ashley accepted President Eliot's invitation to come to Harvard to occupy the first chair in economic history in the world. Nine years later Ashley returned home to become Professor of

Commerce at the new University of Birmingham, helping to organize the first university school of commerce in the United Kingdom.

Ashley had brought to Toronto and to Harvard not only the latest word concerning the study of economic history in England; he was a representative as well of the German school of historical economists. Schumpeter has described Ashley as conforming 'more than any other English economist to the German professional type of that time.'[1] Ashley maintained close ties with the German academic world. He was a regular correspondent of two of the leaders of the so-called 'younger' historical school—Gustav Schmoller and Lujo Brentano.[2] He dedicated one of his books to Schmoller, assuring the Professor of Political Economy at the University of Berlin that 'I feel that for a dozen years I have received more stimulus and encouragement from your writings than from those of any other.'[3] Schmoller responded and graciously complied with 'my friend' Ashley's subsequent request to write an introduction to his daughter's study of the social policy of Bismarck.[4] Ashley was the only English contributor to the *Festschrift* presented to Schmoller on his seventieth birthday;[5] in 1910, he was awarded the Honorary Doctorate of the University of Berlin, a distinction, his daughter has informed us, 'he was then most certain to prize.'[6]

The conviction of the German historical economists that history could serve as a guide for the formulation of policy had found expression in the formation of the *Verein für Sozialpolitik* —a society Ashley was to describe as the historical school

[1] Schumpeter, *History of Economic Analysis*, p. 822n.

[2] Some of Ashley's letters to Brentano have appeared in the *Journal of Economic History*, XV, No. 1, 1955, pp. 34-43.

[3] William Ashley, *Surveys Historic and Economic* (London, 1900), dedicatory page.

[4] Anne Ashley, *The Social Policy of Bismarck* (London, 1912), Birmingham Studies in Social Economics, No. 3, p. v.

[5] W. J. Ashley, 'The Present Position of Political Economy in England, in *Die Entwicklung der deutschen Volkswirtschaftslehre im neunzehnten Jahrhundert* (Leipzig, 1908).

[6] Anne Ashley, *William James Ashley: A Life* (London: P. S. King, 1932), p. 144.

become militant.[1] In so far as the *Verein* had a common programme, it consisted of a rejection of the individualistic doctrines of Manchester and a reliance upon the state as the guardian of the national welfare. With minor exceptions, all the members of the *Verein* were nationalists, monarchists, and protectionists. From about 1890 until his death in 1917, the dominating influence in the *Verein* was Gustav Schmoller, whose social-politics may be described as 'reformist' state socialism and much of whose analysis resembled that of Karl Marx.[2]

Like Marx, Schmoller—writing in his famous *Grundriss*, which Ashley regarded highly[3]—did not doubt the existence of 'contradictory' class interests and acknowledged the inevitability of class conflicts. Furthermore, again like Marx, Schmoller believed that legal institutions had been designed by the 'higher economic classes' to favour themselves. Such circumstances led to 'class abuse' and 'class dominance,' which Schmoller judged as 'degeneration' since it was 'a part of the essential idea of the soverign power that it is to be used in the interest of the whole society, not in the special interest of a class.' Class dominance led to revolution and it was therefore in the interest of every state to protect the weaker classes. Class abuse could be reduced by a bureaucracy of high standards, standing above the class struggle, and by a vigilant, informed public opinion. To limit class abuse, to wean the working man away from the influence of the revolutionary demagogue and to educate him in the ways of practicable reform, Schmoller and the moderate members of the *Verein* called for state action to protect trade unions, to promote factory legislation, to encourage

[1] W. J. Ashley, 'Socialists of the Chair,' in Sir Robert Palgrave, editor, *Dictionary of Political Economy* (London, 1912-15), III, pp. 437-438.

[2] Light has been cast upon the *Katheder-Sozialisten* by Schumpeter, *History of Economic Analysis*, pp. 800-824; illuminating also is Élie Halévy, *Histoire du socialisme européen* (Paris, 1948), pp. 168-170.

[3] See W. J. Ashley, *An Introduction to English Economic History and Theory* (London: Longmans, 1913), p. xvi. In a prefatory note, Ashley reported that 'the spirit and purpose of the German historical economists are now exhibited for our admiration in the great work of Professor Schmoller, *Grundriss der allgemeinen Volkswirtschaftslehre.*'

collective bargaining and arbitration, and to enact such social reforms as national insurance. The *Verein* has been credited with having helped to formulate Bismarck's insurance scheme of the 'eighties.

The similarities of interpretation between the historical school and the Marxists were striking, and the *Katheder-Sozialisten*, 'Socialists of the Chair,' as the members of the *Verein* were called, took great pains to differentiate themselves by denouncing both Marx's theory of surplus value (the theory of the exploitation of labour which was so crucial in giving to Marxism its revolutionary character) and working-class internationalism. Yet certain likenesses persisted: Schmoller even agreed with Marx as to the inevitability of socialism, though he saw its triumph as a consequence of an alliance between socialism and the German 'bureaucratic and military monarchy,' rather than by revolutionary action of an international proletariat. Schmoller was no defender of capitalism but saw it as a stage in historical development. The programme of the *Verein* was designed to insure that the following stage would be the outgrowth of peaceful evolution, rather than risk the dangers of foreign domination or military dictatorship which were inherent in revolution. Revolution Schmoller regarded as 'always the most precarious of all games of chance.'[1]

A declaration of 'economic faith' recorded in a letter which Ashley wrote to his fiancée sometime between 1886 and 1888 corresponded substantially with the opinions of Schmoller and the *Verein*. The form which Ashley employed to describe his faith was itself significant: he constructed a list of those points of Marxist doctrine with which he agreed and those with which he disagreed. Ashley first described his differences with the socialists. (a) He believed that the theory of surplus value was false. (b) 'What they expect in ten years, I think *possible* in 100.' (c) He wished to emphasize the vices of all classes, not only those of the capitalists. (d) 'What they regard as *obstacles*

[1] Gustav Schmoller, *Grundriss der allgemeinen Volkswirtschaftslehre* (Munich, 1923), II, pp. 562–647. (First edition appeared in 1900.) Part of this material has been translated by Albion W. Small: 'Schmoller on Class Conflicts in General,' *The American Journal of Sociology*, XX, No. 4, 1915, pp. 504–531; the quotations in the text have been derived from this translation.

to *immediate* carrying out of socialist changes, I look on as *educating* influences toward a socialization . . . far in the future; such as factory legislation, trade unions, co-operation, wisely administered poor-law, sanitary aid, etc.' He believed revolutions 'for the present and for the next fifty years probably' were 'useless and therefore criminal.'

Ashley agreed with some of the contentions of the Marxists. (a) He thought their analysis of factory industry correct, believing it the same as that of Ricardo and Cairns: 'these argued that, *given certain conditions*, certain results such as the aggregation of capital, the destruction of smaller employers, the lowering of wages down to the standard of subsistence would follow.' For factory industry, these conditions—'complete freedom of competition, superfluity of labourers, etc.'—are 'being progressively realized, and consequently the results are being created.' (b) He believed that the formation of 'great companies' accompanied by 'the increased importance of the managing director' and the clearer distinction between that part of profit due to skill, and that due to the mere possession of capital pointed toward 'ultimate socialization.' (c) He saw in the changing role of the state, as evidenced in the factory acts, employer's liability laws, and the parcel post, a 'clear tendency toward socialization.' In matters of practical policy, Ashley wished to organize government works on the basis of a fair rather than a competitive wage and to extend state ownership to railways, waterworks, and gasworks, as well as to increase municipal property in land and houses.[1]

In another letter during this period, Ashley wrote with less hesitancy about the coming of socialism. He did not judge it as just 'possible,' he declared that the social organization of production and exchange was 'as certain as the rising of tomorrow's sun.' At this time, he called himself an 'evolutionary socialist,' and, in private conversation, retained this description of his views throughout his lifetime.[2] In later years, he told friends that his only choice had been to 'join the Conservatives and push them forward or join the Labour Party and hold them back.'[3] A proper dilemma for a *Katheder-Sozialist*, and properly resolved by joining the Conservatives.

[1] Quoted in Anne Ashley, *Ashley*, pp. 34–35.
[2] Quoted in *ibid.*, p. 36.   [3] Quoted in *ibid.*, p. 129.

In one crucial respect, Ashley's early declaration of 'economic faith' did not conform to the *Katheder-Sozialist* pattern. The *Katheder-Sozialist*, while admitting the existence of class conflict, desired to have that conflict rendered harmless by such unifying forces as common heredity, language, morality, and religion; the German economists were 'national' socialists. Ashley's upbringing was Liberal; his father, a journeyman hatter of modest means, was a slice of nineteenth-century non-conformity—a Baptist, a teetotaller, and a Free Trader. Ashley's background probably left him immune to the rash of nationalism which had infected so many of his associates; we know that he was one of the few Liberal Fellows at Oxford who did not shift party allegiance as a result of the Home Rule controversy.[1] Ashley's stay in North America, however, transformed the cosmopolitan Free Trader into a nationalist and protectionist and thereby a Liberal into a Conservative and Unionist. It was in the United States that Ashley abandoned his father's sect in favour of Episcopalianism, the American branch of the national church which, upon his return to England, he attended faithfully until death. He lived in the United States of the McKinley and Dingley tariffs and in a Canada in which reciprocity with the United States was the key political issue. When Chamberlain announced his programme of imperial preference in 1903, Ashley came actively to his support fearing, as he told J. H. Clapham, that 'were nothing done,' first 'the economic and then the probable political absorption of Canada by the United States was highly probable.'[2] While never an expansionist, he became a patriot and an imperialist. He asserted that the attitude which judged 'the nation as an indispensable instrument for the ultimate well-being of humanity' was 'consistent with a noble idealism,'[3] and he regarded the British Empire as 'the mightiest of instruments for good' and the 'fairest hope of humanity.'[4]

[1] *Ibid.*, p. 126.

[2] J. H. Clapham, 'Sir William Ashley,' *Economic Journal*, XXXVII, 1927, p. 681.

[3] W. J. Ashley, 'Political Economy and the Tariff Problem,' *Economic Review*, XIV, July 1904, p. 264.

[4] W. J. Ashley, 'The Argument for Preference,' *Economic Journal*, March 1904, XIV, p. 1.

The greater part of the Unionist party was soon converted to Chamberlain's Disraelian—and Bismarckian—programme of protection, imperialism and social reform. The Liberal party and the organized labour movement swung into the defence of Free Trade. So, too, did the leading lights of British political economy, Alfred Marshall among them, who signed a petition denouncing the Chamberlain programme as 'detrimental to the material prosperity of this country.'[1] A few days later H. S. Foxwell wrote a letter to *The Times* noting that 'with scarcely an exception, the historical group of English economists declined to sign the manifesto.' 'The fact,' he continued, 'I venture to think, goes far to justify the position they hold as to the importance of historical study in economics.'[2] Shortly afterward, one by one, the leading British economic historians announced their adherence to Tariff Reform and lent their active assistance to Chamberlain's campaign. The arguments of the economic historians were not widely different from those of the sensationalist tariff press but they gave the tariff cause the kind of intellectual respectability which Free Trade derived from orthodox political economy. The economic historians did, however, defend the Chamberlain programme from different standpoints. Hewins' position, for example, was that of the iron and steel industrialists with whom he associated upon the new Tariff Commission: he was a fairly conventional industrial protectionist.[3] For Mackinder, the founder of geopolitics, the 'key' was power: he saw British predominance threatened by Germany and felt that Tariff Reform would protect Britain's industrial strength and preserve the vitality of her working classes, i.e. her 'man-power.'[4] Cunningham hewed faithfully to the Unionist party line in his polemics, but, beneath the rhetoric, he rested his position on the more solid base of

[1] *The Times*, August 15, 1903, 4b. The Free Trade petition-signers were C. F. Bastable, A. L. Bowley, Edwin Cannan, Leonard Courtney, F. Y. Edgeworth, E. C. K. Gonner, Alfred Marshall, J. S. Nicholson, L. R. Phelps, A. Pigou, C. P. Sanger, W. R. Scott, W. Smart, and Armitage Smith.

[2] *The Times*, August 20, 1903, 10c.

[3] W. A. S. Hewins has presented his position in his *The Apologia of An Imperialist*.

[4] See Chapter VIII, *supra*.

conservatism's traditional conception of organic, national community, a view built upon Tudor and Stuart paternalism and mercantilism.[1]

Ashley's summing-up of the economics of protectionism was certainly acceptable to the Tariff Reformers—he was widely regarded as 'the leading academic defender' of the Chamberlain programme and as 'close' to Chamberlain[2]—but his more individual views, especially those on the 'social' side, were so eccentric that they had to be ignored.[3] They did not fit into the type of campaign the Unionist party was fighting. For instance, his view that the industrial supporters of Chamberlain were acting from motives of self-interest and that it was necessary for the working class to safeguard the tariff from selfish abuse was most unusual. It was the Liberals who spoke of the 'selfish interests' of the manufacturers and the Tariff Reformers who responded by citing the national interest, imperial idealism, and the broadening of employment. Ashley, in equally unorthodox fashion, admitted that Tariff Reform 'may open the door to forms of protection that are unnecessary and undesirable,' and added that 'only a grave sense of the needs of the nation and empire could induce any of us to be ready to face the risk.'[4] Ashley discussed the attitude of the German historical school toward the German tariff:

'They have no illusions which blind them to the selfishness of the class interests involved—whether of the great industrialists or of the agrarians; they realize the dangers, but feel that they have to be faced; that for a State to shirk a duty because it is

[1] See Chapter X, *supra*.

[2] Clapham, 'Sir William Ashley,' p. 681. See Anne Ashley, *Ashley*, p. 127.

[3] In the tariff campaign literature that this writer has read, Ashley's special argument concerning the dependence of national insurance on Tariff Reform appeared but once, in the *Monthly Notes on Tariff Reform*, September 1907, VII, No. 3, p. 91, published by the Birmingham Branch of the Tariff Reform League. Here it was clearly identified as Ashley's view—a rather unusual procedure, since the arguments of the other economic historians became common currency.

[4] W. J. Ashley, 'The Present Position of Political Economy,' *Economic Journal*, XVII, December 1907, p. 489.

difficult and can only be imperfectly performed, would be to abdicate its essential function.'[1]

The British working class must therefore give the tariff a 'discriminating support' or it would be responsible if self-seeking protectionists set policy.[2] Selfishness would be minimized by 'the pressure of competent and well-informed criticism of particular measures.'[3]

On questions of trade unionism and Tariff Reform, Ashley's views were in striking contrast to those of his colleagues in economic history and in the Unionist party.[4] On this matter, too, he was in agreement with the *Verein*. Gustav Schmoller had, we have seen, described the functions of the trade unions as most necessary ones. Many members of the *Verein*—Brentano is a noteworthy example—devoted themselves to the history of trade unionism.[5] From his earliest years, Ashley regarded the unions in this sympathetic light and displayed the greatest interest in their problems; unions were 'the only means' of 'remedying social inequalities.'[6] At Harvard during the violent Homestead Steel Strike of 1892 and the Pullman Strike of 1894, Ashley became seriously disturbed lest such armed clashes between capital and labour be reproduced in England. He became a leading advocate of unionism both in Canada and in the United States.[7] While at Harvard, he joined the Church Social Union (Episcopal) and, as chairman of its publications committee, prepared a pamphlet on the Pullman Strike which

[1] Ashley, 'Political Economy and the Tariff Problem,' p. 266.

[2] W. J. Ashley, 'Argument for Preference,' p. 9.

[3] W. J. Ashley, 'The Present Position of Political Economy,' p. 489.

[4] Cunningham, for example, believed that trade union policies were uniformly prejudicial to the national interest and feared the growing power of the unions. See Cunningham, *Christianity and Politics*, pp. 208-210.

[5] Brentano's scholarly reputation was made by his *Die Arbeitergilden der Gegenwart* (Leipzig, 1871-72).

[6] Quoted in Anne Ashley, *Ashley*, p. 55.

[7] See letter of William Ashley to Richard T. Ely, *c.* 1888, Ely Papers quoted in Joseph Dorfman, *The Economic Mind in American Civilization, 1865-1918* (New York: 1949), p. 124. See also Anne Ashley, *Ashley*, p. 55.

defended the right of the workers to strike in the absence of a system of arbitration.[1]

Ashley urged those who were concerned about the future of trade unionism to consider international trade conditions. German and American steel exports were limiting the profits of British steel manufacturers, he argued, and British producers were already beginning to imitate the anti-trade union activities of their competitors. As international trade rivalry became more and more severe, employers 'will demand, and will have a right to get, a freer hand' in order to compete more effectively. If the working class wished to maintain trade unions, Ashley warned, working men had better support Tariff Reform.[2]

If the Tariff Reform programme were not adopted, British manufacturers in their frantic search for markets would, Ashley proclaimed, drive the country to war. British cotton manufacturers had waged war in 1839 in order to maintain their China trade and were capable of doing so again. If the British working man was interested in preserving the peace, the Birmingham economist once again warned, and it was to his interest to do so since the working man would do the actual fighting in event of war, he had better support Tariff Reform.[3]

Social reform, too, would accompany the success of the tariff programme, Ashley asserted. This was not an unusual argument; one of Chamberlain's early pronouncements had promised old-age pensions derived from tariff revenues. Ashley's point was different; he did not see social reform as dependent upon the expansion of revenues. German national insurance was 'hardly less than a social revolution,' he argued, and Bismarck had only been able to weaken the opposition of German industrialists to insurance by simultaneously offering them a protective tariff. A system of national insurance was possible only 'with the acquiescence and co-operation of the employers' and that acquiescence 'can only be obtained when British employers feel that they can carry on their operations with a reasonable degree of commercial security.' Social reform and a tariff were not only

[1] W. J. Ashley, *The Railroad Strike of 1894* (Cambridge, Mass., 1895), pp. 8-12.

[2] W. J. Ashley, *The Tariff Problem* (London, 1920), pp. 191-192. The book was first published in 1903.

[3] *Ibid.*, p. 197.

not inconsistent, Ashley maintained, but, as the German example
had demonstrated, the former was dependent upon the latter.
'This is a great comfort to those of us who are Social Reformers
first and Imperialists afterwards,' Ashley continued, 'those of us
who, in the present crisis of our national fortunes, are such
ardent Imperialists that we are ready to risk even the real
dangers of tariffs, and to do this just because we are Social
Reformers.'[1]

In these arguments to the working class, Ashley had, perhaps
unawares, painted his portrait of contemporary capitalism. It
was an odd picture for a Conservative: selfish industrialists
seeking to pervert national policy to their advantage; a hard-
pressed British capitalism, backed into a corner by its rivals,
which would not hesitate to smash trade unionism and even to
make war in order to better its competitive position; a capitalism
willing to share some of the 'spoils' of imperial success, in the
form of national insurance, in exchange for the working man's
support of protection. It was a portrait of capitalism that might
have been painted by a Marxist critic—indeed Luxemburg and
Hilferding saw capitalism, in its 'last stage of imperialism,' in
much this light.[2] If we turn back to Ashley's early declaration of
'economic faith,' we recall his agreement with Marxist analysis
of factory industry. He stated then that under conditions of
complete freedom of competition—in this instance, the freedom
of German and American industrialists to compete with British
industry—and of a 'superfluity of labourers,' and so on, certain
results—'the aggregation of capital, the destruction of smaller
employers, the lowering of wages down to the standard of
subsistence would follow.' Unlike the Marxists, and in the
pattern of the *Katheder-Sozialisten*, he advised not revolution,
but class compromise and the blocking of foreign competition
by tariffs and preference.

Ashley gave much consideration to the growth of industrial
combinations while at Harvard. Pre-war England had been less

[1] W. J. Ashley, *The Progress of the German Working Classes in the Last
Quarter of a Century* (London, 1904), pp. 19, vi-vii.
[2] See, for example, Luxemburg, *op. cit.*, *passim*, and especially pp.
446-453. This book was originally published in 1913. Hilferding's
work on finance capital was published in 1910. Ashley, therefore,
anticipated some of the points of their more definitive formulations.

affected by the trust movement than either Germany or the
United States, and English Liberal economists associated her
comparative freedom from trusts with Free Trade, warning that
the adoption of Tariff Reform would end this immunity.
Defenders of the tariff appeared to agree with this view and
preferred not to deal with this charge. Ashley attacked the
problem boldly; for him, as for the Marxists, trusts were no
'merely temporary' phenomenon, not simply a consequence of
protection, they were an inevitable part of capitalist development. He saw gigantic trusts looming in England's industrial
future whether or not protection were adopted. Competition
led to crises and unemployment; crises, for Ashley as for the
Marxists, were produced 'automatically, by the "normal"
working of the competitive system.' At the present stage of
capitalist development, Ashley wrote, the normal crises were
made even sharper by—and once more the Marxists would have
agreed—'the increasing use of fixed capital.' These crises led
unfailingly to industrial combination.[1]

Yet Ashley's attitude toward the trust was hardly Marxist
or that of British and American middle-class opinion. He
described trusts, in the light of the agonies of competition in
America, as 'simply an attempt to lessen and, if it may be, avert
altogether the disastrous and harassing effects of cut-throat
competition.'[2] Schmoller wrote similarly of trusts as both
inevitable and, if regulated by statute and guided by informed
public opinion, beneficial.[3] Ashley adopted a moral position on
the trust which he felt 'proceeds from the good side of humanity,
the impulse toward mutual assistance and the desire for stability,
as well as from the less attractive side, the pursuit of gain.'[4]

Industrial combinations were beneficial to the working class,
Ashley asserted. Competition—both internal and external—
was driving wages to the subsistence level and was responsible
for unemployment. International competition would be
restricted by the programme of Tariff Reform. After that, 'our

[1] W. J. Ashley, 'American Trusts,' in *Surveys Historic and Economic*,
pp. 378-384.
[2] *Ibid.*, p. 385.
[3] For Schmoller on trusts, see *Grundriss*, I, pp. 537-556.
[4] W. J. Ashley, *The Economic Organisation of England* (London:
Longmans, 1935), pp. 188-189. Originally published in 1914.

main hope must rest,' Ashley reported, 'in the limitation of internal competition among employers by the growth of capitalistic combination.'[1] Combination would guarantee for the working man that 'continuity of employment and steadiness in the rate of remuneration' which were 'really more important than temporary high wages.'[2] In one respect, the workers would be disadvantaged. It would be more difficult to bargain with the the industrial combination than it had been with the small concern. Ashley's solution was that the working men, too, should form combinations.

For Ashley, as for Schmoller, there was no doubt concerning the existence of contradictory class interests. Cunningham and other 'advanced' Conservatives were at this time, backing schemes of co-partnership and profit-sharing.[3] Although Ashley wished social reconciliation, not conflict, he rejected as un-realistic all attempts to bring about class harmony which took as their starting point the identity of interest between employer and employee. Trade unionism, based as it was on 'a solidarity, or community of interest, between all the workmen of a trade, face to face with, if not in opposition to, all the employers of the trade'—that was the true principle and the sound one since it did not attempt to detach employees from 'the common interests of their class.' Ashley warned employers not to attempt to destroy this principle of unionism. 'The weakening of unionism,' Ashley insisted, 'paradoxical as it may sound, weakens the necessary basis for industrial peace in the only direction in which it is likely to be secured nowadays, i.e. the direction of collective agreement.'[4]

Ashley puzzled about the form which the national economy of the future would and should take. In discussing the Standard Oil monopoly in the United States, he admitted that development had reached the point where 'on the purely economic and administrative side, there could be little objection to the Government taking over the business,' but added significantly,

---

[1] W. J. Ashley, 'The Present Position of Social Legislation in England,' *Economic Review*, October 1908, XVIII, p. 397.

[2] Ashley, 'American Trusts,' p. 386.

[3] See Cunningham, *The Causes of Labour Unrest*, p. 18.

[4] W. J. Ashley, 'Profit-Sharing,' *Quarterly Review*, CCXIX, 1913, pp. 522, 530, 524, and *passim*.

'if only there were a Government politically capable of the task.'[1]
The future society he did see was based upon the corporative
theories which were being revived and widely discussed on the
continent and which Ashley, alone among the English economists, upheld. Ashley believed that the future would see great
national organizations of employers engaged in collective
bargaining with great national organizations of working men.
Such a situation already existed in certain British industries and
would become more general. This Ashley regarded as the
'natural response' to economic conditions.[2] 'Society,' Ashley
wrote in 1914, 'is feeling its way with painful steps towards a
corporate organisation of industry on the side alike of employers
and employed; to be then more harmoniously, let us hope,
associated together—with the State alert and intelligent in the
background to protect the interests of the community.'[3] It was a
natural conclusion for this English *Katheder-Sozialist*, working
with tools of economic analysis wielded by the Marxists but
toward the non-revolutionary goals of the German historical
school.

Many of Ashley's arguments to persuade the working class
to accept Tariff Reform were bad politics and consequently
ignored. British Conservatism eschewed specious theory and
turned more naturally to Hewins' industrial protectionism,
Mackinder's warnings concerning German might, and Cun-
ingham's 'national' economics. Although he acknowledged
himself a disciple of German historical economics, Ashley never
did publicly call himself a disciple of *Katheder-Sozialismus* as
well. Such an admission might easily have further limited his
political influence in pre-war Britain. Although Ashley had a
much more profound understanding of the importance of orthodox economic analysis than had Schmoller and the German
school,[4] it was to the Germans that he owed that special point
of view which differentiated him from his English colleagues
and it was largely from them that he derived the insights which
enabled him to prophesy our present age of oligopoly.

[1] Ashley, 'American Trusts,' p. 387.
[2] Ashley, *Economic Organisation of England*, pp. 189-190.
[3] *Ibid.*, pp. 190-191.
[4] See Schumpeter, *History of Economic Analysis*, pp. 822-823n.

XII

LORD ROBERTS AND
ROBERT BLATCHFORD

'Universal conscript military service, with its twin brother universal suffrage, has mastered all Continental Europe— with what promises of massacre and bankruptcy for the 20th century!'

HIPPOLYTE TAINE, *Les Origines de la France Contemporaine*, 1891

'Have you thought of the physical improvement which conscription would bring about in the manhood of the country? What England wants is chest! (*he generously inflates his own.*) Chest and Discipline. I don't care how it's obtained.'

GRANVILLE BARKER, *The Voysey Inheritance*, 1905

ROBERTS—A BARRACKS SOCIAL-IMPERIALIST

The international situation caused imperialists of both parties to reconsider the basis and organization of the British Army during the time between the war in South Africa and 1914. During the Boer War, many weaknesses in the structure of both the War Office and the Army were recognized by both politicians and military men. Many military men became rather interested in conscription, a system in practice in most of the continental countries and upon which the much heralded German army based its strength. After the war, Lord Roberts—who had become a popular hero during the fighting—campaigned, under the auspices of the National Service League which had been founded in 1901, for a programme which called for four years of training for all British young men between the ages of 18 and 30. The 'four years' were to consist of two months of instructional training in the first year and a fortnight in each of the three following years. Even the comparative moderation of the programme did not exempt it from the attacks of the anti-conscriptionists and from the hostility arising from the widespread feeling among all classes that conscription was somehow 'un-British.' Organized labour, in particular, loathed

conscription, as did the international socialists of the I.L.P.
'National' Socialists like the Fabians and Robert Blatchford
were convinced of the need for military training of some sort,
although the Fabians leaned to the militia formula, the 'nation-
in-arms' concept of the continental socialists, rather than the
'barracks' formula of the professional soldiery.

After the South African war, two Unionist Secretaries for
War—St John Brodrick, who accepted the post in 1901, and
H. O. Arnold-Forster, who supplanted Brodrick in 1903—made
efforts to reorganize the War Office and to make the army
conform to modern—that is, to German—standards. In the
Liberal government which took office at the end of 1905, R. B.
Haldane became war minister. Haldane continued the reforms
initiated by his Unionist predecessors and advanced forward,
in the same direction, with vigour and considerable success.
He even succeeded in creating a General Staff for the Army,
after the German model, thus giving the army 'a brain.' The
contribution to British armed strength of which the Liberal-
Imperialist Secretary was most proud was the creation of the
Territorial Force by the Army Bill of 1907.

By the provisions of this bill, young men between 18 and 24
were encouraged to join the Territorial Force and to undergo a
training period of about a fortnight a year for four years.
Officers' Training Corps were set up in the public schools and
universities. The ultimate goal of the Force was 300,000 men.
The Cobdenites within the Liberal party and the government's
Labour party allies were not pleased by this Liberal-Imperialist
army scheme but were persuaded that its voluntary principle
was preferable to conscription which top military opinion and
many Tariff Reformers preferred and which they might otherwise have secured. The advocates of conscription gave the
scheme some grudging support as a step in the right direction.
The *Daily Mail* was employed by the War Office to help recruit
for the new force. In its enlistment appeals the War Office took
advantage of the trade depression which began at the end of 1907
and lasted for about a year; many unemployed joined the Force.
At the end of 1908, the Territorial Force numbered 188,000;
by the beginning of 1910, 276,000.[1]

[1] Halévy, *History of the English People*, VI, pp. 154-232.

Despite this growth in Britain's armed might, Lord Roberts continued to maintain that, although the Territorial Force was better than nothing, what the country required was 'national service.' Just as the nation appeared to detest the word protection so did it abhor 'conscription,' which made the proponents of those causes soften their labels by such terms as 'Tariff Reform' and 'national service.' But to Roberts, the distinction between the two was not only verbal but technical. He understood by conscription the shipment overseas of men called into the service—this, indeed, had been the programme of the National Service League under the presidency of the Duke of Wellington, in 1904, before Roberts had assumed charge. This policy had been changed as a concession to the Field-Marshal. The programme of the League had become support for universal service and training of citizens for home defence, which would free the regular, professional army for overseas commitments and provide an officer reserve for emergency expansion.

Roberts believed that only a professional force could cope with imperial military problems—and who had more expert knowledge on this matter? Born in India, the son of a General in the service of the East India Company, he had, after his education at Eton and Sandhurst, returned to India to serve with the Bengal Artillery. Roberts had helped in the suppression of the Indian Mutiny of 1857, in the course of which action he had won the Victoria Cross. Then had come many years of service in India and active fighting in Afghanistan. In 1885, his service in India was crowned by his elevation to the post of Commander-in-Chief in India. In 1892, he was created Baron Roberts of Kandahar, and in 1895, Field-Marshal. He was his country's foremost military officer. When it became clear, by December 1899, that the war in South Africa was not going well, Roberts was appointed to the supreme command, with Kitchener as his chief of staff. Roberts proved to be precisely what the South African military situation required; the tide of battle turned; England was set on the road to victory.

When Baron Roberts returned to England in January 1901, he was greeted with a shower of praise and gratitude by his countrymen. He was received by Victoria who conferred upon him a new title—he became Viscount St Pierre and Earl Roberts of Pretoria. Roberts was admitted to the Order of the Garter and parliament granted him £100,000 for his services. The great hero of the British Empire was named Commander-in-Chief of the British Army. It was early in 1904 that Earl Roberts retired from active duty with the Army and set out on the last campaign of his life.

It was an intensely personal campaign. Roberts delivered himself entirely to the cause and was regarded as somewhat of a crank as a result. One of his pet projects, for example, was the rifle club. In 1905, he urged the formation of rifle clubs by means of which Englishmen might become as skilled marksmen as their medieval ancestors, the bowmen victors of Agincourt. He toured the country warning his listeners that British security could only be protected by armed strength. South Africa had demonstrated the weaknesses of the Army. Would not action now be taken to raise the large numbers of trained, skilled soldiers which were needed to defend the country and the Empire?

Speakers were dispatched to all parts of the country by the National Service League to campaign in support of Roberts. Tours to study the Swiss system of national service were arranged by the League and special efforts were made to have Labour M.P.'s and trade union officials join these tours. Roberts' speeches were published and widely distributed. By the end of the decade, the League's and Earl Roberts' appeals appear to have been heard by many in the country despite the silence of the parliamentary politicians. By 1908, Roberts, as President of the Society of Miniature Rifle Clubs, was able to announce that more than 1,000 clubs, most of them new ones, had become affiliated to the national society. *The Times*, the *Daily Telegraph*, the *Daily Mail*, and the *Spectator* were offering the National Service League their regular support. By 1909 the League, which had had but 4,000 members when Roberts had taken charge in 1904, had 35,000 members.[1]

Roberts and the National Service League made special appeals to the working class, known to be especially antagonistic to conscription or any form of 'militarism.' Roberts warned the working man that his prosperity depended upon the import of raw materials for him to work up into finished goods and that

[1] See David James, *Life of Lord Roberts* (London: Hollis & Carter 1954) and Walter Jerrold, *Field-Marshal Earl Roberts* (London, 1914).

he could not live without imported foodstuffs. Without a strong
army and navy, he asserted, these necessary imports would be
imperilled in the event of war.[1] This was no mere 'party
question,' Roberts maintained, it was 'a National question':
'it is my absolute belief that, without a military organisation
more adequate to the certain perils of the future, our Empire
will fall from us and our power will pass away.'[2] In a famous
speech delivered in Manchester, in October 1912, Roberts gave
the working man a shrill warning concerning the danger of
Germany: 'The German Socialist, it is said, will not make war
upon his French or his English comrade,' Roberts began. This
was nonsense. 'Gentlemen,' he continued, 'it is to the credit of
the human race that patriotism, in the presence of such organisa-
tions, has always proved itself superior to any class or any
individual.' The alternatives were simple: Englishmen must
either 'abandon our Empire, and with it our mercantile wealth'
or 'we must be prepared to defend it.'[3]

Lord Roberts' strictures upon Germany in his Manchester
address gave rise to much criticism of the Field Marshal himself,
especially on the part of the Liberal press. It also provided the
occasion for Robert Blatchford, a former non-commissioned
officer in the British army, to comment in his socialist weekly,
The Clarion, upon the campaign of the National Service League.
'Lord Roberts is a great general and an honourable man,'
Blatchford wrote in a leading article on 'The Mis-Ruling
Classes.' 'The sincerity of his patriotism is above suspicion.
Logically, also, he is impregnable. He sees that in an armed
Europe an unarmed England is a danger. He believes, and so
do I, that the best way to preserve the peace is to be prepared
for war. He sees that the Empire is threatened; he knows that
the Empire is not secure. . . .' Lord Roberts saw Germany as the
force endangering the Empire. The real danger, however,
Blatchford asserted, was that 'the masses of the people are
anti-patriotic and anti-militarist.' Lord Roberts, therefore,

[1] Earl Roberts, *Fallacies and Facts; An Answer to 'Compulsory Service'*
(London, 1911), pp. 69-72.
[2] Earl Roberts, *National Security, Speech delivered in House of Lords,*
November 23, 1908, (n.p., n.d.), p. 15.
[3] Lord Roberts, 'A Nation in Arms,' Speech in Manchester, October
1912, pp. 8, 9.

'might as well ask for the moon as ask for universal service.'
Why was the working class opposed to conscription? 'The
masses will not have it' because 'they do not trust the so-called
ruling classes.'[1]

Roberts felt obliged to reply to this assertion—and did so in
good social-imperialist fashion. 'In a democratic nation,'
Roberts wrote, 'the working classes are themselves the ruling
classes,' and furthermore 'the interests of England and of the
Empire are their interests.' Since this was the case, the English
working classes must secure for themselves the historic 'right'
and 'inalienable privilege' of all ruling classes—'service in war.'
'Such service,' Roberts concluded, sounding very much like the
continental socialists and even like Blatchford himself, 'is the
only mark of the true and perfect citizenship.'[2]

This was not the first time that Earl Roberts had spoken such
words. The previous year, 1911, he had written a letter to *The
Times* urging the Unionist party to formulate a 'constructive
policy' on 'Social Reform and National Defence,' two problems
which were 'intimately connected,' and a 'satisfactory solution'
of which had to 'precede any real strengthening of Imperial
bonds.' 'The conditions amid which millions of our people are
living,' he wrote, 'appear to me to make it natural that they
should not care a straw under what rule they may be called upon
to dwell, and I can well understand their want of patriotic
feeling.' Could there be a more cogent expression of the fears
of the social-imperialist?

Roberts called for the increase of the school-leaving age, for
education in patriotism, for instruction in the habits of 'order,
obedience, and discipline.' Such educational reform and 'Social
Reform is a preliminary to any thorough system of national
defence.' 'With how much more confidence,' Roberts proclaimed,
'should we be able to appeal to the young men of this nation and
the Empire to do their duty as citizen soldiers if we had the
certainty that they regarded England, not as a harsh stepmother,
but as a true motherland . . . if we could further appeal to them
to defend the nation and the Empire, because within its bounds
they can live nobler and fuller lives than on any other spot on

[1] *The Clarion*, November 1, 1912, p. 1.
[2] See Earl Roberts, *Lord Roberts' Message to the Nation* (London,
1912), pp. 39-40.

earth!' Yet 'to tens of thousands of Englishmen engaged in daily toil, the call to "sacrifice" themselves for their country must seem an insult to their reason; for those conditions amid which they live make their lives already an unending sacrifice.'

Roberts called to the Unionists to take the lead on this issue. 'No party,' he warned, 'can long continue in power which relies for its prestige solely upon fomenting class hatreds—that is, by dividing the State against itself.'[1] This was a warning not only to the Unionists, but to the Cobdenites and to the Socialists. One professed 'socialist,' Blatchford, enthusiastically agreed with Field-Marshal Roberts' views in practically every particular. In fact, he seemed to go far beyond Roberts in his appreciation of military virtues.

ROBERT BLATCHFORD—SOCIALIST OF THE BARRACKS

In 1891, Robert Blatchford left the staff of the *Sunday Chronicle*, on which he had been employed since 1885, to found a new weekly paper, *The Clarion*. This journal was to become the most successful socialist publication in Great Britain during the period before the war of 1914, and its editor was the leading spokesman for the rank-and-file working-class socialists, a group whose interest in pub and track was at least as great as its resentment of 'the upper classes.'

An able, craftsmanlike writer, Blatchford wrote in short sentences and short paragraphs, with rhythm, with clarity, and with courage, all qualities which made instant appeal to his British working-man readers. His briefs for Socialism—*Merrie England*, followed by *Britain for the British*—were immensely popular. They were translated into many tongues and their sale in Great Britain and the United States alone reached a total of over two million copies. One of Blatchford's biographers has written that *Merrie England* alone 'has made more converts to English Socialism than all other Socialist publications

---

[1] *Ibid.*, pp. 43-45; see also Socialist Labour Party, *Compulsory Military Service* (Glasgow, 1912?), for a verbatim record of a debate between a speaker for the National Service League and a Marxist opponent.

combined.'[1] Another has described him as the man who created
the army which followed the great leaders of British socialism.
Blatchford, he continued, 'can manufacture Socialists more
quickly than anyone else,' and makes 'more Socialists than any
other rival establishment.'[2]

Blatchford did not have any of the backgrounds that might
customarily have been expected in a successful journalist—even
a working-class journalist. A man of the people, Blatchford had
had no formal education, and, most surprisingly, aside for a brief
time in his youth when he worked as a brushmaker, he had not
even experienced the life of the working classes. Before turning
to journalism, he had served as an enlisted man in the British
army, joining as a private and leaving as a sergeant of the
103rd Dublin Fusileers. In later life he confessed 'I *had* to
go for a soldier; it was written,' and 'I love the Army. . . .
I love a rifle as one loves a living thing. I was happy in the
Army. . . . I got nothing but good by it. I really don't know
how much I owe to it.'[3] Blatchford's view of the great influence of his military experience upon him was essentially a
sound one.

Socialist though he was, Blatchford was one of the chief
critics of the newly formed Labour party. He disliked the
complete subservience of the Labour Party leadership to
Liberalism, especially in matters of international policy. For
ex-soldier Blatchford, anti-patriotic, cosmopolitan Cobdenite
Liberalism was an enemy of major proportions, was, in fact, the
very antithesis of what he understood by 'socialism,' and he
fought against it throughout his life. In the month before
the first of the two general elections of 1910, Blatchford
characterized both the Liberals and the leaders of the Labour
Party as 'hopeless.'[4] Two weeks earlier he had written that he
would regard the return of a Labour majority as a 'calamity.'[5]
After the election of 1931, Blatchford expressed his pleasure at
Labour's defeat because 'I believe they would have disrupted the

---

[1] A. Neil Lyons, *Robert Blatchford* (London, 1910), p. 89.
[2] Quoted in *Ibid.*, p. 102.
[3] Robert Blatchford, *My Life in the Army* (London: Blatchford, 1915),
pp. 9, 14.
[4] *The Clarion*, December 31, 1909, p. 1.
[5] *The Clarion*, December 17, 1909, p. 1.

British Empire. I dreaded their childish cosmopolitanism. . . .'[1]
Blatchford had none of the illusions concerning the international
brotherhood of workers that were the common property of his
Labour party comrades, nor did he share their sentimental
pacifism, their anti-imperialism, their noble, if futile, cosmopolitanism. 'We were Britons first and Socialists next,' was
his frequent boast concerning himself and his *Clarion* colleagues.[2]
In the course of the years, Blatchford revealed himself an
advocate of economic nationalism, imperialism, militarism,
jingoism, and an uncompromising opponent of parliamentarian-
ism and the party system.

Yet all the while he regarded himself—and was regarded by
others—as a socialist. Blatchford's special combination of
hostility not only to capitalism but to such offshoots of bourgeois
predominance as cosmopolitan anti-militarism and liberal
democracy was not unusual on the continent. In France, for
example, he would have found asylum with Maurras and
L'Action Française—he would probably have been an anti-
capitalist monarchist and undoubtedly an anti-Dreyfusard.
In Austria, he would have joined the Christian Socialists of
Vienna's Mayor Lueger in opposition to the Social-Democrats.
But in England, he was a man of the 'left,' not perhaps by
choice, but because the 'right' was not sufficiently broad—nor
corrupt—to admit a man of his social background and
sympathies. Unlike France, all classes in England had accepted

[1] In a letter, in 1931, to his good friend and *Clarion* associate, Alex
M. Thompson, Blatchford spoke of the difference between *Clarion*
socialism and that of the Independent Labour Party:

> You remember that from the first the Clarion crowd and the Hardie
> crowd were out of harmony. It was a repetition of the old hostility
> between the Roundheads and Cavaliers. The Labour Leader people
> were Puritans; narrow, bigotted, puffed up with sour cant. We both
> disliked them, because we were both Cavaliers. They were
> nonconformist, self-righteous ascetics, out for the class war and the
> dictation by the proletariat. We loved the humour and colour of the
> old English tradition. You know it was so. You know we never
> could mix.

quoted in Laurence V. Thompson, *Robert Blatchford, Portrait of an
Englishman* (London, 1951), p. 230.

[2] Robert Blatchford, *My Eighty Years* (London, 1931), p. 199.

the parliamentary regime of the limited monarchy, all classes
had been won over by the basic precepts of 'liberalism,' even
Labour party socialists and 'true blue' Conservatives. Not that
there were not men of the right, contemporaries of Blatchford,
who had not tired of the parliamentary game. Viscount Milner,
the hero of the South African War, was one of these.[1] There
were, furthermore, others—like Earl Roberts—who came close
to Blatchford's 'socialism of the barracks.' Yet there was a
certain broad area of agreement in British politics which left
Blatchford in a comparatively isolated position on many basic
issues.

England experienced a great crisis of conscience at the turn
of the century—the Boer War. The left, almost to a man, under
the leadership of two future Liberal prime ministers—Campbell-
Bannerman and Lloyd George—defended the Boers against
British imperialism. Not so socialist Robert Blatchford. In
February of 1899, Blatchford assessed both imperialism, and
what he called 'the Peace Palaver,' and concluded 'that Imperialism lives by deeds, while the Peace Palaver is all words.'
Imperialism could point to impressive accomplishments: the
greatest empire the world had ever known, peopled by hundreds
of millions of subjects. The best qualities of the British nation
had gone into the building of that empire. The peace palaver he
judged as nothing but 'volumes of sermons, pious resolutions,
and some miles of newspaper articles consisting chiefly of
insincere fine writing.' What Blatchford urged was the necessity
of 'a large and efficient fleet, of strengthening the defences of
our empire, and of making our army as fit as science and
discipline can make it.'[2] When the South African War began, in
the latter part of 1899, ex-sergeant Blatchford rushed to the
colours. He heaped scorn on the Cobdenites, his 'cosmopolitan
friends, who are so cosmopolitan that they can admire every
country but their own, and love all men except Englishmen.'
He joshed the Socialists who, while 'despising military glory,
are yet so eloquent over the marksmanship and courage of the
Boers.'[3] They were 'smug, self-righteous prigs.'[4] These

[1] See Chapter IX, *supra*.
[2] *The Clarion*, February 4, 1899, p. 33.
[3] *The Clarion*, October 28, 1899, p. 337.
[4] *The Clarion*, November 4, 1899, p. 346.

P

socialists had better understand that they could not have it both
ways; they must either be willing to give up their colonies or to
fight for them. 'To give them up would be difficult and dangerous
to us, and not good for the colonies.' To defend them, Britain
must have a powerful army and navy, and 'if we have soldiers
and ships it will not be wise nor just to call those soldiers
murderers, nor to wish for their defeat, nor to grudge them
thanks for their gallantry.'[1] Blatchford was an old soldier. His
'whole heart is with the British troops'; he loved Tommy
Atkins. 'When England is at war,' he declared, 'I'm English.
I have no politics and no party. I am English.'[2]

The Liberals cherished the ideal of international Free Trade—
clearly practicable only in a peaceful world. The Labour Party
—indeed all the principal European socialist parties—supported
international Free Trade. Blatchford saw no peace and seeing
himself, here too, as 'English' rather than a cosmopolitan,
espoused economic nationalism as the 'nobler' ideal. He devoted
much of his two larger works, *Merrie England* and *Britain for
the British*, to hammering at British Free Trade. One of his
favourite arguments was that Free Trade had made it impossible
for Britain to feed herself and that this boded ill for the preservation of the Empire. The logical and inevitable result of the Free
Trade legislation, he wrote, had been the destruction of British
agriculture. Buying in the cheapest market and selling in the
dearest had robbed Britons of much more than the $\frac{1}{4}$d. they
saved on each loaf of bread: 'We lose the beauty and health of
our factory towns; we lose annually some twenty thousand lives
in Lancashire alone . . . we lose the stamina of our people;
and—*we lose our agriculture*.'[3] The last loss was especially
serious in time of war, when despite the supremacy of the British
fleet, England could be brought to the point of starvation
because of her dependence for her food upon foreign nations.[4]

During the tariff agitation initiated by Chamberlain in 1903

[1] *The Clarion*, November 11, 1899, p. 354.

[2] *The Clarion*, October 21, 1899, p. 332.

[3] Robert Blatchford, *Merrie England* (London, 1895), p. 33.

[4] Robert Blatchford, *Britain for the British* (Chicago, 1902), pp. 99,
101, 118, 115-116.

Blatchford's distrust of the factory system and attachment to the
life of agriculture often reminds us of the great nineteenth-century

as part of a Bismarckian and imperialist programme for England, the position of Blatchford and the *Clarion* on the issue of protection was ambiguous. The Liberal *Fortnightly Review*, in an article hostile to Tariff Reform, tried to identify Tariff Paternalism and Socialism and affirmed that protection 'finds an enthusiastic supporter in Mr Blatchford, whose Socialist sermons in the *Clarion* are read by thousands of working men every week.'[1] In the House of Commons, Claude Hay, a prominent Tariff Reformer, quoted, with approval, a *Clarion* article written by R. B. Suthers—Blatchford's chief colleague and a frequent mouthpiece for Blatchford's views—on the investment of British capital abroad.[2] Actually neither Blatchford nor the *Clarion* formally backed Joseph Chamberlain's tariff movement. The announced goals of the Tariff Reformers—the revival of British agriculture, a self-supporting British Empire, a producer-oriented rather than a consumer-oriented economics—met, however, with the *Clarion's* full approval. Considerably before the opening of Chamberlain's Tariff Reform campaign directed toward this very goal, Blatchford had urged that Britons work toward a self-sustaining Empire.[3] Nor had the *Clarion* any sympathy with 'the Fetish of Cheapness,'[4] the doctrine of low Tory Democrat William Cobbett. Writing to his typical British workman, John Smith, Blatchford says:

'Oh, John, John, you silly fellow, have you no eyes? These are some of the reasons why I don't love the factory system. . . . The thing is evil. It is evil in its origin, in its progress, in its methods, in its motives, and in its effects. No nation can be sound whose motive power is greed. No nation can be secure unless it is independent, no nation can be independent unless it is based upon agriculture.' (Blatchford, *Merrie England*, p. 35; see also *Clarion*, August 19, 1899, p. 257).

Manchester had made entirely lop-sided the balanced economic structure of the old England Blatchford loved.

[1] Autonomous, 'Pinchbeck Protectionism' in *Fortnightly Review*, 80/74:732, November 2, 1903; see also G. S. Street, 'Socialists and Tories,' in *Fortnightly Review*, 85/79:626-629, April 2, 1906.

[2] *Parliamentary Debates*, Fourth Series, CLIL, 879-880, February 26, 1906.

[3] *The Clarion*, August 19, 1899, p. 257.

[4] A. M. Thompson and R. B. Suthers, 'Our Point of View,' *Clarion*, July 3, 1903, p. 4.

prices for consumers which the Cobdenites cited as one of the advantages of Free Trade. In *Merrie England* Blatchford had constructed this syllogism: 'Now cheap goods mean cheap labour, and cheap labour means low wages. You have nothing but your labour to sell, and you are told that it will pay you to sell that cheaply.'[1]

'Tariff Reform, rightly used,' wrote R. B. Suthers, Blatchford's *Clarion* associate, 'might be a weapon. Yes, a Trusty weapon if you like, well worth our attention.' But the tariff must be formulated along 'national' lines and 'not by the votes and gold of interested individuals.' If there were a real Labour party, a party which truly represented the interests of all of labour, then it might be able, in a Tariff Reform parliament, to prevent the gerrymandering of the fiscal system. But there was no such party, only 'a sectional Labour Party professing to be guided by Socialists, and reclining in the arms of the Free Trade Party.'[2] Blatchford summed up the matter in the *Clarion*: 'I do not believe in Free Trade; and I do not believe in Tariff Reform—as Tariff Reform will be applied by the Tories.'[3] On this great question the Tories were not to be trusted; but a socialist government would find a tariff a natural, efficient, and necessary instrument.

Blatchford—like Earl Roberts—devoted the years preceding the war to trying to arouse his countrymen against the German menace. Alarmed at German war preparations and at the failure of the British people to appreciate their significance, and

[1] Blatchford, *Merrie England*, p. 92.

[2] R. B. Suthers, 'Socialism and Tariff Reform,' *Clarion*, January 21, 1910, p. 5; Suthers presents the same general point of view in his volume collection of *Clarion* articles, *My Right to Work* (London, 1906).

[3] *Clarion*, December 17, 1909, p. 1. The *Clarion* protested when a majority of the London County Council, including John Burns, and J. Ramsay MacDonald, voted against a recommendation that the steel for the construction of the Vauxhall Bridge be British-made. The Council majority believed it would be less expensive to purchase steel abroad. The British producer, wrote Thompson and Suthers in the *Clarion*, wants protection. 'The Liberals have no Protection to offer. . . . The Tories offer Protection, but it is Protection of "vested interests." . . . But Socialism offers the only Protection that is worth the workers' consideration. . . .' (*Clarion*, July 3, 1903, p. 4.).

convinced that Germany was aiming at nothing less than the destruction of the British Empire, which he regarded as the most serious calamity that could befall world civilization, Blatchford set out to warn Britons that Germany's goal was conquest and world-domination, a policy bound to clash with 'the traditional policy of Britain . . . the extension of the Empire and the maintenance of the balance of power in Europe.'[1] Yet, Blatchford inquired, what had been the reaction of the British people to this challenge? Sloth, apathy, factional dispute. The Liberals and the men of the Labour Party persisted in thinking of the Germans as 'pacific and dove-like.'[2] The socialists of the Labour party even went so far as to entertain a theory of joint action by the British and German working classes in case of war, a theory Blatchford called 'one of those harmless games with which some Labour statesmen amuse themselves in dull days.'[3] Someone had to sound the alarm, to state the case 'in the teeth of the anti-militarist and anti-patriotic masses.' In a series of articles, published by the Tory *Daily Mail*, Blatchford warned 'that unless the British people are ready to fight and pay and work as they have not fought and paid and striven for a hundred years— if ever—the Empire will assuredly go to pieces and leave us beggared and disgraced under the conquest of a braver, better trained, and better organised nation.'[4]

Why was it so difficult to arouse the government to this vital issue of survival? Government had been paralyzed by the party system. Ineffective factionalism was an inevitable part of parliamentary government. In saying this, Blatchford went far beyond Lord Roberts. The rejection of parties as 'purposeless factions,' of party politicians as frauds and cheats, of the parliamentary machinery as clumsy, inefficient, and in some mysterious way, undemocratic, were arguments characteristic of contemporary syndicalists, communists, and 'fascists' who preferred the operation of the leadership and plebescite principles to the parliamentary one. Such an attitude toward liberal democracy was found frequently among continental national socialists.

Fairly early in his journalistic career, Blatchford described

[1] Robert Blatchford, *Germany and England* (New York, 1914), pp. 3-5, 7-8, 12.
[2] *Ibid.*, p. 20.   [3] *Ibid.*, pp. 41-42.
[4] *Ibid.*, p. 50; see also *Clarion*, August 6, 1909, p. 1.

himself as no Republican but a 'Democrat' which, he wrote, 'is much better.'¹ His 'Democracy' had a Rousseauian flavour. He had no use for parliaments or for parliamentary action which, he felt, 'is not worth the trouble and expense it will entail.'² He sneered at manhood suffrage. 'For some reason not present to the practical Radical mind,' he wrote, 'votes seem to produce only representatives who are not representative, or carpet-baggers—with nothing in their bags.'³ If he did not 'care a cigar stump for elections, nor for Parliament,' he was a strong advocate of the adoption of a system of Initiative and Referendum.⁴ Only in that way could the clear collective-voice of the nation be heard and the will of Britons be done in Britain.

Before the election of January 1910, Blatchford wrote of his disgust with the failure of the Government to take effective action to meet an expanding Germany. 'I can recognize nothing but angry cries of Partisanship and class antagonism,' he complained. 'The Referendum would help to sort out the tangled issues. But we have no Referendum. Lacking that we have chaos.'⁵ The party politicians, he believed, should not discuss such non-essential matters as the Budget, the House of Lords, Tariff Reform, or Free Trade. They ought to 'go to the country with a plain warning of a great impending danger' and ask for the public sacrifices which were vitally necessary 'for the safety of the Empire and for the preservation of our trade, our honour, and our independence.' He himself, were he a candidate for election, would campaign on a programme of 50 million pounds for the Navy, compulsory military service, elementary military training for all schoolboys over 10. He would appeal to all employers to hire British subjects in preference to foreigners. Party politics were so much talk. The empire was in danger and 'it cannot be saved by talk: it can only be saved by sacrifice and work.' 'This warning,' Blatchford concluded, 'is not written by a politician; it does not come from a Socialist, nor from a Liberal, nor from a Tory; it comes from an Englishman.'⁶

¹ *Clarion*, November 11, 1899, p. 354.
² *Clarion*, February 25, 1899, p. 57.
³ *Clarion*, February 18, 1899, p. 49.
⁴ *Clarion*, February 4, 1899, p. 33.
⁵ *Clarion*, December 17, 1909, p. 1.
⁶ Blatchford, *Germany and England*, pp. 69-74.

If not parliamentary government, what? Blatchford's solution was one which was to become painfully familiar in the second quarter of the twentieth century. The nation, he wrote, required a leader: 'What the British nation stands most in need of in this portentous hour is a *man*.' Looking about Blatchford saw nothing but party politicians and 'purposeless factions.' Germany —his enemy—was also his model: 'The German nation is homogeneous: organised. Their Imperial policy is continuous. . . . Their principle is the theory of blood and iron.'[1] They had their leader, their man. Blatchford had selected his '*man*.' '*The* man,' he wrote, 'is Lord Kitchener.'[2] It was, it seems, inevitable that ex-sergeant Blatchford's *man* should be a Field-Marshal of the British Army, Roberts' chief of staff in South Africa.

As a result of his *Daily Mail* articles on the 'German menace,' Blatchford was called 'Jingo' and 'scaremonger' by his internationalist-minded socialist comrades. The Liberals sneered at 'the Tories under their new Socialist leader' and accused Blatchford of treachery, of having 'sold out.'[3] This last charge was most difficult for Blatchford to swallow. He might be a 'jingo,' even though he persistently denied the justice of such an epithet. But traitor, and worse still, traitor to the Liberals? In the *Clarion* of December 31, 1909, he wrote:

'I have never been a comrade of the Liberals. I have never marched under the Liberal banner. I have always opposed the Liberals. I was irreconcilably opposed to *Liberalism* before I became a Socialist. . . . I am a Socialist. I believe that the nation should be a family. . . .
I ask my fellow-citizens to lay aside their Liberalism and their Toryism, and to deal with an Imperial danger as Britons.'

'Let us,' he concluded, 'first make the family safe as a family, and then we can settle our domestic differences within the shelter of the family defences.'[4]

Blatchford indeed was no 'comrade of the Liberals.' He was an imperialist, a militarist, a nationalist, a protectionist—everything the pre-war British Radical was not. He opposed even the political forms of Liberalism—parliaments and parties—

[1] *Ibid.*, p. 106.   [2] *Ibid.*, p. 92.
[3] Liberal Publication Department, Leaflet No. 2303.
[4] *Clarion*, December 31, 1909, p. 1.

preferring referendums and strong men. Blatchford was a 'socialist' in that he wished to improve the condition of the working class—but, it would seem, this so that England might be made stronger in struggling with foreign enemies. He believed, furthermore, that the British working class was dependent upon Britain's empire for its prosperity. In 1903, the *Clarion* had written that 'next to the question of the Condition of the Poor, that of our future relations with the British Empire beyond the Seas is the most important and vital to the British workers.'[1] What was good for the British Empire was good for the British working man. At times of national emergency, petty class interests must be forgotten, and all Englishmen had to close ranks and meet the common foe in battle. Blatchford set the ideal of the nation as a family against the atomistic cosmopolitanism of the Liberals. As an imperial-socialist he insisted that the need to protect the nation-family against other nation-families, principally Germany, was an object far more important than the class struggle of the international socialists.

He wished all Britons to develop a family spirit, a spirit of comradeship, and he believed that the only way in which this could be done was by means of a system of universal military training. What Lord Roberts had deemed necessary to meet an emergency, Blatchford erected into one of the positive goals of his socialism. Such a system of military training would be 'the salvation of the British race,' he expostulated. The Army, he wrote, 'trains men in comradeship, it infuses what I call the collective spirit.'[2] For Blatchford, Germany was a perfect example of what happened when the collective spirit was organized on a national scale, and Imperial Germany must be the model for Imperial Britain. The Germans had achieved this goal as a result of military training. This military-collective spirit 'gives power and coherence to the people of Germany,' he maintained. 'The German nation is an army. The British nation is a mob of antagonistic helpless atoms.' The German nation was like a regiment, he wrote, and he added:

'A regiment is very much more than a crowd of men all dressed in the same uniform. It is a regiment. It has that which a mob

[1] *Clarion*, May 22, 1903, p. 4.
[2] Blatchford, *Germany and England*, pp. 87-90.

never has: a collective mind, a collective soul. The 10th Infantry Brigade is a very different thing from a crowd of 3,000 young men in khaki; it is an organism; all of its units are parts of a whole; all its units move and feel and act together. It is not what so many civilians often call it—a machine. A machine has no soul; but a brigade of soldiers has a soul. When it marches all its 6,000 legs move as one. When it charges all its bayonets are in line. When it sings it has one great thrilling voice. It is alive; it is an organism; it is the 10th Infantry Brigade.'[1]

The British nation, Blatchford was convinced, must be constructed on the model of the 10th Infantry Brigade.

Blatchford's politics should be understood in the light of the military model of his socialism. His concern for British agriculture resulted from his desire that Britain achieve complete independence in case of war; an army must be certain of its supplies. Just as it would be impossible to run an army if it were divided into military factions, so parties only interfered with the efficient operation of the national army. A strong military leader, like Kitchener, was far superior to blundering, carpetbagging party politicians. The British nation must be like a regiment, it must be a living, breathing organism, with a collective mind and a collective soul. It must be a strong, well-disciplined army, ready to meet the challenge of other strong national armies.

In fighting for socialism, ex-sergeant Blatchford was not suggesting mutiny. He was simply voicing a non-commissioned officer's cynical disrespect for bumbling majors and colonels—though not necessarily for generals like Kitchener—and demanding bigger rations and greater liberties for the great mass of enlisted men of the 10th Infantry Brigade. The sum of Blatchford's message was this: 'The masses must be better educated, better governed, better trained and better treated, or the Empire will go to pieces . . . when the poor rot, the Empire is rotten. We cannot make soldiers and sailors out of weeds. . . . If the Empire is to stand we must have a healthy, and an educated and a united people.' Only in this way, Blatchford concluded, 'can we maintain an Empire upon which the sun never sets.'[2]

[1] *Ibid.*, pp. 90-92.
[2] *Clarion*, December 31, 1909, p. 1.

XIII

CONCLUSION

SUMMARY

In England, by 1914, the working classes found themselves relatively prosperous, and, after years of close collaboration with the Liberal party, fairly well protected by laws which not only guaranteed trade union security, but also provided national insurance and old-age pensions. In this way, the British working classes were 'nationalized,' were given their 'stake' in the state, just as the German working class had been nationalized in the decades following the enactment of Bismarckian social reform, and the Italian working class had been 'incorporated' into the nation by the pre-war Giolittian programme. When war came in 1914, the 'proletariats' of all the European nations had become convinced that the working classes of the losing nations would suffer far more than those of the victors. They consequently tossed aside sentimental socialist internationalism and became patriots. The elaborate programmes of the social-imperialists had justified themselves as the proletariats, heretofore hostile to the state, rushed to the national battle standards.

There had been two principal forms of social-imperialism in England. One had emphasized the need to maintain the empire and had asserted that the welfare of the working class depended upon imperial strength. The second had emphasized the condition of the working classes as the basis of imperialism, the need for a healthy and vigorous imperial race, and had suggested that it would be impossible to defend and maintain the empire without such a base. The first argument was to be found—expressed or implied—in the writings of all the social-imperialists and imperial-socialists; it served as virtually the sole argument for the Tariff Reform League and Joseph Chamberlain. The second was adopted not only by the Liberal-Imperialists—who made it their chief campaign point—but it also appeared prominently in the writings of such Tariff Reformers as Milner and Mackinder, and in the tracts of the

Fabians. Both Milner and Mackinder appear to have subscribed to both social-imperial equations and to have accepted the full social-imperial creed of the interdependence of imperialism and social reform.

The social-imperialists—both Free Trade and Tariff Reform —and the imperial-socialists adhered in common to certain canons of belief. First of all, they were nationalists who vied with each other in the intensity with which each proclaimed himself a Briton. They were imperialists. In varying degrees, they recognized the new power forces which were in operation in the twentieth century and urged Great Britain to ready her army and navy, and so conduct her foreign policy as to meet the, for them, inevitable challenge of German power. For this reason, they scoffed at Cobdenite or socialist proclamations of international friendship. Both social-imperialist and imperial-socialist declared their hostility to the nation-dividing class antagonism which they believed international socialists and cosmopolitan Cobdenites alike fostered. The 'national interest' rather than the interest of any group within the nation was set as the only legitimate goal. (In certain instances, however, it appeared that the Tariff Reform social-imperialists believed that the national interest and the declared interest of the organized working class were inevitably at opposite poles.) They all condemned the *laissez-faire*, do-nothing philosophy of nineteenth-century government; both imperialism and social-reform were positive programmes of state action. They all regarded social-amelioration as a prime objective for a stronger Britain and a stronger Empire. They called for 'organization' and 'efficiency': the two words are used again and again by Pearson, by the Fabians, by the Liberal-Imperialists, by Milner, and by Mackinder. 'Efficiency' had many meanings: a sound industrial system, a united Empire, a vigorous people, a state of military and naval preparedness.

There were, no doubt, important differences between the Tariff Reform and Free Trade social-imperialists, and between both these groups and the imperial-socialists. They differed on the question of trade policy, which led to many other points of variance. For instance, a chief villain of the Tariff Reformer (and of the imperial-socialist)—as for many of the continental social-imperialists—was the cosmopolitan financier, whose interests were defended by the Liberal-Imperialists. They differed in their programmes of social reform and in the means they proposed for raising new revenues. But in spite of these differences, they—social-imperialists and imperial-socialists—constituted a fairly harmonious, self-conscious group, self-conscious in that they were aware of the numerous articles of faith which bound them together and which separated them from the *laissez-faire*, cosmopolitan Radical. The existence of the Coefficients Club is evidence of this.

Schumpeter and the Marxists have treated social-imperialism as an attempt by the imperialist classes to dupe the working class, as a well-thought-out plot of entrepreneurial capitalism to deceive the working class into the support of imperialist schemes which could only work to their long-term disadvantage. This thesis was formulated largely on the basis of continental —primarily German—rather than British social-imperialism. The analysis was founded upon the specious cry of German and Italian social-imperialism that the 'proletarian nation,' e.g., Germany or Italy, ought to rise up and overthrow capitalistic, plutocratic nations, e.g., Great Britain. Whereas German imperialism was an aggressive force at this time, however, British imperialism was inevitably defensive. British social-imperial politics may not have been exclusively motivated by concern for the interests of the working class. There was little doubt, for example, that Chamberlain, an imperialist, and a Birmingham industrialist, had used social-imperial arguments to persuade the working class to accept the sacrifice of higher food prices and thus halt 'impending' disintegration of the empire—and of the midlands metal industries; or that the Tariff Reform League has used the ideals of social-imperialism to get the support of the working class for protection. But it would be unjust and inaccurate to attribute such 'chauvinistic' or 'selfish' motives as operating alone as a motivating force in the development of social-imperial concepts, to regard social-imperialism as exclusively a hypocritical manipulative device to gain the support of the working-class electorate.

In many respects, the social-imperialists saw the needs of the time more clearly than their opponents. In the face of Labour party support for a programme of protection and preference in the 'forties and 'fifties, can it be stated categorically, as

Schumpeter has, that the Chamberlain programme would necessarily have worked to the long-term disadvantage of the working man? Nor can we say that there was no sincere interest in the condition of the working classes. Some social-imperialists, in fact—William Ashley, for instance—arrived at their position largely because of their concern for the welfare of the working man. Similarly, it would be unfair to class Milner's conception of a 'nobler Socialism' as an unconscious elaboration of a selfish capitalist scheme for worker support. It would be equally unjust to so label Mackinder's unfortunately accurate description of the new world forces which would operate in the twentieth century. Although William Cunningham hued more strictly to the Chamberlain position, his social-imperialism was largely a resurrection of the older, *pre-capitalist* ideal of community, of an organic national life, rather than an ideological expression of a capitalist plot.

There are large differences between British and continental social-imperialism. As already noted, such concepts as 'proletarian' nation were entirely alien to Great Britain, for Marxist terminology was unknown to the British working class, and Britain could hardly regard herself as a proletarian nation. Also, the highly aggressive note of German and Italian social-imperial writings was largely absent from British social-imperialism. In fact, it might even be argued that the form which neo-mercantile imperialism took in England stemmed from the conviction—after the Boer War—that new colonial expansion would be difficult. Tariff Reform imperialism was formulated primarily as a means of defence of what Britain already possessed, and Free Trade imperialism after the war in South Africa was based on 'peaceful,' economic penetration. Continental social-imperialists had ranted of national and racial missions, and these notions were not entirely absent from the thoughts of some British imperialists—of the Social-Darwinist Pearson, or the South African triangle, Milner, Chamberlain, and Rhodes, who all wrote and spoke of the glories of the British race and of its imperial mission. But a country which was the commercial and industrial hub of a great world market could not be expected to feel the passionate national fervour, or to nourish the fierce national resentments of a submerged Balkan province or of a climbing nation with an empire still to be achieved. It was therefore rather a pragmatic, balance sheet tone of defence which animated even Tariff Reform social-imperialism.

Continental social-imperialists had largely adopted corporative economics. This was a logical, if extreme, reaction against nineteenth-century individualism and was the embodiment of the concept of identity of interest of all producers—worker and capitalist. Among the British social-imperialists only Ashley approached full corporative theory. Nor did British social-imperialists condemn democracy and parliamentary institutions with the fervour of their continental comrades. True, social-imperialism was the doctrine of the organizers, of efficiency, and as such was bound to regard democracy as slow-moving and at times slow-witted. Pearson, Mackinder, and Milner, for example, held serious reservations concerning the effectiveness of parliamentary institutions. With the Fabians these considerations were supplemented by vague neo-Hegelian philosophical considerations concerning the subordination of the individual to the state. Only Robert Blatchford approached some of the continental social-imperialists—like Maurras and Corradini—in the violence of his attack on democratic government. On the whole the democratic tradition in England ran too deep.

The objective of the social-imperialists was the conversion of the British working class to one of the two competing systems of imperialism. The political philosophy of the organized working class at the beginning of the twentieth century was a blend of the international cosmopolitan creed of Cobdenism and the doctrines of international socialism, both very much anti-imperialistic. In the newly formed Labour party, in the Independent Labour party, and in the Trades Union Congress, cosmopolitanism and internationalism were predominant. Although hardly a substantial political force during this period, middle-class Cobdenism still managed to retain a foothold among the teetotalling, nonconformist faithful of the Liberal party, and was still expounded by such intellectuals as J. A. Hobson, the sociologist and economist, and by such journalists as H. W. Massingham, the editor of the Liberal weekly *The Nation*. But the voice of Cobdenite Radicalism within the Liberal government, where the making of foreign policy and the readying of Britain's armed might were in the hands of imperialists, was seriously muted.

The Tariff Reformers appealed for support against Cobdenism on the basis of more work at better pay. They failed. The working class, faced with a choice between two different kinds of imperialism and between two different kinds of social-imperialism, chose Liberal, Free Trade imperialism and social-imperialism rather than the Chamberlain programme. The support of organized labour for the Liberal party can be attributed to many causes: the less blaring, therefore partially disguised imperialism of the Liberal-Imperialists (further disguised by the presence of Radical anti-imperialists in the Liberal-Imperialist led government), the fear of the stomach tax, hostility to the Tories because of House of Lords' attacks upon the trade unions, the class bias of the Unionist argument against the Budget as well as the Liberal appeal to workers' class prejudice (tax the 'dukes'), the attraction of the Liberal programme of social reform, and the general prosperity of the decade before the war of 1914. The fact that the attempt of the Tariff Reform social-imperialists to arouse concern over the impending disintegration of the empire by tying worker prosperity to imperial unity and strength failed ought not to be interpreted as a vote against imperialism—whatever might have been in the mind of the individual voter. The working-man voter's effective choice was limited, and, in point of fact, he chose to continue the old forms of imperialism, to which he attributed his present prosperity and which was providing a full programme of social reform, rather than accept the new Chamberlain model.

LLOYD GEORGE'S 'COALITION' OF 1910

The British novelist, C. P. Snow, has written of a conversation that he had with David Lloyd George during the 'thirties. Snow had asked the former Prime Minister what he believed history would say of him and Lloyd George had replied:

'I think our wars will seem rather local affairs to posterity, because the centre of gravity of the world is going to change, if it hasn't changed already. I am inclined to think that, if they are interested in me at all, they will be interested because, in the first country to be highly industrialised, I did something to mollify class conflict—and whether they approve or not, will depend on whether they believe that was a good thing to do.'[1]

Lloyd George had not, during the period preceding the war, publicly subscribed to the social-imperialist creed. Although principally responsible for the social programme of the Liberal-Imperialist led government, the Welsh Liberal had led the Radical pack of pro-Boers during the South African War and had fought for social reform against Dreadnoughts in the cabinet crisis of 1909. Yet when war with Germany came, both parties turned to him, to the 'anti-imperialist' Lloyd George, to head the war-time government, a coalition backed principally by the Unionist party. The question which presents itself is, of course, how this could have occurred if Lloyd George's views had remained those of Radical anti-imperialism. It is all too easy to regard Lloyd George as an opportunist, and such an explanation can be made to jibe with many of the facts. Indeed, in Lloyd George's case there is a rather large grain of truth imbedded in such a view. Yet it is not a fully satisfactory one. Perhaps we can better understand Lloyd George and—more important— the political mood of Great Britain during this period before the War of 1914 if we explore the story of Lloyd George's 'other coalition,' a coalition that never was to be.

When this coalition was presumably only a glint in the mind's eye of its eventual initiator, it emerged, full-blown, in the novels of that remarkable writer, the Liberal M.P. Hilaire Belloc. In Belloc's *Mr Clutterbuck's Election*, published in 1908,[2] were incorporated not only its author's many well-known, and highly unattractive, prejudices but a description of an England of the future, an England with two new political parties. The first of these imaginary groups was called the 'National Party.' In what seemed like the purest nonsense, Belloc pictured the National party as a consequence of the acceptance of a modified tariff by the Liberal majority and by the Unionist Free Traders as well as the acceptance of Home Rule for Ireland on the part of the majority of the Unionist party. The chief leaders of the

[1] C. P. Snow, 'London Diary', in *New Statesman*, February 23, 1957, LIII, No. 1354, p. 227.

[2] Hillaire Belloc, *Mr Clutterbuck's Election* (London, 1908), *passim*.

two traditional parties, in Belloc's fantasy, had thus accepted what each had publicly dedicated himself most fervently to oppose. The second party was called the Opposition—it could not agree on a more satisfactory name. It was composed of the unreconstructed Free Traders and die-hard Orangemen. In a later novel, *Pongo and the Bull*, published in 1910, Belloc's readers found themselves in the same political spectrum, with a new element—the 'Straights,' a socialist party clearly modelled upon the Fabians. The Straights, we are told, 'were willing and quite sincerely willing to support the general programme of armament and of Imperial policy for which the National party now stood.' For his part, the leader of the National party was 'not only willing as a politician, but naturally inclined as a thinker to follow their advice upon the details of social-reform.'[1]

What Hilaire Belloc had depicted in the National party was the party of national efficiency which the Fabians had tried to form when they assembled the Coefficients. It was a party which might have found favour in the eyes of Joseph Chamberlain who, we recall, had been speaking of a 'National party' as early as the 'seventies. With its lofty method of transcending the issues of practical politics in favour of a united approach on problems of armament, imperial policy, and social reform, the National party of Belloc's novels was the party of social-imperialism. It was a party which the Cobdenites dreaded—and which the cynical Belloc, the author of the *Servile State*, anticipated with grim foreboding. For Belloc, the co-author, with Cecil Chesterton, of *The Party System*, in 1911, such deceitful compromises were an inescapable part of parliamentary democracy. Belloc's attack on the 'system' was much along the lines of Robert Blatchford, that is, defence of the democracy of 'general will,' accompanied, in the continental manner, by an attack on elections, parliaments, and political parties. Parties for Belloc were meaningless instruments between which there was 'no difference of economic interest or of political principle.' As a result of the party system, statesmen paid no attention to the wishes of the electorate. It was not at all the people who mattered under the party system, it was 'the Governing Group,' and the leaders of both parties were members of this group—or

[1] Hilaire Belloc, *Pongo and the Bull* (London, 1910), p. 48, and *passim*.

Q

were soon absorbed by this group. The principles which the member of the governing group supposedly held were quite 'unreal' to him although real enough to the voters. That was why 'governments suddenly abandon causes which they have enthusiastically espoused, and why Oppositions tolerate such abandonment and lend themselves to such manoeuvres.'[1]

Shortly before the writing of *The Party System*, a 'conference' had been called, in mid-1910, of both the Unionist and the Liberal leaders. The purpose of this conference had been the solution of the constitutional impasse into which England had been hurled by the Lords' rejection of the Lloyd George budget. This conference, Belloc was to assert, was not entirely unique —on a less formal level, it constituted 'the normal method of governing the country.'[2] The inter-party discussions of the conference of 1910 were a matter of public intelligence. In a most private and secretive manner, on the topmost levels, another kind of discussion was in progress, the objective of which would have come as no real surprise to the authors of *The Party System*, and the details of which would have confirmed the prophecies of the author of *Pongo and the Bull*, had they but known of them.

In mid-October, in 1910, Lloyd George approached F. E. Smith, one of the leaders of the Unionist party, with an extraordinary proposal. As a means of solving the many thorny problems with which the nation was faced, Lloyd George suggested the formation of a Coalition government composed of the 'moderate' wings of the Liberal and Unionist parties. Smith immediately brought the Leader of the Opposition, A. J. Balfour, into the discussions—and, soon afterward, such Unionist stalwarts as Austen Chamberlain and Andrew Bonar Law. For his part, Lloyd George was speaking on behalf of five of his cabinet colleagues: the Liberal Chancellor of the Exchequer had secured the agreement of the Prime Minister, H. H. Asquith, of Lord Haldane, of Sir Edward Grey, of Lord Crewe and of Winston Churchill to the terms upon which the Liberals would accept a coalition government. The Liberal chiefs proposed that the Conservatives join them on a programme which would set

[1] Hilaire Belloc and Cecil Chesterton, *The Party System* (London, 1911), pp. 8-9, and *passim*.
[2] *Ibid.*, pp. 54-55.

up a system of national military training, much like the Swiss militia system; which would put the Navy on a 'satisfactory footing'; which would at once grant tariff preference to the colonies on the duties immediately available as well as set up an inquiry into what further duties might be imposed in the national and imperial interest; which would deal with the problems of the Poor Law and set up a system of national insurance—which last, in Austen Chamberlain's words, 'if done by common agreement, could be done better and cheaper than if done by one Party.' A virtually complete amalgam of both Liberal and Tariff Reform social-imperialisms. All that Lloyd George and the Liberal-Imperialists sought from the Unionists in exchange for this multitude of concessions was a policy of devolution within the United Kingdom which would give Ireland her parliament.

F. E. Smith and Austen Chamberlain were enormously pleased. Smith's explanation of Lloyd George's proposal was simply, *quem Deus vult perdere prius dementat.* We must remember, in viewing the terms set forth by the Liberals, that, with the exception of Lloyd George, those Liberals who had subscribed to the secret proposal were all self-acknowledged imperialists. Prompted, perhaps, by their mounting fears for the safety of the Empire, the Liberal-Imperialists appeared willing to throw over their Radical Cabinet colleagues, just as Chamberlain had thrown over Gladstone on the issue of Irish Home Rule in the 'eighties, and to deny almost all traces of the creed of Cobdenite cosmopolitanism which had characterized Liberalism for over half a century. The Unionists appeared quite willing to accept all this, and quite understandably. What stuck in their throats was the provision of Home Rule for Ireland. Balfour hesitated and the Unionist party-whip, Akers-Douglas, expressed the view that the party would not support a coalition on such a basis—and so the proposal fell through.[1]

Lloyd George's coalition proposal of 1910 was more than a

[1] This would-be coalition is discussed in David Lloyd George, *War Memoirs* (London, 1933), I, pp. 32–41; Austen Chamberlain, *Politics From Inside*, pp. 191–193; 283–294, 576–577; Earl of Birkenhead, *Frederick Edwin, Earl of Birkenhead* (London, 1933), I, pp. 203–209. Also see S. J. Hurwitz, *State Intervention in Great Britain* (New York, 1949), pp. 22–25.

curious fulfilment of the fantasy-prediction of Belloc's novels.[1]
In these proposals, we may see the socio-political programme of
perhaps the most enlightened section of the British governing
classes at a crisis-time in British history. It was a time of crisis,
a period of domestic violence (suffragette, Orangeman, and
syndicalist), and of heightening fears of Imperial Germany. In
his *War Memoirs*, Lloyd George described the conditions which
had led to his proposal of a party truce in 1910—conditions
which, perhaps because of the failure of his proposal, persisted
until the coming of war in 1914:

'The shadow of unemployment was rising ominously above the
horizon. Our international rivals were forging ahead at a great
rate and jeopardising our hold on the markets of the world.
There was an arrest in that expansion of our foreign trade
which had contributed to the phenomenal prosperity of the
previous half-century, and of which we had made such a
muddled and selfish use. Our working population, crushed into
dingy and mean streets, with no assurance that they would not
be deprived of their daily bread by ill-health or trade
fluctuations, were becoming sullen with discontent. Whilst
we were growing more dependent on overseas supplies for
our food, our soil was gradually going out of cultivation.
The life of the countryside was wilting away and we were
becoming dangerously over-industrialised. Excessive indulgence
in alcoholic drinks was undermining the health and efficiency
of a considerable section of the population. [Furthermore,] A
great Constitutional struggle over the House of Lords
threatened revolution at home, another threatened civil war at
our doors in Ireland. [Abroad,] great nations were arming

---

[1] Even the 'Straights,' in the form of the Labour Party, were asked to
join the Coalition. Lloyd George, with an unerring ability to recognize
the coalition personality, approached J. Ramsay Macdonald, rather
than either George Barnes, the leader of the parliamentary party, or
Arthur Henderson, the chairman of the party. Macdonald tentatively
accepted a position in the forthcoming coalition cabinet but Henderson
wisely refused to consider the matter. We might of course see this
proposal as anticipatory of both the Lloyd George coalition government of 1916 to 1922 and of J. Ramsay Macdonald's National
Government of 1931-35. See Mary Agnes Hamilton, *Arthur Henderson*
(London: Heinemann, 1938), p. 74.

feverishly for an apprehended struggle into which we might be drawn by some visible or invisible ties, interests or sympathies.

Lloyd George's agonizing final question was: 'Were we prepared for all the terrifying contingencies?'[1]

Lloyd George's picture of conditions at home was an amalgam of the complaints of the Radicals, the Liberal-Imperialists, and the Tariff Reformers. From the last mentioned had come the picture of Britain's loosening hold on her export markets and the resulting unemployment, from them and from men like Robert Blatchford had come the steady insistence that Free Trade had dealt a death blow to the countryside and that England was becoming dangerously dependent on overseas food, from the Radicals had come the fear that drink was proving the ruination of a good part of the working class, and from the Liberal-Imperialists the warning of the dangers of slum-dwellings to the breeding of an imperial race. But there was a single undercurrent, a single strand which united the seemingly disparate elements. Fear. The 'shadow of unemployment' rises 'ominously'; the working class was 'becoming sullen with discontent'; there was a threat of 'revolution at home' and of 'civil war' in Ireland. And across the North Sea Germany was planning new mischief. These were the circumstances—wrote Lloyd George—which had led to his proposals and, presumably, to their acceptance by the imperialist members of the Liberal cabinet. These were the circumstances under which the leading members of what Belloc has described as the 'Governing Group' of England negotiated for the end of party warfare, for the shelving of traditional party war-cries—whether addressed to the nonconformist conscience or to Irish Protestant prejudice—in the interest of preparing England for the coming international struggle. Only in this way, the Liberal-Imperialists felt, and the leading Tariff Reformers appeared to agree, could the revolutionary dangers of a discontented working class be averted while, at the same time, England's vital defences might be strengthened to meet foreign attack. The members of the governing group, regardless of party-label, recognized social-imperialism as the necessary policy.

Yet somehow the politics of social-imperialism did not quite

[1] Lloyd George, *op. cit.*, I, p. 35.

jibe with the code and rules of the English party system. English politics was a gentlemanly game played by gentlemen. The naked social-imperial appeals to the working class made by continental social-imperialists would have stuck in the throats of Asquith, or Grey, or Rosebery, or Balfour, or even Joseph Chamberlain. Chamberlain was in many ways most extreme in his statements—yet even he had half-apologized for the 'squalid argument.' The Unionist Party permitted such extra-party organizations as the Tariff Reform League to say what it itself had refused to say—we have noted Balfour's wincing over the slogan 'Tariff Reform Means Work for All.' Nor, to cite another example, did the Liberal statesmen clearly depict the social-imperial meaning of their decision to prove social reform compatible with Free Trade by their programme of taxing the new 'unearned' wealth of the urban landlords, though their supporters in the Labour party had intuitively grasped this. The English political system just was not set up to admit the sort of demagogic social-imperialism which, in the years to come, Hitler and Mussolini were to spout on the continent. As a consequence, perhaps, the leading exponents of social-imperialist theory in England were men who did not or could not play the party game—men like Milner, who had called himself a political Ishmaelite, or academicians like Ashley, Mackinder, or Cunningham. It somehow seems very English that this attempt to form a social-imperial party was defeated by the veto of the Unionist party whip who understood that the Tory squires would not have countenanced the 'betrayal' of the Orangemen.

SIR OSWALD MOSLEY:
THE FULFILMENT OF SOCIAL-IMPERIALISM?

When the war of 1914 came to England, the Labour Party supported the government—as of course did the Fabians and Robert Blatchford. Only a small number of socialists, principally those who constituted the Independent Labour Party, withheld their approval. The ILP leadership—men like J. Ramsay Macdonald, Philip Snowden, and J. Bruce Glasier—was Radical in outlook. Their devotion to Free Trade and to peace stemmed from Bright and Cobden rather than from the internationalism of Marx and Engels. It was much these same sentiments which were to lead such Radicals as E. D. Morel, J. A. Hobson, L. T. Hobhouse and others to found the Union of Democratic Action, once war came, and to campaign for a negotiated peace without victory. Disgusted with the war policies of Liberalism, first under Asquith and then under Lloyd George, who finally formed his coalition in 1916, many of these pacifistic Radicals left Liberalism altogether and joined the I.L.P. and the Labour Party, to which the I.L.P. was affiliated. Partially as a result of their influence, the post-war Labour Party once again took up the internationalist cause and even elected J. Ramsay Mac-donald, who had been denounced as a war-time 'traitor,' as its leader.

Labour experienced a large increase in numbers in the post-war years and this sealed the doom of the Liberal Party, which never again formed a government. The former Prime Minister Asquith became the leader of a faction rather than a party. Liberalism was dead and Labour was its heir, and the heir to the Cobdenite tradition of anti-imperialism. The national inheritance into which Labour party governments were ultimately to come had been diminished, however, by a kind of international death duty. Many of Great Britain's foreign investments had been liquidated to pay for the war against Imperial Germany. Lancashire was being increasingly hard-pressed by Japanese and Indian competition. The United States was supplanting Great Britain as the leading creditor nation. The world found itself, by the late 'twenties, labouring under the burden of the most serious of industrial depressions. These new conditions at last persuaded many cosmopolitan Free Traders that a change in fiscal policy had become essential. Throughout this time, the Tories had continued to speak of the benefits of protection, and the newspapers of Canadian-born Lord Beaverbrook—especially the leading organ of imperial protectionism, the *Daily Express*— had constantly upheld the cause of imperial preference. But, during the early years of international depression, even Liberals —the long-time fighter for Free Trade, John Maynard Keynes, for example—were speaking cautiously about the desirability of adopting a 'revenue' tariff. Labour Cobdenism, however, went deep. It was the 'socialist' Chancellor of the Exchequer Philip Snowden who now stubbornly battled for the 'principle' of Free Trade. In 1930, there occurred a struggle within the

Labour cabinet between Snowden's Cobdenite orthodoxy and the advocates of 'socialist protectionism.' The leader of the protectionists was Sir Oswald Mosley, then Chancellor of the Duchy of Lancaster. Snowden was finally defeated, but not by Mosley. A 'National' Government led by Macdonald adopted a tariff in 1932, and later in the same year in Ottawa, Great Britain and her self-governing dominions constructed the imperial preferential system for which Chamberlain had struggled. Snowden's cabinet opponent, Oswald Mosley, had a different role to play. He became the intellectual heir of the most extreme wing of Chamberlainism, of protectionist social-imperialism, and as such he emerged as the founder of the British Fascist Party.

The continental social-imperialists, as has been mentioned earlier, were the intellectual predecessors of the fascist movements (and even of the 'National Bolshevism' of the Stalin era) which became so important in the period between the wars. Hitler's 'National Socialism,' Mussolini's Fascism, and the Vichy regime of Pierre Laval and Marshal Pétain were substantially indebted to the social-imperialism of Schmoller and Stocker, of Labriola and Corradini, and of Maurras and Sorel. Great Britain, too, had its fascist party, a party whose doctrine resembled that of continental fascism much more than the British social-imperialism of thirty years earlier had resembled its continental counterpart. This was perhaps in part attributable to changes which had taken place in England's condition in the interim, but it partly resulted in British fascism's remaining a crank-movement which was reduced to imitating German and Italian fascism but was incapable of achieving their success. Yet despite much obvious emulation of continental older brothers, British fascist doctrine was firmly rooted in home soil.

The leader of British fascism was and is Sir Oswald Mosley. Mosley, a scion of an old and respected landed family, was a young serviceman who served in the trenches in Flanders and had returned to run in the Conservative interest for Harrow in the 'khaki election' of 1918. Upon being asked to define his policy on this occasion, he had replied 'Socialistic Imperialism.'[1] Mosley won Harrow. There then followed a series of remarkable

[1] Quoted in *Mosley: The Facts* (London, 1957), p. 92.

shifts and accomplishments which drew national attention to the young man. In 1922, Mosley left the Conservatives to become an 'Independent.' In 1924, he joined the Labour Party and challenged Neville Chamberlain in what had practically become a family seat. By 1929, he was the acknowledged leader of the socialist forces in the Birmingham area and had been named the Chancellor of the Duchy of Lancaster in the new Macdonald Cabinet. Already Beatrice Webb, who had previously marked out Joseph Chamberlain, H. H. Asquith, and R. B. Haldane, as 'coming men,' saw Mosley as a future national leader. For her, as early as 1924, he was 'the perfect politician who is also a perfect gentleman.'[1] Many of the younger socialist members, a group which included John Strachey and Aneurin Bevan, were attaching themselves to his leadership, most especially to his famous 'Birmingham proposals' of 1925 which had called for direct socialist action, in particular against the outposts of finance, instead of the do-nothing behaviour of the Macdonald forces.[2] These proposals and Mosley's efforts to spark the Labour party brought upon him the same fierce opposition of the propertied which Joseph Chamberlain had earned by his 'ransom' speech over forty years earlier.

The comparison to Chamberlain is most appropriate. The Birmingham Socialist M.P. who had, while yet a Conservative, declared his policy to be 'Socialistic Imperialism,' put forth, in 1930, a series of proposals designed to remedy the problem of unemployment. These proposals were proper 'Brummagem' ones involving protection against foreign imports and a turning to imperial markets and to an extension of the home market rather than a continued pressing for foreign markets. Mosley was in full revolt against Liberal orthodox economics and the gold standard, then so highly regarded by Chancellor of the Exchequer Snowden. After a row in which Snowden had called him a 'pocket Mussolini,' Mosley resigned from the cabinet and from the Labour party, forming a 'New Party,' and taking with him not only Bevan and Strachey, but such notables as Harold Nicolson, C. E. M. Joad, and Osbert Sitwell. Within a year,

[1] Beatrice Webb, *Beatrice Webb's Diaries, 1912-1924* (London: Longmans, 1952), p. 242.
[2] See Oswald Mosley, *Revolution by Reason* (London, 1925); see especially pp. 7-8.

these men were to desert Mosley as the New Party's leader began to speak more and more about 'National Socialism,' with an increasing emphasis upon the component of nationalism, and seemed quite ready to give up his more socialistic proposals to obtain the support of such men of property as motor-car magnate, Sir William Morris.[1]

In late 1931, Mosley united his New Party with fascist groups, which had been formed earlier, into the British Union of Fascists and affirmed the ideological identity of his movement with those of Mussolini and Hitler in Italy and Germany. Like them he denounced the control of the world by international finance, by 'Wall Street, and its sub-branch in the City of London,'[2] and set out to accomplish for Great Britain the 'self-contained' and self-sufficient Empire toward which Joseph Chamberlain had directed his efforts three decades earlier. Just as Bernard Shaw had enthusiastically greeted the Chamberlain campaign for Tariff Reform and was to find kind words for Mussolini, he wrote of Mosley as 'one of the few people who are writing and thinking about real things, and not about figments and phrases. You will hear something more of Sir Oswald before you are through with him. I know you dislike him, because he looks like a man who has some physical courage and is going to do something; and that is a terrible thing.'[3] Others who associated themselves more clearly with the new British Fascist party were men who believed they recognized in Mosley and his programme the ideal for which they had fought in the years before the war. Carlyon Bellairs, one of the original dozen members of the Fabian-formed Coefficients, who had been converted from Liberal-Imperialism to Tariff Reform by Chamberlain, was now an open advocate of Mosley's views. Ralph D. Blumenfeld, who had formulated the slogan of 'Tariff Reform Means Work For All,' and had helped to convert the publisher of the *Daily Express*, Arthur Pearson, to Tariff Reform, and who now was the Chairman of

---

[1] See A. K. Chesterton, *Oswald Mosley, Portrait of a Leader* (London, 1937), *passim*; Cecil F. Melville, *The Truth About The New Party* (London, 1931), pp. 28-31, 42-45 and *passim*; James Drennan, *B.U.F.*; *Oswald Mosley and British Fascism* (London, 1934), *passim*.

[2] Oswald Mosley, *Tomorrow We Live* (London, 1939), p. 3.

[3] Quoted in *Mosley: The Facts*, p. 25.

that paper as well as a founder of an active Anti-Socialist Union, became associated with Mosley. One of the more vigorous of the Tariff Reform stalwarts in the pre-war House, an ex-Confederate leader, and now a member of the upper chamber, Lord Lloyd, gave moral support to the British Union.[1]

Lest it be thought that the support of these social-imperialists of the turn of the century was given upon false or inadequate grounds, we need only turn to the many speeches and writings of Sir Oswald Mosley, who can be said to have combined virtually all of the salient views of virtually all of the social-imperialists whom we have discussed, and to have welded them into a British fascism. Whereas the earlier social-imperialists had spoken *sotto voce*, Mosley shouted, but the elements of his doctrine were the same as theirs.

Mosley was a compound of Joseph Chamberlain and Robert Blatchford, primarily, with healthy admixtures of Karl Pearson, and with somewhat lesser contributions from others we have discussed. In a Cambridge Union debate, as early as 1924, for example, he described the army and navy, in terms reminiscent of the *Clarion's* editor, as 'Socialist institutions because they have the spirit of the protection of the community, which is the Socialist spirit.'[2] Of course, Mosley and Blatchford shared a common distrust of the parliamentary and party system. This paragraph from a Mosley speech of August 1937 could as easily have been uttered by the imperial-socialist editor:

'Such are the lessons of division, arising from the war of parties and the war of class, which have set Britons at each others' throats so that disunion may rivet on their necks the yoke of their financial masters. Thus Merrie England in an age which could be golden, fades away in the smoke of the sweat shop and the slum, and the green beloved country becomes the play-ground of the stock-jobber, while the sturdy yeoman lines up in the unemployment queue. . . .'[3]

[1] See Labour Research Department, *Who Backs Mosley* (London, 1934), pp. 11-12; also Frederic Mullaly, *Fascism Inside England* (London, 1946), p. 62.

[2] Quoted in Labour Research Department, *op. cit.*, p. 5.

[3] Quoted in *Mosley: The Facts*, p. 90.

Mosley's debt to Joseph Chamberlain's turn-of-the-century arguments is clearly visible in the British fascist leader's speech delivered in October 1936:

'But how are we to judge any system? Surely by the condition of the people. Today we have in England low wages, long hours, rotten houses, unemployment and poverty corrupting our people—all absolutely unnecessary! With the vast imperial resources which are the heritage of this country . . . the problems of poverty and want can easily be solved by a government empowered by the people to carry out their will. While democratic governments are giving away the Empire which our fathers won, our people are abandoned to poverty and unemployment. Yet the Empire belongs to you, the people of Britain! The hands of Englishmen won this great Empire which has been the glory of the world; their sacrifice and heroism gained it for us. . . . Arise and enter your own, and be great, happy and wealthy once again! Arise in your thousands and work with us. . . .'[1]

Mosley did not publicly acknowledge his debt to Chamberlain and to Blatchford, despite his obvious paraphrasings from their writings and speeches. His struggles with the Chamberlain family in Birmingham were perhaps too recent for him to do anything but denounce Conservative protection. His grounds for doing so were the same as those which had prevented Blatchford and the *Clarion* from joining Chamberlain's Tariff Reform campaign, despite their approval of protection. The Conservatives, Mosley asserted, 'have handed over the fiscal system of the country to a struggling committee of appointed businessmen who are vested with wide powers, but are endowed with inadequate information and with no machinery.' Like Blatchford, and his *Clarion* colleague R. B. Suthers, Mosley called for 'scientific' protection, protection which was 'made conditional upon industrial efficiency' and 'upon good wages to the workers.'[2] Mosley had joined socialism to protectionism as Blatchford, Suthers, and Bernard Shaw had urged.

Mosley's slogans were the same as those of Chamberlain and Blatchford. Mosley, too, called for a policy of the 'self-

[1] *Ibid.*, p. 90.
[2] Oswald Mosley, *The Greater Britain* (London, 1932), p. 90.

contained Empire,' and urged that 'we build an Empire system that rests on the simple principle that the British people shall consume what the British people produce.' 'Nothing shall be imported into Britain,' Mosley declared, 'which can be produced within Great Britain . . .[this] will give employment to nearly a million and a half of our people. In addition, British industry will be free on the home market from the cheap foreign competition, which to-day holds down wages and diminishes the extent and purchasing power of the home market.'[1] In urging that immigration be stopped, he repeated the most famous of Blatchford's slogans: 'Britain for the British,' he declared, 'is our motto.'[2]

The German National Socialists espoused the cause of 'productive' industrial capital and denounced 'parasitic' finance capital of the 'international bankers,' whom the older German social-imperialists had thought of as predominantly British, and whom the Nazis of the 'twenties and 'thirties thought of as Jewish. Like the Nazis, Mosley, too, denounced 'international Jewish finance,' in particular as it was represented by Wall Street. New York's new position in international banking had made it possible for British fascism to adopt, at least in part, the posture of 'proletarian nation' which German and Italian social-imperialism had been able to assume more naturally. Yet, despite the aping of the Germans and Italians, Mosley's opinions on this matter had to be substantially different, given the rather special nature of Great Britain's position. It was therefore thoroughly rooted in the special arguments of earlier English social-imperialism. In confirmation of the view of both Hobson and Schumpeter that protection was the inevitable basis for imperialism, Mosley roundly denounced the 'usurious' imperialism of Free Trade and adopted, rather fully, the neo-mercantile imperialism of the Tariff Reformers, which we have described above.

Great Britain's refusal of offers of imperial preference and her emphasis upon foreign trade as a more desirable alternative, Mosley held to be 'for the sole reason that the process is a means

[1] Oswald Mosley, *Blackshirt Policy* (London, 1934), p. 30; and Mosley, *Tomorrow We Live*, pp. 41-42.
[2] Oswald Mosley, *Fascism: 100 Questions Asked and Answered* (London, 1936), Question No. 94.

of collecting the usury of the City of London.' For this reason, 'an Empire system is sacrificed,' that is, 'solely because the British Government and our economic system are debt collectors for the City of London.' Imports, produced by sweated foreign labour, which displaced English labour, were simply the interest payments to the usurers.[1] In a speech in 1930, he inquired as Mackinder had earlier: 'Why is it so right and proper and desirable that capital should go overseas to equip factories to compete against us, to build roads and railways in the Argentine or in Timbuctoo, to provide employment for people in those countries. . . .'[2] In a book published in 1937, Mosley spoke of the 'conspiracy' which taught the British people 'to believe that to send steel to a remote country to build a bridge over a far away river, and to send bicycles for savages to ride over the bridge . . . is a transaction of sound economy and finance.'[3] As recently as 1956, although much of Mosley's programme has changed since the war of 1939, the British fascist spoke of the choice between 'a bankers'' and 'a producers'' economy, between 'an isolated island, giving to the whole world special-ised services like banking and insurance, and a producers' economy, which meant entering a larger economic unit.'[4] In 1937, he had spoken of the 'top-heavy structure' of the British economy[5] and two years later, repeating the earlier arguments of Austen Chamberlain and Sir Gilbert Parker against tertiary industry, he called for 'the elimination of overlapping and redundant distributive services, and the reabsorption of such labour . . . back into productive industry.'[6]

Mosley took up the theme of class harmony exposited by all the earlier social-imperialists in opposition to the doctrines of class struggle of the socialists. 'International finance and international Socialism,' he maintained in 1939, 'march openly hand in hand.' Disaster would be the only result of 'supporting international socialism in an age when only National Socialism can work.'[7] The solution to the problem of class conflict lay in the corporate state. 'Class war will be eliminated,' he wrote,

[1] Mosley, *Tomorrow We Live*, p. 45.
[2] Quoted in Drennan, *op. cit.*, p. 134.
[3] Mosley, *Tomorrow We Live*, p. 39.
[4] Quoted in *Mosley: The Facts*, p. 255.   [5] *Ibid.*, p. 92.
[6] Mosley, *Tomorrow We Live*, p. 53.   [7] *Ibid.*, pp. 67, 31.

'by permanent machinery of government for reconciling the clash of class interests.'[1] In his support of corporativism, Mosley was almost entirely dependent on continental social imperialism, although we have noted that Ashley had touched on the issue. (Within the last few years, though curiously not in the 'thirties, Mosley has brought back one of the other pet-projects of the tariff social-imperialists. Once again in confirmation of Hobson's view, Mosley has adopted the position that indirect rather than direct taxation was the preferable financial method for his corporative state. 'A man should be taxed not on what he earns but on what he spends,' he declared in 1956. 'All direct taxation of earnings would be eliminated. . . . We propose a combination of expenditure tax and indirect taxation.'[2] Clearly the prosperous 'fifties were a more appropriate time to campaign upon such a fiscal programme than the depressed 'thirties.)

Like Milner and Rhodes, Mosley, during the 'thirties, intoned that 'we believe profoundly in our own British race which has created the Empire.' This statement was followed by one bearing a more modern ring, though certainly reminiscent of Karl Pearson. 'We have created that Empire,' Mosley asserted, 'without race mixture or pollution. . . . It should only be necessary by education and propaganda to teach the British that racial mixtures are bad.'[3] Pearson's influence is even more clearly apparent in the fascist leader's emphasis upon the need to

'secure the production of children by the fit. . . . At present, birth control is known and practised by the relatively well off. It is largely unknown and less practised by the very poor. The result is exactly the reverse of the national interest. . . . The unfit will be offered the alternatives of segregation sufficient to prevent the production of unfit children, or voluntary sterilisation.'[4]

Mosley laboured hard during the years preceding 1939 to persuade the middle and the working classes to accept his programme. He made a special effort to entrench himself in

[1] Mosley, *The Greater Britain*, p. 28.
[2] Quoted in *Mosley: The Facts*, p. 138, and *passim*.
[3] Mosley, *Fascism: 100 Questions*, Question No. 93.
[4] *Ibid.*, Question No. 76.

Lancashire, the site of the cotton industries which had, by their support of Free Trade, contributed so much to the defeat of the Chamberlain programme thirty years before. Now, a hard-pressed Lancashire was more ready to listen to talk of protection than it had been earlier and the Mosley programme promised Lancashire the exclusion of all foreign textiles from entrance into any part of the empire, most particularly the exclusion of Japanese cottons from India, and the forcible removal of all Indian tariffs against Lancashire cottons. But the Lancashire working class turned down Mosley's 'offer' of India, setting him down as 'an employers' man.'[1] This was the reaction of the British working class generally. He was regarded as 'un-British,' especially after the reports of fascist meetings at which opponents of Mosley were severely beaten. Nor did Englishmen take to the private armies of the fascists, with their uniform black-shirts, and their strange salutes. It seemed all very 'foreign,' a mere imitation of the Nazis and Fascisti, and the Mosley party therefore was destined to remain a movement of a small minority.

Mosley insisted that his movement was not at all 'foreign,' that, like Liberalism and Socialism before it, it was an inter-national movement, that it espoused a doctrine which all countries were finding more appropriate to the conditions of the twentieth century. He did not but easily could have demonstrated that, from the point of view of programme and doctrine, 'fascist' principles were directly derived from the views and principles and platforms of some of the most respected names in British politics, science, and scholarship. He could have pointed to the presence within his ranks, or as friendly to his cause, such former associates of Joseph Chamberlain as Bellairs, Lloyd, and Blumenfeld, and have observed that even J. L. Garvin, Chamber-lain's friend and biographer, had had some kind words for him.[2] He made no such claims. Perhaps if he had he would have been disowned by such survivors of the old Chamberlain social-imperialism as H. J. Mackinder and Leopold Amery. They, too, would have regarded Mosley's movement as something quite 'foreign.'

[1] See William Rust, *Mosley and Lancashire* (London, 1937), p. 2 and *passim*.

[2] See quote in A. K. Chesterton, *op. cit.*, p. 93.

For, in the larger sense, despite the evidence linking his programme with that of earlier social-imperialism, Sir Oswald Mosley's British Fascist Union was indeed alien to the British scene. In his denunciation of parliamentary institutions, he had joined Blatchford and Belloc, both of whom also fell outside of the normal pattern of British political life. Mosley's extremist presentation of the 'national socialist' case went against British libertarian traditions, as did his para-military organization with its violent methods. His admiring self-subordination to Hitler and Mussolini went against the British grain. Perhaps more important than any of these matters, the condition of Great Britain was still substantially different from that of Germany, or Italy, or any of the eastern European countries which went fascist during the period between the wars. Great Britain had not been defeated in the War of 1914, and, despite the fact that America was supplanting her as the leading financial power, she—with her great Empire—could still not regard herself, or be regarded, as a have-not country. Finally, many of the heterodox solutions to the problems of *laissez-faire* capitalism which had been proposed by the social-imperialists of the turn of the century were already being applied by calmer, more moderate men than the fascist leader. The Cobdenite orthodoxy —represented at this time by men like Philip Snowden—was doomed to be defeated not by a 'pocket Mussolini,' but by renegade international socialists like J. Ramsay Macdonald and by heterodox Liberals like John Maynard Keynes.

EPILOGUE

The Labour Party's foreign policy in the 'thirties still bore the marks of socialist anti-imperialism and pacifism, and its domestic programme was probably—at this time of depression and of Laski and Strachey—more subject to the influence of the class-warfare doctrines of Marxism than previously. Yet, clearly, Labour policy today is quite different. In so far as the primary objective of the social-imperialists of half a century ago was the conversion of organized Labour from class warfare and international proletarian solidarity to the 'national' interest, they can be said to have succeeded. The roots of this development were, as already indicated, complex and dependent on the

R

great changes which had occurred in the nineteenth and early twentieth centuries. So far as Labour's present attitudes are concerned, there were also more immediate determining circumstances. For one thing, the war of 1939 had indeed been a war for survival, and a German victory would have meant disaster for all classes. Further, participation in government, from 1940-1951, acquainted Labour with the realities of power, and, after 1945, with the overwhelming reality of a disillusioningly frank Soviet imperialism, a prospect which could only help to snuff out the remaining, already flickering, sentiments of socialist internationalism. To complete the picture, prosperity in the 'fifties, marked by three Conservative electoral victories, greatly dampened the socialism of class-warfare.

With a nationalist, Ernest Bevin, as Foreign Secretary, internationalism was relegated to the back-benches during the Labour governments of 1945-51. In fulfilment of long-standing promises, and in response to strong immediate pressure, the Labour government did act to give dominion status to India and Pakistan and freedom to Burma; yet it held on to other parts of the empire with at least as much tenacity as the succeeding Tory governments. It fell to Labour's share to bring Roberts' dream of national service to fruition, since conscription proved necessary to maintain an occupation army in Germany. In Opposition, after 1951, an image of the old internationalism flourished briefly in the group surrounding Aneurin Bevan, but the dominant leadership, as well as the rank-and-file, supported the 'national' policy of the government, while reserving its right to 'deplore' excesses, such as the Suez expedition, or to speak in favour of accommodation, when Tory policy seemed too unbending. With increasing awareness of dependence upon America, the area of freedom to determine foreign policy, especially in a time of nuclear warfare, became so narrow that Labour came to believe that it could not, even if it would, manage affairs significantly differently from the Conservatives. Soon Aneurin Bevan himself was converted to the dominant view.

On occasions, the old Radical spirit flared—over 'brutalities' in Cyprus, for example. But the country was unsympathetic, and the Labour leaders deplored in subdued tones, in contrast to the violent Radical protests over the Jamaica 'massacres,' in

1865, the Boer War, and the firing at Amritsar. Labour was dependent on an electorate which, now that peacetime conscription had enlisted their sons in the armed services, was as little disposed as Blatchford had been to hear the acts of British troops maligned. Nor was Labour prepared to defend Free Trade, as in the past. Lancashire's workers now demanded protection against imported cottons, and, furthermore, it was better understood, as Blatchford and the Fabians had asserted earlier, that socialism—a planned, national economy—required the regulation of foreign trade and of capital transfers. The most dire foreboding of the Tariff Reformers had been justified. If the dominions did remain loyal for more than two decades longer without preference, revealing that Free Trade talk of imperial sentiment was not thoroughly unrealistic, there was no question but that England was no longer a power of the first rank, though it was very doubtful whether the adoption of the Chamberlain programme in 1903 would have substantially altered this outcome. Labour's traditional foreign policy could not but be affected by this development.

Labour's new foreign policy views were matched by its new position in domestic affairs. The Labour government of 1945 had embarked on a programme of nationalization, and had acted to effect a more equitable distribution of national wealth by an extension of social services. But nationalization alone was to prove not very attractive. The traditional cry of socialism had been 'equality.' While this appeal—the Conservatives described it as an appeal to greed—had been a stirring one during bad times, it seemed out of place in the relative prosperity of the 'fifties. After two defeats, a 'new Socialism' was being advocated, a domestic counterpart to the changing front in international affairs, a 'national' socialism in opposition to the class-conscious, egalitarian doctrine of Keir Hardie, a 'socialism' reminiscent of the still-born Fabian party of national efficiency, and even of the views of Joseph Chamberlain.

The 'new Socialism' berated Conservatism in much the same terms as the Tariff Reformers had attacked Free Trade. The short-sighted policies of a capitalism, concerned only with private profit while neglecting the national interest, were contrasted with Socialism's concern for planned expansion—so that Britain might maintain her position among the industrial powers. The Tories were chastized for encouraging the export of capital and the trade unions were urged to postpone wage claims so that more money would be free for productive investment. The 'new Socialism' sought to transform socialist economics: the egalitarian, social-revolutionary aspects, predominant as recently as 1950, were now overshadowed by the economics of industrial expansion and of the 'national interest'—a reversion to the Fabian model.[1]

[1] On the 'new Socialism,' see R. H. S. Crossman, 'London Diary,' *The New Statesman*, November 29, 1958, p. 751. Wrote Crossman in describing the programme upon which Labour expected to fight a forthcoming general election: 'What strikes me is that this new Socialism has been shaped by two men whose names are largely unknown to the general public. They are Dr. Thomas Balogh and Professor Richard Titmuss. Balogh is the Galbraith of British economics, and for years has been pungently pointing out the evils of ostentatious waste and industrial stagnation. But, unlike his American counterpart, he has been able to proceed from negative criticism of the affluent society to the positive concept of planned expansion which is the central idea of the new Socialism.' See also the exposition of this concept in Thomas Balogh, *The New Statesman*, November 15, 1958, p. 662. Wrote Balogh, in a jeremiad much like those of Joseph Chamberlain: 'The seven years of Tory rule have left Britain a much weaker country, knocked out of third place among industrial powers of the world by Germany, about to be pushed down to fifth place by China. This period, moreover, has left Britain far less able to grapple with the future . . . [it has] not been used decisively to increase investment, and thus to strengthen our competitive position in the struggle for economic coexistence with far stronger and more menacing powers. It has left the Commonwealth weakened, economic expansion at home has stopped. . . .' Balogh further denounced the Tory budgets which 'have encouraged the export of capital'; suggested that 'the trade unions, moreover, must understand that premature claims for higher wages will inevitably wreck any programme of broad and quickening social advance.' Just two years of a 'lull' in wage claims would mean 'another £600 million would be free to flow toward investment: our productive investment would thus be doubled, bringing our relative rate up to that of Germany or Russia.' If necessary, tax concessions 'to investment must be given to foster those industries whose expansion and increased efficiency is needed to meet increasing demands for capital and durable consumer goods and to meet foreign competition'—especially steel, chemicals, and machine tools.

The social-imperialism of the twentieth century had united, in altered and sometimes distorted forms, three central tendencies of the century preceding—socialism, nationalism, and even democracy, if not necessarily parliamentary democracy, at least that dependence upon public acceptance which characterizes mass industrial societies. It had, however, turned fully against libertarian individualism, that is, nineteenth-century liberalism, and had had no truck with the generous sentiments of internationalism which had inspired both liberalism and socialism. It was indeed the absence of the specifically 'liberal' elements which characterized its special versions of socialist, nationalist and democratic concepts, and which left it open to the distortions we have noted in the period between the wars.

Today, the Cobdenites and the international socialists are virtually extinct breeds. 'War is a sport,' Bernard Shaw wrote in his last play. 'It used to be the sport of kings. Now it is the sport of Labour Parties.' And, certainly, the victory of collectivism over individualism has become one of the hallmarks of our time. To paraphrase Sir William Harcourt, all nations have become, more or less enthusiastically, social-imperialist now. If this is so, it would be futile to denounce a phenomenon which has possibilities for good as well as for evil. Nazism—German 'national socialism'—was a most pernicious form of the doctrine, a largely successful attempt to call into being a state like the warrior states of antiquity. This Nazi version was, and unfortunately still is, a tempting programme for nations which regard themselves as relatively penurious and exploited. But social-imperialism is no more inevitably 'fascism,' than individualism is inevitably anarchy. The great positive accomplishment of less virulent forms of social-imperialism has been the victory over the dangers of open class-warfare in the industrialized West. Having seen some of the fruits of contemporary social-revolutions, we can better understand the fears of the social-imperialists at the beginning of the century and appreciate their efforts to conciliate the dissatisfied classes. Yet, when the alternative to class warfare—and in the case of some social-imperialists, the desired alternative—was the era of international wars in which we are living, we cannot suppress a shudder, or fail to pay proper respects to their opponents who upheld what was, in large part, the more admirable ideal, that of peace and friendly intercourse between nations, an ideal, furthermore by no means incompatible with the pacific adjustment of differences between social classes.

In the West, we still have the will to circumvent the dangerous tendencies of social-imperialism—that is, we still believe that individual liberty and peace, and consequently individualistic democracy and internationalism are worthwhile. We will not easily submit to the process which threatens to create a world of efficient camp-states, of warrior nations with nuclear armaments. There are, of course, many obstacles. In time, it must prove possible to duplicate, on an international scale, the decision taken in the first quarter of the century within the advanced nations of the West. It must prove possible to satisfy the poorer nations of Asia and Africa so that their peoples will not be persuaded to follow the path taken by the so-called 'have-not' nations of central Europe, during the 'thirties, a much more dangerous course in our day. Technological progress can provide the plenty required to resolve international tensions created by too great disparities in wealth *between* nations as it already has significantly resolved such tensions *within* the nations of the West. Fortunately, there seems to be awareness of the problem and of the nature of its solution. We can only hope that there will be enough time and determination.

SELECTED BIBLIOGRAPHY

It seems wise to outline briefly the general principles upon which the selection of books to be listed was made. The number of works which passed through my hands during the course of the research was sizeable, largely because the conflict over the tariff stimulated so much fervour, and, consequently, so many hundreds of published items— newspaper and magazine articles, leaflets and pamphlets, and many, mostly rather pedestrian, books. Clearly, I did not examine all these, but I did a great many. It did not seem useful to list these works individually; I have noted below the general categories of periodical, serial, and pamphlet materials investigated, and refer the reader to footnote references for specific items actually quoted.

I have also declined to list any but the most useful of the biographies, general histories, and general discussions of the politics and ideas of the period. There are a number of more specialized books which proved useful for limited purposes, but did not seem sufficiently significant for inclusion, though many of them are cited in footnotes. Certain of the men whose ideas are discussed were very prolific, and little that they wrote had not some pertinence, but I have tried to confine bibliographical listings to only their most relevant writings, and I have employed this principle with the writings of the less prolific as well.

Periodicals, Serials, Pamphlets, etc.

Blackwood's Magazine.
Contemporary Review.
Fortnightly Review.
Independent Review.
National Review.
Nineteenth Century and After.
The Round Table.
Socialist Review.
Westminster Review.

The Clarion.
The Nation.
The New Statesman.
The New Statesman and Nation.
The Spectator.

The Times.

Annual Register.

Dictionary of National Biography.
Directory of Directors.
Parliamentary Debates.
Who's Who.

Cobden Club Leaflets and Pamphlets.
Fabian News.
Free Trade Union Leaflets.
Liberal League Publications Leaflets.
Liberal Magazine.
Liberal Publication Department Leaflets and Pamphlets.
Monthly Notes on Tariff Reform (Birmingham Series).
Monthly Notes on Tariff Reform (London Series).
Rural Labourers' League Publications.
Tariff Reform League (Leaflet Series).
Tariff Reform League (Cartoon Series).
Tariff Reform League (Industrial Series).
Trade and the Empire Series (Imperial Tariff Committee, Birmingham).
Unionist Free Food League Pamphlets.
United Empire Trade League Publications.

Fabian Annual Reports.
Reports of the Independent Labour Party Conferences.
Reports of the Labour Party Conferences.
Reports of the Labour Representation Committee Conferences.
Reports of the Trades Union Congress Conferences.

Primary

AMERY, L. C. M. S. *My Political Life.* London: Hutchinson, 1953-1955.

AMERY, L. C. M. S. *The Problem of the Army.* London: Edward Arnold, 1903.

ARNOLD-FORSTER, H. O. *English Socialism of To-day: Its Teachings and Its Aims Examined,* London: Smith, Elder, 1908.

ASHLEY, ANNE. *The Social Policy of Bismarck.* Birmingham: Birmingham Studies in Social Economics, 1912.

ASHLEY, W. J. *The Adjustment of Wages: A Study in the Coal and Iron Industries of Great Britain and America.* London: Longmans, Green, 1903.

ASHLEY, W. J. 'The Argument for Preference.' *Economic Journal.* XIV, March, 1904, pp. 1-10.

ASHLEY, W. J. *The Christian Outlook: Being the Sermons of an Economist.* London: Longmans, Green, 1925.

ASHLEY, W. J. *The Economic Organisation of England.* London: Longmans, Green, 1935.

ASHLEY, W. J. *Industrial Unrest; A Practical Solution.* London: John Murray, 1914.

ASHLEY, W. J. *An Introduction to English Economic History and Theory.* New York: Longmans, 1894.

ASHLEY, W. J. 'Political Economy and the Tariff Problem.' *Economic Review.* XIV, July 1904, pp. 257-278.

ASHLEY, W. J. 'The Present Position of Political Economy.' *Economic Journal.* XVII, December 1907, pp. 467-489.

ASHLEY, W. J. 'The Present Position of Political Economy in England' in *Die Entwicklung der deutschen Volkswirtschaftslehre im neunzehnten Jahrhundert.* Leipzig: Duncker and Humblot, 1908.

ASHLEY, W. J. 'The Present Position of Social Legislation in England.' *Economic Review.* XVIII, October 1908, pp. 391-411.

ASHLEY, W. J. 'Profit-Sharing.' *Quarterly Review.* CCXIX, October 1913, pp. 509-530.

ASHLEY, W. J. *The Progress of the German Working Classes in the Last Quarter of a Century.* London: Longmans, Green, 1904.

ASHLEY, W. J. *The Railroad Strike of 1894.* Cambridge, Mass.: Church Social Union, 1895.

ASHLEY, W. J. 'Socialists of the Chair' in Sir Robert Palgrave (ed.), *Dictionary of Political Economy.* London: 1912-1915.

ASHLEY, W. J. *Surveys Historic and Economic.* London: Longmans, 1900.

ASHLEY, W. J. *The Tariff Problem.* London: P. S. King, 1920.

ASQUITH, H. H. *Fifty Years of Parliament.* London: Cassell, 1926.

ASQUITH, H. H. *Speeches by the Earl of Oxford and Asquith, K. G.* London: Hutchinson, 1928.

BALFOUR, A. J. *Mr Balfour on Imperial Preference.* London: Tariff Reform League, 1910.

BELLOC, HILAIRE. *Mr Clutterbuck's Election.* London: T. Nelson, 1908?.

BELLOC, HILAIRE. *Pongo and the Bull.* London: Constable, 1910.

BELLOC, HILAIRE, AND CHESTERTON, CECIL. *The Party System.* London: Stephen Swift, 1911.

BIRKENHEAD, EARL OF. *Frederick Edwin, Earl of Birkenhead.* London: Thornton Butterworth, 1935.

BLATCHFORD, ROBERT. *Britain for the British.* Chicago: Charles H. Kerr, 1902.

BLATCHFORD, ROBERT. *Germany and England: The War That Was Foretold.* New York: Edward J. Clode, 1914.

BLATCHFORD, ROBERT. *Merrie England.* London: Clarion Newspaper, 1895.

BLATCHFORD, ROBERT. *My Eighty Years.* London: Cassell, 1931.

BLATCHFORD, ROBERT. *My Life in the Army*. London: Amalgamated Press, 1915?

BLUMENFELD, R. D. *The Press in My Time*. London: Rich and Cowan, 1933.

BLUMENFELD, R. D. *R. D. B.'s Diary, 1887-1914*. London: William Heinemann, 1930.

BLUMENFELD, R. D. *R. D. B.'s Procession*. New York: Macmillan, 1935.

BOOTH, CHARLES, JR. *Fiscal Policy and British Shipping from the Free Trade Point of View*. Liverpool: Henry Young, 1909.

BRIDGES, JOHN A. *Reminiscences of a Country Politician*. London: T. Werner Laurie, 1906.

CHAMBERLAIN, AUSTEN. *Down the Years*. London: Cassell, 1935.

CHAMBERLAIN, AUSTEN. *Politics from Inside: An Epistolary Chronicle, 1906-1914*. London: Cassell, 1936.

CHAMBERLAIN, JOSEPH. *Mr Chamberlain's Speeches* (edited by Charles W. Boyd). New York: Houghton Mifflin, 1914.

CUNNINGHAM, WILLIAM. *Alien Immigrants to England*. London: Swan Sonnenschein, 1897.

CUNNINGHAM, WILLIAM. 'Back to the Land.' *Economic Review*. XVII, October 1907, p. 389.

CUNNINGHAM, WILLIAM. *The Case Against Free Trade*. London: John Murray, 1911.

CUNNINGHAM, WILLIAM. *The Causes of Labour Unrest and the Remedies For It*. London: John Murray, 1912.

CUNNINGHAM, WILLIAM. *Christianity and Economic Science*. London: John Murray, 1914.

CUNNINGHAM, WILLIAM. *Christianity and Politics*. New York: Houghton Mifflin, 1915.

CUNNINGHAM, WILLIAM. *Christianity and Social Questions*. London: Duckworth, 1910.

CUNNINGHAM, WILLIAM. *The Church's Duty in Relation to the Sacredness of Property*. Cambridge, Mass.: Church Social Union, 1895.

CUNNINGHAM, WILLIAM. *The Common Weal*. Cambridge: Cambridge University Press, 1917.

CUNNINGHAM, WILLIAM. 'The Economic Basis of Universal Peace— Cosmopolitan or International?' *Economic Review*. XXIII, January 1913, pp. 7-13.

CUNNINGHAM, WILLIAM. '*Economic Change*' in *Cambridge Modern History*. Cambridge: Cambridge University Press, 1902. I, pp. 493-531.

CUNNINGHAM, WILLIAM. 'English Imperialism.' *Atlantic Monthly*. LXXXIV, July 1899, pp. 1-7.

CUNNINGHAM, WILLIAM. *An Essay on Western Civilisation in Its Economic Aspect*. New York: G. P. Putnam, 1913.

CUNNINGHAM, WILLIAM. 'The Failure of the Free Traders to Attain Their Ideal.' *Economic Review*. XIV, January 1904, pp. 39-53.

CUNNINGHAM, WILLIAM. *The Growth of English Industry and Commerce in Modern Times*. Cambridge: Cambridge University Press, 1892 and 1912.

CUNNINGHAM, WILLIAM. 'Nationalism and Cosmopolitanism in Economics' in Report of the Sixty-First Meeting of the British Association for the Advancement of Science held at Cardiff in August, 1891. London: John Murray, 1892.

CUNNINGHAM, WILLIAM. *Political Economy and Practical Life*. Boston: Church Social Union, 1895.

CUNNINGHAM, WILLIAM. *Politics and Economics; An Essay on the Nature of the Principles of Political Economy, Together with a Survey of Recent Legislation*. London: Kegan Paul, Trench, 1885.

CUNNINGHAM, WILLIAM. *The Progress of Capitalism in England*. Cambridge: Cambridge University Press, 1916.

CUNNINGHAM, WILLIAM. 'The Progress of Socialism in England.' *Contemporary Review*. XXXIV, January 1879, pp. 245-260.

CUNNINGHAM, WILLIAM. *The Rise and Decline of the Free Trade Movement*. Cambridge: Cambridge University Press, 1905.

CUNNINGHAM, WILLIAM. *Strikes*. Boston: Church Social Union, 1895.

FABIAN SOCIETY. *Fabianism and the Fiscal Question; An Alternative Policy*. London: Fabian Tract No. 116, 1904.

GRIFFITH-BOSCAWEN, A. S. T. *Fourteen Years in Parliament*. London: John Murray, 1907.

HALDANE, R. B. *Autobiography*. New York: Doubleday Doran, 1929.

HALDANE, R. B. *Universities and National Life*. London: John Murray, 1911.

HARBEN, H. D. *The Endowment of Motherhood*. London: Fabian Tract No. 149, 1910.

HAYCRAFT, JOHN BERRY. *Darwinism and Race Progress*. London: Swann Sonnenschein, 1895.

HEADLEY, F. W. *Darwinism and Modern Socialism*. London: Methuen, 1909.

HEWINS, W. A. S. *The Apologia of An Imperialist: Forty Years of Empire Policy*. London: Constable, 1929.

HOBHOUSE, LEONARD T. *Social Evolution and Political Theory*. New York: Columbia University Press, 1911.

HOBSON, J. A. *The German Panic*. London: Cobden Club, 1913.

HOBSON, J. A. *Imperialism: A Study.* London: George Allen and Unwin, 1938.

HOBSON, SAMUEL GEORGE. *Pilgrim to the Left; Memoirs of a Modern Revolutionist,* London: E. Arnold, 1938.

KIDD, BENJAMIN. *The Control of the Tropics.* New York: Macmillan, 1898.

KIDD, BENJAMIN. *Individualism and After.* Oxford: Oxford University Press, 1908.

KIDD, BENJAMIN. *The Science of Power.* London: 1918.

KIDD, BENJAMIN. *Social Evolution.* London: Macmillan, 1894.

LAW, A. BONAR. *The Fiscal Question.* London: National Review Office, 1908.

LLOYD GEORGE, DAVID. *War Memoirs.* London: Odhams Press, 1933.

MACDONALD, J. RAMSAY. *Tariff-Ridden Germany.* London: *The Daily News,* 1908?

MACDONALD, J. RAMSAY. *The Zollverein and British Industry.* London: Grant Richards, 1903.

MACKINDER, HALFORD J. *Britain and the British Seas.* London: Heinemann, 1902.

MACKINDER, HALFORD J. *Democratic Ideals and Reality: A Study in the Politics of Reconstruction.* London: Constable, 1919.

MACKINDER, HALFORD J. 'The Geographical Pivot of History.' *Geographical Journal.* XXIII, April 1904.

MACKINDER, HALFORD J. 'The Great Trade Routes.' *Journal of the Institute of Bankers.* XXI, March, 1900, pp. 137-155; May 1900, pp. 266-273.

MACKINDER, HALFORD J. 'Man-Power As A Measure of National and Imperial Strength.' *National Review.* XLV, March 1905.

MACKINDER, HALFORD J. *The Modern British State: An Introduction to the Study of Civics.* London: George Philip, 1914.

MACKINDER, HALFORD J. *Money-Power and Man-Power: The Underlying Principles Rather Than the Statistics of Tariff Reform.* London: Simpkin, Marshall, Hamilton, Kent, 1906.

MACKINDER, HALFORD J. *The World War and After.* London: G. Philip, 1924.

MACNAMARA, THOMAS J. *Tariff Reform and the Working Man.* London: Hodder and Stoughton, 1910.

MACNAMARA, THOMAS J. *The Political Situation: Letters to a Working Man.* London: Hodder and Stoughton, 1909.

MAXSE, LEOPOLD J. 'Germany on the Brain, or The Obsession of a crank.' *Gleanings from the National Review.* London: National Review, 1915.

Memoranda, Statistical Tables, and Charts Prepared in the Board of Trade with Reference to Various Matters Bearing on British and Foreign Trade and Industrial Conditions; 1903 Cd. 1761. LXVII. 253.

MILNER, ALFRED, 1ST VISCOUNT. *Arnold Toynbee: A Reminiscence.* London: E. Arnold, 1901.

MILNER, ALFRED, 1ST VISCOUNT. *The British Commonwealth.* London: Constable, 1919.

MILNER, ALFRED, 1ST VISCOUNT. *The Nation and the Empire.* London: Constable, 1913.

MILNER, ALFRED, 1ST VISCOUNT. *Our Imperial Heritage.* London: Tariff Reform League, 1910.

MILNER, ALFRED, 1ST VISCOUNT. Six lectures on Socialism reprinted in the *National Review,* January-June 1931.

MORLEY, JOHN. 'The Issues At Stake' (a speech). London: Liberal Publications Department, 1904.

MOSLEY, OSWALD. *Blackshirt Policy.* London: 1934.

MOSLEY, OSWALD. *Fascism: 100 Questions Asked and Answered.* London: B. U. F. Publications, 1936.

MOSLEY, OSWALD. *The Greater Britain.* London: B. U. F. Publications, 1932.

MOSLEY, OSWALD. *Revolution by Reason.* London: Blackfriars Press, 1925.

MOSLEY, OSWALD. *Tomorrow We Live.* London: Greater Britain Publications, 1939?

MOSLEY, OSWALD. *Mosley: The Facts.* London: Euphorion Distribution, 1957.

PARKER, GILBERT. *The Land For the People: Small Ownership and Land Banks.* London: *Daily Express,* 1909?

PARKER, GILBERT. *A National Policy: Our Fiscal System and Imperial Reciprocity.* Gravesend: Standard, 1903?

PEARSON, KARL. *The Chances of Death and Other Studies in Evolution.* London: E. Arnold, 1897.

PEARSON, KARL. *Darwinism, Medical Progress and Eugenics.* London: University of London, 1912.

PEARSON, KARL. *The Ethic of Free Thought.* London: A. & C. Black, 1901.

PEARSON, KARL. *The Function of Science in the Modern State.* London: University of London, 1919.

PEARSON, KARL. *The Grammar of Science.* London: A. & C. Black, 1900.

PEARSON, KARL. *The Life, Letters, and Labours of Francis Galton.* Cambridge: Cambridge University Press, 1914-1930.

PEARSON, KARL. *National Life from the Standpoint of Science.* London: A. & C. Black, 1905.

PEARSON, KARL. *Nature and Nurture: The Problem of the Future*. London: University of London, 1910.

PEARSON, KARL. *The Problem of Practical Eugenics*. London: University of London, 1912.

PEARSON, KARL. *The Scope and Importance to the State of the Science of National Eugenics*. London: University of London, 1911.

PEARSON, KARL. *Social Problems: Their Treatment, Past, Present and Future*. London: University of London, 1912.

ROBERTS, EARL. *Lord Roberts' Message to the Nation*. London: John Murray, 1912.

ROBERTS, EARL. 'A Nation in Arms.' Speech delivered in Manchester, October 1912.

ROBERTS, EARL. 'National Security.' Speech delivered in House of Lords, November 23, 1908.

ROSEBERY, EARL. *Miscellanies: Literary and Historical*. London: Hodder and Stoughton, 1921.

RUSSELL, BERTRAND. *Portraits from Memory and Other Essays*. London: Allen and Unwin, 1956.

SCHMOLLER, GUSTAV. *Grundriss der allgemeinen Volkswirtschaftslehre*. Munich, 1923.

SHAW, G. BERNARD (ed.) *Fabian Essays*. London: Allen and Unwin, 1948.

SHAW, G. BERNARD. *Fabianism*. London: Fabian Tract No. 233, 1930.

SHAW, G. BERNARD (ed.) *Fabianism and the Empire: A Manifesto by the Fabian Society*. London: Grant Richards, 1900.

SHAW, G. BERNARD. *An Unsocial Socialist*. London: Constable, 1932.

SMALL, ALBION W. (translator.) 'Schmoller on Class Conflicts in General.' *American Journal of Sociology*. XX, 1915, pp. 504–531.

SNOWDEN, PHILIP. *The Chamberlain Bubble; Facts About the Zollverein with an Alternative Policy*. London: Independent Labour Party, Tracts for the Times, No. 1, 1903.

SOCIALIST PARTY OF GREAT BRITAIN. *Socialism Versus Tariff Reform*. London: S.P.G.B., 1912.

SOCIOLOGICAL SOCIETY. *Sociological Papers*. London: 1905.

SPENCER, HERBERT. *A Rejoinder to Professor Weismann*. New York: 1894.

SUTHERS, R. B. *My Right to Work: Free Trade; Protection or Socialism?* London: Clarion Press, 1906.

WEBB, BEATRICE. *Our Partnership*. London: Longmans, Green, 1948.

WEBB, SIDNEY. *The Decline in the Birth Rate*. London: Fabian Tract No. 131, 1907.

WEBB, SIDNEY. 'Lord Rosebery's Escape from Houndsditch.' *Nineteenth Century and After*. CCXCV, September 1901, pp. 366-386.

WEBB, SIDNEY. *Twentieth Century Politics: A Policy of National Efficiency*. London: Fabian Tract No. 108, 1901.

WELLS, H. G. *Experiment in Autobiography*. London: Gollancz, 1934.

WELLS, H. G. *The New Machiavelli*. London: John Lane, 1911.

Secondary

ASHLEY, ANNE. *William James Ashley: A Life*. London: P. S. King, 1932.

BEER, MAX. *A History of British Socialism*. London: Allen and Unwin, 1948.

BÉRARD, VICTOR. *British Imperialism and Commercial Supremacy*. London: Longmans, Green, 1906.

BERLAU, ABRAHAM J. *The German Social Democratic Party, 1914-1921*. New York: Columbia University Press, 1949.

BLACKER, C. P. *Eugenics. Galton and After*. London: Gerald Duckworth, 1952.

BORGESE, G. A. *Goliath: The March of Fascism*. London: Gollancz, 1938.

BOWEN, RALPH H. *German Theories of the Corporative State, with Special Reference to the Period 1870-1919*. New York: Whittlesey House, 1947.

BRIE, FRIEDRICH. *Der Einfluss der Lehren Darwins auf den britischen Imperialismus*. Freiburg in Baden: 1927.

BROWN, BENJAMIN H. *The Tariff Reform Movement in Great Britain, 1881-1895*. New York: Columbia University Press, 1943.

BUKHARIN, NIKOLAI. *Imperialism and World Economy*. New York: 1929.

BUTHMAN, WILLIAM C. *The Rise of Integral Nationalism in France, with Special Reference to the Ideas and Activities of Charles Maurras*. New York: Columbia University Press, 1939.

CHESTERTON, A. K. *Oswald Mosley, Portrait of a Leader*. London: Action Press, 1937?

CLAPHAM, J. H. *An Economic History of Modern Britain*. Cambridge: Cambridge University Press, 1930-1938.

CLAPHAM, J. H. 'Sir William Ashley.' *Economic Journal*. XXXVII, 1927.

CLARK, COLIN. *The Conditions of Economic Progress*. London: Macmillan, 1951.

COATES, T. F. G. *Lord Rosebery, His Life and Speeches*. London: Hutchinson, 1900.

COLE, G. D. H. *British Working Class Politics, 1832-1914.* London: Routledge, 1941.

COLE, G. D. H. *A Short History of the British Working Class Movement, 1789-1947.* London: Allen and Unwin, 1952.

COLE, G. D. H., AND POSTGATE, RAYMOND. *The British Common People, 1746-1938.* New York: Alfred A. Knopf, 1939.

COLE, MARGARET (ed.) *The Webbs and Their Work.* London: Frederick Muller, 1949.

CRANKSHAW, EDWARD. *The Forsaken Idea; A Study of Viscount Milner.* London: Longmans, Green, 1952.

CREWE, THE MARQUIS OF. *Lord Rosebery.* London: John Murray, 1931.

CUNNINGHAM, AUDREY. *William Cunningham; Teacher and Priest.* London: S. P. C. K., 1950.

DANGERFIELD, GEORGE. *The Strange Death of Liberal England.* New York: Harrison Smith and Robert Haas, 1935.

DARK, SIDNEY. *The Life of Sir Arthur Pearson, Bt., G.B.E.* London: Hodder and Stoughton, 1922?

DAWSON, W. H. *Bismarck and State Socialism;* (An Exposition of the Social and Economic Legislation of Germany Since 1870). London: Swan, Sonnenschein, 1890.

DE ROUX, MARIE. *Charles Maurras et le Nationalisme de l'Action Française.* Paris: Bernard Grasset, 1927.

DRENNAN, JAMES. *B.U.F.; Oswald Mosley and British Fascism.* London: John Murray, 1934.

DUGDALE, BLANCHE E. C. *Arthur James Balfour, First Earl of Balfour.* London: Hutchinson, 1936.

EARLE, EDWARD MEADE (ed.) *Nationalism and Internationalism.* New York: Columbia University Press, 1950.

ENSOR, R. C. K. *England: 1870-1914.* Oxford: Clarendon Press, 1936.

FAY, C. R. *Great Britain from Adam Smith to the Present Day.* London: Longmans, Green, 1948.

FOXWELL, H. S., AND KNOWLES, LILIAN. 'Archdeacon Cunningham' (Obituary). *Economic Journal.* XXIX, September 1919, pp. 382-393.

GALLAGHER, JOHN, AND ROBINSON, RONALD. 'The Imperialism of Free Trade.' *Economic History Review.* VI, August 1953, pp. 1-15.

GARVIN, JAMES LOUIS. *The Life of Joseph Chamberlain.* London: Macmillan, 1932, 1933, 1934. (Volume IV in 1951 by Julian Amery, after Garvin's death).

GILBERT, E. W. 'The Right Honourable Sir Halford J. Mackinder, P.C., 1861-1947.' *Geographical Journal.* CX, January 1948, pp. 94-97.

GRETTON, R. H. *A Modern History of the English People, 1880-1922.* London: Secker, 1930.

GULLEY, ELSIE E. *Joseph Chamberlain and English Social Politics.* New York: Columbia University Press, 1926.

HALÉVY, ÉLIE. *Histoire du socialisme européen.* Paris: 1948.

HALÉVY, ÉLIE. *A History of the English People in the Nineteenth Century.* London: Ernest Benn, 1949.

HALPÉRIN, VLADIMIR. *Lord Milner et l'évolution de l'impérialisme britannique.* Paris: Presses Universitaires de France, 1950.

HAYES, CARLTON J. H. *British Social Politics.* Boston: Ginn, 1913.

HAYES, CARLTON J. H. 'Influence of Political Tactics on Socialist Theory in Germany, 1863-1914' in Charles E. Merriam and Harry E. Barnes (eds.), *A History of Political Theories; Recent Times.* New York: Macmillan, 1924.

HECKSCHER, ELI F. *Mercantilism.* London: Allen and Unwin, 1935.

HILFERDING, RUDOLF. *Das Finanzkapital, Eine Studie über die jüngste Entwicklung des Kapitalismus.* Vienna: 1910.

HO, PING-TI. 'Land and State in Great Britain, 1873-1910: A Study of Land Reform Movements and Land Policies.' (An unpublished Columbia University Ph.D. Thesis, 1950.).

HOFFMAN, R. J. S. *Great Britain and the German Trade Rivalry, 1875-1914.* Philadelphia: University of Pennsylvania Press, 1933.

HOLLAND, BERNARD. *The Life of Spencer Compton, Eighth Duke of Devonshire.* London: Longmans, Green, 1911.

HOVDE, BRYN J. 'Socialistic Theories of Imperialism Prior to the Great War.' *Journal of Political Economy.* XXXVI, 1928, pp. 713-758.

HUMPHREY, RICHARD D. *Georges Sorel, Prophet Without Honor: A Study in Anti-Intellectualism.* Cambridge, Mass.: Harvard University Press, 1951.

HURWITZ, SAMUEL J. *State Intervention in Great Britain: A Study of Economic Control and Social Response, 1914-1919.* New York: Columbia University Press, 1949.

JAMES, DAVID R. *Lord Roberts.* London: Hollis and Carter, 1954.

JERROLD, WALTER. *Field-Marshal Earl Roberts.* London: W. A. Hammond, 1914.

JONES, G. P., AND POOL, A. G. *A Hundred Years of Economic Development in Great Britain.* London: Duckworth, 1948.

KEYNES, JOHN MAYNARD. *The Economic Consequences of the Peace.* London: Macmillan, 1920.

KOEBNER, RICHARD. 'The Concept of Economic Imperialism.' *Economic History Review.* II, 1949, pp. 1-29.

S

LANGER, WILLIAM L. *The Diplomacy of Imperialism, 1890-1902.* New York: Alfred A. Knopf, 1935.

LENIN, N. *Imperialism; The Highest Stage of Capitalism.* New York: 1939.

LIST, FRIEDRICH. *Nationalism System of Political Economy.* Philadelphia: 1856.

LOEWENSTEIN, F. E. 'The Shaw-Wells Controversy of 1904-1908: A Chapter of Fabian History.' *Fabian Quarterly.* April 1944, pp. 15-20.

LORIA, ACHILLE. 'Les deux notions de l'impérialisme.' *Revue économique internationale.* III, 1907, pp. 459-477.

LUXEMBURG, ROSA. *The Accumulation of Capital.* New Haven: 1951.

LYONS, A. NEIL. *Robert Blatchford.* London: Clarion Press, 1910.

MACCOBY, SIMON. *English Radicalism, 1886-1914.* London: Allen & Unwin, 1953.

MADDOX, WILLIAM P. *Foreign Relations in British Labor Politics.* Cambridge, Mass.: Harvard University Press, 1934.

MALLALIEU, W. C. 'Joseph Chamberlain and Workmen's Compensation.' *Journal of Economic History.* X, May 1950, pp. 45-57.

MEGARO, GAUDENS. *Mussolini in the Making.* London: Allen & Unwin, 1938.

MELVILE, CECIL F. *The Truth about the New Party.* London: Wishart, 1931.

MICHELS, ROBERTO. *Le proletariat et la bourgeoisie dans le mouvement socialiste italien particulièrement des origines à 1906.* Paris: 1921.

MULLALY, FREDERIC. *Fascism Inside England.* London: Claud Morris Books, 1946.

NEUMANN, FRANZ. *Behemoth: The Structures and Practice of National Socialism, 1933-1944.* London: Gollancz, 1942.

ORRY, ALBERT. *Les Socialistes Indépendants.* Paris: Riviere, 1911.

PEARSON, E. S. *Karl Pearson, An Appreciation of Some Aspects of His Life and Work.* Cambridge: 1938.

PEASE, EDWARD R. *The History of the Fabian Society.* London: Allen and Unwin, 1925.

PETRIE, CHARLES. *The Chamberlain Tradition.* London: L. Dickson, 1938.

PIPKIN, CHARLES. *Social Politics and Modern Democracies.* New York: Macmillan, 1931.

RENNER, KARL. *Marxismus, Krieg und Internationale.* Stuttgart: 1917.

RITCHIE, DAVID G. *Darwinism and Politics.* New York: 1889.

ROSTOW, W. W. *British Economy of the Nineteenth Century.* Oxford: Oxford University Press, 1948.

SALOMONE, A. WILLIAM. *Italian Democracy in the Making*. Philadelphia: University of Pennsylvania Press, 1945.

SCHMOLLER, GUSTAV. *The Mercantile System and Its Historical Significance*. New York: 1910.

SCHUMPETER, JOSEPH A. *Business Cycles; A Theoretical, Historical, and Statistical Analysis of the Capitalist Process*. New York: McGraw-Hill, 1939.

SCHUMPETER, JOSEPH A. *History of Economic Analysis*. New York: Oxford University Press, 1954.

SCHUMPETER, JOSEPH A. *Imperialism and Social Classes*. Oxford: Blackwell, 1951.

SCOTT, W. R. 'William Cunningham, 1849-1919.' *Proceedings of the British Academy, 1919-1920*. London: Oxford University Press, 1920?

SNELL, JOHN L. 'Socialist Unions and Socialist Patriotism in Germany, 1914-1918.' *American Historical Review*. LIX, October 1953, pp. 66-76.

SPENDER, J. A., AND ASQUITH, CYRIL. *Life of Herbert Henry Asquith, Lord Oxford and Asquith*. London: Hutchinson, 1932.

THOMAS, J. A. *The House of Commons, 1832-1901: A Study of Its Economic and Functional Character*. Cardiff: University of Wales Press Board, 1939.

THOMPSON, LAURENCE V. *Robert Blatchford: Portrait of An Englishman*. London: Victor Gollancz, 1951.

TSIANG, TINGFU FULLER. *Labor and Empire:* A Study of the Reaction of British Labor, Mainly as Represented in Parliament to British Imperialism since 1880. New York: Columbia University Press, 1923.

TYLER, J. E. *The Struggle for Imperial Unity* (1868-1895). London: Longmans, Green, 1938.

WEBB, SIDNEY AND BEATRICE. *The History of Trade Unionism*. London: Longmans, Green, 1920.

INDEX

GEORGE ALLEN & UNWIN LTD
*London: 40 Museum Street, W.C.*1

Auckland: 24 Wyndham Street
Bombay: 15 Graham Road, Ballard Estate, Bombay 1
Buenos Aires: Escritorio 454-459, Florida 165
Cape Town: 109 Long Street
Calcutta: 17 Chittaranjan Avenue, Calcutta 13
Hong Kong: F1/12 Mirador Mansions, Kowloon
Karachi: Meherson's Estate, Wood Street, Karachi 2
Mexico: Villalongin 32-10, Piso, Mexico 5, D.F.
New Delhi: 13-14 Ajmeri Gate Extension, New Delhi 1
São Paulo: Avenida 9 de Julho 1138-Ap. 51
Singapore: 36c Princep Street, Singapore 7
Sydney, N.S.W.: Bradbury House, 55 York Street
Toronto: 91 Wellington Street West

RUSSIAN POLITICAL INSTITUTIONS

DEREK J. R. SCOTT

This book is intended primarily to meet the need of university students for a good account of the political institutions of the Soviet Union in terms similar to those used in their study of other countries. Though the unique comprehensiveness of the Soviet state's concerns, to which the book draws attention, precludes a formally comparative approach, the ways in which its business is done can be explained, as elsewhere, by the country's circumstances and historical experience.

The first chapter indicates something of these circumstances and experience and of the motives of the Soviet state. The second explains the manner in which the distinctive institutional form of the Soviet state came into being and the process by which it assumed some of the conventional state machinery. The third examines this conventional state and its unconventional functions in a Russian Communist setting. The fourth concerns the structure and operation of the complex device called the Party. The fifth, in turn, examines the means evolved for the fulfilment of the state's main task, the management of the fully nationalized economy as a single concern, and the other main systems of control, including the judicial system. The sixth chapter suggests briefly how priorities of tasks are decided upon, obligations determined and their performance secured.

Minerva Series. Demy 8vo. 21s. net.

INTERNATIONAL INSTITUTIONS

PAUL REUTER

Broadly speaking institutions are the organizations, the traditions and the basic rules of a particular society. Between nations a similar series of traditions has developed and it is possible to assess the continuity and the variety of international societies as they have existed in recent history and as they exist and work today.

The introduction defines the elements of international society in terms of the accepted principles of group psychology. Part One considers the origins of present-day international institutions. Part Two deals with the structure of the day to day relations between States and the means of recognizing changes within a State. Part Three is concerned with International Organizations. Professor Reuter gives first a brief introduction to their evolution and classification and then gives a full analysis of the major juridical problems they raise. Finally he examines the United Nations and the principal regional organizations.

Although the study of international institutions is firmly based on a foundation of law, it is also a matter of importance for sociology, history and politics. This carefully prepared book is of prime importance for all deeply concerned with these subjects.

Minerva Series. Demy 8vo. 28s. net. Cheap edition 20s. net.

FREE ELECTIONS

W. J. M. MACKENZIE, M.A., LL.B.

Professor Mackenzie sets out compactly the facts and arguments which have to be considered in designing and running electoral systems. The book was written primarily as a result of his experience in lecturing about this subject during two visits to Africa in 1952 and 1956, but the establishment and growth of free elections are important in many other countries, and Professor Mackenzie is not only concerned with the problems of emergent states in Africa and Asia.

The book is in four parts: Votes and Candidates; Methods of Voting; Administration and Adjudication; and Electoral Morality and its Enforcement.

It concludes with a chapter on the pathology of elections. The object of this arrangement is to give a balanced account, covering on the one hand qualifications and voting systems, which have been much discussed, and on the other hand less 'political' questions of administration and control, which are of equal importance in the working of an electoral system, and are equally illumined by Professor Mackenzie's erudition and experience.

Minerva Series. Demy 8vo. Cloth edition 15s. net, Paper edition 12s. 6d. net.

THE USE OF ECONOMIC STATISTICS

C. A. BLYTH

This is an elementary introduction to the sources of economic statistics and their uses in answering economic questions.

The author's approach is novel in that he introduces statistical methods as tools to be used in examining economic problems. Each chapter deals with a typical problem of applied economics and explains in detail the statistical sources and methods required. Emphasis is placed upon the framing of hypotheses, the selection of appropriate statistics and the testing of the hypotheses by inspection. The economic problems—such as the present position of the cotton industry; the effect of hire purchase controls upon car sales; the extent to which prices have risen since the war; etc.—are so chosen and arranged that statistical subjects are presented to the student in an understandable way.

The book has two special merits: by dealing with real problems, it avoids the arid presentation of statistical methods based upon 'cooked-up' examples; and it tries to teach the student to ask worthwhile questions.

Minerva Series. Demy 8vo. 28s. Cloth. 22s. paper.

THE BRITISH ECONOMY, 1920–1957

A. J. YOUNGSON

The greater part of this book consists of an attempt to describe and account for the course of British economic development since the end of the post-war boom in 1920, a subject which has hardly been tackled at any length or in any convenient form. The coverage is general, but the author pays particular attention to changes in the industrial structure, to international trade, financial policy and fluctuations in the level of activity. The final section is devoted to a fascinating discussion of government economic policy throughout the period, in which the author seeks to trace the relation between policy and the ideas put forward at the time by economists such as Pigou, Robertson and Keynes. The picture which emerges of economic development and policy as a whole in the past thirty-seven years will greatly contribute to our general understanding of current problems.

Demy 8vo. 28s. net.

THE BRITISH BUDGETARY SYSTEM

SIR HERBERT BRITTAIN, K.C.B., K.B.E.

The Budget is now much more important than it was before the last war, for two main reasons. First, we have come to recognize its influence in the shaping of the country's general economic policy. Secondly, the scope and the size of both the current and capital parts of the Budget have been greatly enlarged: on the current side by the rise in the level of the Central Government's expenditure, and on the capital side by the extent to which the Exchequer now has to finance new State enterprises of various kinds.

Sir Herbert Brittain writes with expert knowledge, for until June 1957 he was Second Secretary in charge of Home Finance and Supply in the Treasury. His book is the first to describe the British Budgetary System in this new setting. It is essentially expository and seems likely to become a standard work which will be indispensable to teachers and students in a field relating both to the national economy and to public administration—the author has been conscious while writing of the needs both of economists and of students of administration.

One very useful aim of the book is to guide the reader at each point to the appropriate official accounts, reports and other documents which reflect the actual operation of the system which the book describes.

Demy 8vo. 25s. net.

THE LONDON SCHOOL OF ECONOMICS
AND ITS PROBLEMS 1919–1937

LORD BEVERIDGE

During the eighteen years from 1919–1937 when Sir William Beveridge was its Director, the London School of Economics enjoyed its greatest period of expansion. The achievements of this period were described and welcomed as its 'refoundation' by Sidney and Beatrice Webb, who had founded it in 1895.

The years between the wars presented a number of problems discussed in this book, such as those of finding space in the heart of London, of the proper scope and method of economics, of academic self-government, and of political activity by university readers of social sciences. The Director also could not avoid calls for service outside the school, for the government of the University of London, or of a social and personal character. His account of these pre-occupations emphasises some of the differences between life in London then and now.

In his last chapter arising out of a lecture given by him at the School to celebrate the Centenary of the Webbs, the author tells of his forty years of friendship with Sidney and Beatrice Webb, using letters between him and them not published hitherto—friendship unaffected by differences of political opinion. Demy 8vo. 21s. net.

NATIONALIZED INDUSTRY AND
PUBLIC OWNERSHIP

WILLIAM A. ROBSON

Most of the books, articles and pamphlets on the subject of nationalization are so prejudiced that they are of little value except as ammunition for political warfare. Professor Robson's new book is primarily an inquiry into the working of the British nationalized industries during the past ten years. He examines, with the aid of a wealth of material, the organization and management of these industries, how far they are subject to competition, their labour relations, their financial policies, their research and development programmes, their consumer councils, their relations with Ministers and Parliament, the political influences to which they are subject, and their general performance. He considers also the ideas and proposals which have recently been put forward about the manner in which publicly-owned industries should be run and the aims they should pursue. The final chapter discusses some of the alternatives to nationalization which have been advanced. Sm. Royal 8vo. 50s. net.

GEORGE ALLEN & UNWIN LTD